D0948313

IN PURSUIT OF THE ALMIGHTY'S DOLLAR

In Pursuit of

THE
ALMIGHTY'S
DOLLAR

A HISTORY OF MONEY

AND AMERICAN PROTESTANTISM

James Hudnut-Beumler

THE UNIVERSITY OF NORTH CAROLINA PRESS

Chapel Hill

© 2007 THE UNIVERSITY OF NORTH CAROLINA PRESS

All rights reserved

Designed by Amy Ruth Buchanan

Set in Minion by Keystone Typesetting, Inc.

Manufactured in the United States of America

This book was published with the assistance of the William R.
Kenan Jr. Fund of the University of North Carolina Press.

The paper in this book meets the guidelines for
permanence and durability of the Committee on
Production Guidelines for Book Longevity of the
Council on Library Resources.

Library of Congress Cataloging-in-Publication Data

Hudnut-Beumler, James David.

In pursuit of the Almighty's dollar : a history of money and
American Protestantism / by James Hudnut-Beumler.

p. cm.

Includes bibliographical references and index.

ISBN-13: 978-0-8078-3079-6 (cloth: alk. paper)

1. Economics—Religious aspects—Christianity. 2. Money—
Religious aspects—Christianity. 3. Protestantism—United
States—History. 4. Protestant churches—United States—History.
5. Protestant churches—Doctrines—History. 6. Stewardship,
Christian. 7. United States—Church history. 8. Money—
United States—History. I. Title.

BR115.E3H78 2007

241′.680882804—dc22

2006021910

A Caravan book. For more information, visit
www.caravanbooks.org.

11 10 09 08 07   5 4 3 2 1

In memory of my father,

Arthur K. Beumler,

who lived much of the story

about which I write.

CONTENTS

Illustrations, Tables,
and Figures

TABLES

FIGURES

PREFACE

In a world of rapid change, a Protestant Sunday morning worship service gives the appearance of rocklike immutability. Much of what historians have been able to describe about services of worship in 1750 could still be seen in the year 2000. Not all is as it seems, however. Over the last 250 years, tremendous changes have taken place in the institutions of American religious life. This is a book about those transformations.

Most historical writing reflects the time in which it was produced. *In Pursuit of the Almighty's Dollar* is the product of an era when many religious bodies are faltering because of a lack of support while others are growing, economically and in terms of numbers of adherents. It is a time when making ends meet is a widespread anxiety. What drives the analysis presented here is a concern for understanding the ways in which something may change in history, without its outward identity shifting. The historical perspective of the book is, broadly speaking, economic: under examination here are finance, capital, labor, the nature of the firm, and issues of scope and scale in American Protestantism over more than two centuries. We usually do not look at religious activity through economic lenses, but occasionally we should, since when we do, we see some things in the history of religious life to which we are typically blind.

Consider how much any commercial activity has changed over the last 250 years. For example, in the production of clothing, markets have emerged and disappeared; technology has radically changed how materials are made and at what cost; capital formation has led to the virtual disappearance of homespun garments; the labor for clothing production first moved into factories, then organized, and then was largely replaced by people working in less developed countries for a fraction of the wages previously paid. Moreover, the ways in which apparel products are brought to market and the ways in which the whole process is financed have changed drastically even in the last quarter century.

At first glance, religion in its most familiar congregational form, by contrast to clothing production, appears to be an island of immutability. But initial impressions can be deceiving. The idea that the business of religion alone has changed not a bit in the last quarter millennium is misguided. Indeed, if we begin by accepting the premise that, underneath the obvious continuities, religious life has developed in remarkable ways in the United States, we can then see new aspects of familiar phenomena. In this regard, religion is not unlike higher education: colleges still have the names William and Mary, Yale, Harvard, Princeton, and Dartmouth, but their scale and the scope of their activities would make it difficult for the college masters and students of 1750 to recognize their schools. In fact, some of the enduring features of American religious life—its basic congregational organization, for example—are all the more remarkable for their resilience.

S ome of my colleagues have asked whether a loaded phrase like "paying for God" is necessary to the interpretation. My answer to their queries is important for readers as well, for as I delved further into the documents and data, the story proved to be one fraught with both material and spiritual anxiety. Clergy, in particular, throughout the period studied were anxious about their place in their communities. Resentful of the need to raise their own support, they repeatedly invoked God, ecclesiastical tradition, and scriptural evidence to promote giving to the churches they served. At the same time, they exhibited an abiding sincerity in their belief that this is the way things should be, that God ought to be served and humanity uplifted by the Christian church. As for the laity, they both cooperated with and resisted the plans of the clergy, by giving and withholding, by participating and by staying away when called. It is in this climate of mixed this-worldly and otherworldly hopes, expectations, and results that the history I recount took shape. In the end, I hope readers will agree that it is precisely the tension between the spiritual and the material requirements of religious life in the American setting that accounts for the singular ways and means that have been embraced to carry out organized religious life in this country over the last two centuries.

This book emerges from the "if I would truly know a man I would rather look at his checkbook than his diary" school of historical inquiry. A somewhat more elegant description would term this an exercise in the study of practices. The practices in question are the acquisition and expenditure of resources in Protestant congregations over a long span of time. This book treats getting and spending as material facts of religious social life that tell us what mattered to religious elites and ordinary adherents at various points in time. I originally set out to make the narrative an economic history, either proceeding according to a strict chronology or moving topically through the different actors and categories that economists use when examining the social enterprise—capital, labor, the nature of the firm, finance, and so forth. In going over the historical record, however, I found that the most striking aspect of the story was the ever-changing but persistent rhetoric by which successive generations of clergy sought to raise the resources to support the ministries of their churches. What I call the "great privatization," that is, the relocation of religion from a public good to a private, voluntarily supported good, so overshadowed the American Protestant experience as to generate both a body of rhetoric and a genre of practical religious thought substantial enough to bear the narrative frame of this book. In economic terms, therefore, five major chapters focus on the question of the financing of American Protestantism. Seeking money for ministry is only one part of the story. The way Protestants have spent their money, particularly on labor (mostly ministerial labor) and buildings, has also revealed the changing shape of American church life. Indeed, noticing that there are changes in spending is necessary lest we believe that every minister who ever asked for support was seeking to support the same thing, or that every member of the clergy who complained about his (or later her) salary was equally disadvantaged in fact.

The five large chapters telling how money was sought for ministry are complemented by four shorter chapters: one on the Protestant ministry as a profession, another on the experience of minister's wives with that profession, and two chapters on the church buildings Protestants have constructed and adapted and how that major category of expense discloses the functional ecclesiologies and theologies of the communities that build them. Readers might be tempted to gloss over the labor and capital chapters, but I urge them to linger at these interludes since the pursuit of the Almighty's dollar at diverse points in this country's history was highly dependent on how churches and their leaders felt those dollars needed to be spent. To borrow again from the language of economics, the financing story is intimately related to the evolving nature of the firm.

This is the history of a mentality across many years. The rise of this mentality is evident at the narrative's starting point in 1750, when competition for Protestant adherents began in the aftermath of the Great Awakening. The thought patterns went through many changes and transformations, but I would argue that the culmination of the process can be seen in the U.S. Catholic bishops' 1992 Pastoral Letter on Stewardship. What was once a distinctively Protestant way of thinking about money in the church had become the American way of thinking about giving to and supporting churches. This book is also an examination of the materialization of religion. Materialization is inevitable. Embodied people engage in their religion in physical places, utilizing material means. In the national setting of the United States, materialization took on novel and interesting forms. The Protestant story is instructive because these forms were the quintessentially American expressions of religion that not only were the religion of the majority, but also came to be the culturally dominant way of structuring and supporting an organized religion in a voluntary society.

Who counts as a Protestant? "Does your book include evangelicals, fundamentalists, and Pentecostals, or only old-line groups?" I have been asked. The simplest answer to that inquiry is to say that I have tried to let the sources guide both my definition of a Protestant and whom to include at each stage of the book. Until the middle of the twentieth century, many of these groups we now distinguish from mainline Protestantism were not numerous and were difficult to separate out from the so-called mainline traditions. In more recent years—as the reader will see in the last chapters of the book—more conservative and evangelical voices have grown greatly in volume. When it comes to raising and spending money in the Lord's work, however, evangelicals, fundamentalists, dispensationalists, Pentecostals, and mainline Protestants preach, talk, and act very much alike. Indeed, while beliefs, theologies of worship, patterns of church leadership, and moral orthodoxies have divided Americans into thousands of discrete types of Protestants, the practices of raising money based on a few biblical precedents and the weight of past cultural patterns unite these types of Protestants far more than standard accounts of American religious history would lead us to believe. In a dramatic way, being in the "church business" makes all American Protestants more like one another than they themselves would think. This is just one of the ironies of American Protestant church life. Over the course of this book, at least three other such ironies will be encountered:

1. The very clergy who raised money "for God" had to do so knowing that a large portion of that money would fund their own salaries. This led to a more intense spiritualization of giving than was true in the European churches from which most of the American churches were descended.

2. The spiritualization of giving and spending for godly pursuits not only helped fund congregations and support their ministers; it also financed the so-called benevolent empire of voluntary societies and helped constantly enlarge the conception of the Protestant church's appropriate activities, whose expanded scope and scale then drove the need for yet more funds.

3. The voluntary nature of church financing in the United States provided the means by which individual congregations and denominations could secure their own future and also guaranteed that competing religious entities would have exactly the same means.

As in so much else when it comes to American religion, *In Pursuit of the Almighty's Dollar* is a tale of the best of intentions, unintended consequences, and surprising outcomes. At the start, the reader would be well advised to put aside what she or he "knows" about the ways churches raise and spend their money and to enter the mind-set of late colonial America.

ACKNOWLEDGMENTS

Since this a book about money, it is only appropriate that I seek to discharge some debts.

A sabbatical and much of the research was financed through the help of a generous grant from the Lilly Endowment, Inc., and I was consistently encouraged by the senior program director, Fred Hofheinz, and the vice president for religion, Craig Dykstra.

Across the years, I have had encouragement from a wide range of scholars in the historical and theological disciplines. Robert Wood Lynn shared a love for the early nineteenth-century materials that I use in this work. Seven other scholars associated with the Material History of American Religion Project, which I directed in the late 1990s, read drafts, offered pointers, and helped account for further authorial choices. Dan Sack provided innumerable hours of support as associate director of the project and never failed to be an outstanding sounding board for new approaches to the questions I sought to ask. Robert Orsi asked me early on whether I disliked the clergy about whom I wrote, leading me to the insight that I did not dislike people who raised money for religious causes so much as I felt for them because of the terrible ironies expressed in their lives through their appeals. Diane Winston helped me recognize the right tone to use in bringing the voices of the religious actors to print. Colleen McDannel asked where the people were in some of my building illustrations and thereby inspired the chapter in this book on the testimonies of ministers' wives, the missing people in far too many discussions of the Protestant churches. Marie Griffith, Leigh Schmidt, David Watt, Judith Weisenfeld, and David Morgan rounded out a group of early conversation partners whose enthusiasms reassured me in the pursuit of my inquiry that no topics were off limits in the study of American religion.

At Vanderbilt, my colleagues Kathleen Flake, James Byrd, and Dale Johnson have offered helpful comments and readings along the way. Jane Gleim and

Sherry Willis, each of whom typed large parts of this history in installments, sometimes kept me going by wanting to know what came next and at other times by telling me great stories from their own church experiences that confirmed the central thesis and showed me that others had observed some of what I had seen along the way.

Libraries and librarians at Christian Theological Seminary in Indianapolis, Emory University (Pitts Library), Columbia Theological Seminary, and Vanderbilt University were indispensable, as were the dozens of people who passed me pamphlets and promotional literature they had run across in which they thought I might be interested.

As always, my wife, Heidi, deserves special thanks for encouraging me and letting me hole up in a crowded home office to construct this book.

IN PURSUIT OF THE ALMIGHTY'S DOLLAR

PROLOGUE

Sunday Morning 1750

The most public day of the week arrives. From Massachusetts to Georgia, people in England's American colonies come together to spend the morning at their community's church. In all but the largest cities, there is no choice in the matter of which church to attend. There is but one church for the settlement, be it a rural Anglican parish in Virginia, or in an urbanized settlement of German Lutherans just outside Philadelphia. People do not choose their churches; their churches are closely bound up with what it means to be part of a community. Churches are public institutions in the way that schools would later be regarded. A church building itself is the largest, and usually only, public assembly space in a town. Decisions about fixing roads and dividing land are made in this meeting house. Men were elected to the vestry, or council, or as justices of the peace in this place. Taxes and rates are set to support the public's business, and no business is more universally important in colonial America than divine worship. On this day, other business affairs were left outside the church's doors, though their presence was evident even in worship.

The Lord's Day began in earnest with the sounding of a church bell or a town crier summoning the community to church. In New England most townsfolk live no farther than several hundred yards from the church, a practice required by law in the seventeenth century and continued in common practice in the eighteenth century. In the urban centers of Boston, Newport, New York, Philadelphia, and Charleston, the distances to church are even shorter. In rural areas of Virginia and the Carolinas, one may be a considerable distance from the church, but bells carry long distances in an age free of mechanized noise. Moreover, at the crossroads where the parish church stands, community is to be had, a gathering of kindred men or women, friends, rivals, other youth, servants, a relief from the monotony of one's own household and a reminder of a larger world beyond daily work.

Inside the church the public is also on display, not in a leveled democracy of souls equal before God, but in seating patterns that reveal social and moral standing in the world. Though community funds have built the church in one way or another, and rates (or taxes) have brought monies in support of the minister, the pews are likely rented to families according to rank to assure a place for their members. Where this is not done, the pews are still "dunned" by vestrymen or selectmen, who assign the pews to those worthy by the community's standards. Not infrequently men and women sit in separate sections of the church, but within this gendered arrangement the social order is still mirrored. Invariably, a place of honor near the pulpit is reserved for the minister's wife. Other prominent pews are auctioned or assigned to leading lay leaders or trustees who contribute generously and represented the prominent and wealthy families of the town. Some good spots are set aside for widows esteemed for their piety rather than their current means. The rest of respectable society from high to low estate fills out its pews in increasing distance from the pulpit, table, and, in winter, heat from a common stove (if there was one). Whole pews are rented by families without a single church member in their number, for divine worship is understood to be an obligation of the healthy whether or not one qualifies for membership. The wealthy furnish their pews to their own liking, adding improvements as they see fit, including more comfortable seats, armrests, and hand- and foot-warming stoves. All of these conveniences help sustain churchgoers through services lasting upwards of two hours, with sermons seldom lasting less than an hour irrespective of the minister's church background. Only in the remote corners of the church building are there any free and unassigned seats set aside for the poor or for slaves, who are likewise expected to attend services, but reminded of their indigence when they do.

The minister himself was a public man. Always called "Mister," a title derived from "My Sir" and reserved for the gentry and college graduates, the clergy thought of themselves as public officers and as the intellectual elites of their communities. Though other men in their congregations held more property and possessed more finery, few could equal their ministers in education or learning. Even after the Great Awakening of the 1730s and 1740s brought with it an increased emphasis on the personal piety of the clergy, the colonial clergy were overwhelmingly college trained and given to pride in their learning alongside their faith.

The minister was a public man in yet another sense, for his income was in all places a public matter. In New England, the Congregational minister was called by the church's members, but employed by the town. In New York, the Anglican clergy were in the keeping of an established church, but Presbyterians on Long Island and Dutch Reformed Christians in the Hudson River Valley and in Brooklyn used the power of the Crown and their status as recognized dissenters to compel local citizens to pay their clergy. Even in Pennsylvania, Lutherans had made use of town finances to pay their ministers. In Virginia, Restoration era laws had established the annual right of clergy to "16,000 pounds of tobacco plus their lawful perquisites" for marriages and funerals as support due them from their parish members. In 1749, the Virginia General Assembly gave Anglican rectors the right of permanent induction into their parishes, a kind of life tenure by which means they possessed their jobs and "livings," or income, as a property right that could not be taken away through mere action of a vestry, no matter how wealthy or powerful its planter members might be.

If colonial clergy as a class appear to the modern eye to have been respected and well provided for by their communities, it is because they were. The New England divine Jonathan Edwards received £840 in 1748 (the equivalent of approximately $72,000 in 2000 dollars, and nearly three times that amount in economic standard of living equivalence).[1] On the other hand, colonial records bear abundant witness to the fact that sometimes results regarding ministerial support fell short of a community's intentions or a clergyman's expectations. Sometimes these payment problems reflected a church-minister dispute; sometimes they signaled a failure on the part of the town to get its fiscal act together; and sometimes they were the result of a general downturn in economic activity that made it difficult, if not impossible, to pay the promised sums. On the other hand, the disputes can, at times, reflect an unrealistic sense on the part of the clergy of their true economic worth. Thus one must be careful about crediting too much the complaints of colonial-era clergy like Cotton Mather who wrote, "Only milk and ministers are cheap in New England."[2]

Historians knowledgeable about relations between ministers and people in particular places know that disputes over the payment of salaries occurred throughout the colonial era. Arguing that a sea change took place in the support of the ministry between 1750 and 1800, as does this book, will prompt the historian to ask, "So what changed?" Nothing and everything. Nothing changed in the sense that clergy out of favor with their people had trouble collecting all of their promised wages. Nothing changed in the sense that people and towns where money was tight often were slow to pay their obligations to the clergy, much as people are slow to pay any bills they can put off when money is tight.

Everything changed in a crucial switch in definition of who "the people" were who were obliged to support a minister and church. The definitional shift occurred so slowly over more than a half century that the change was not viewed for what it was until midway into the nineteenth century. Nevertheless, the path from public to private support of religion proceeded in one direction only in the years after 1750. The colonial revivals, starting with the Great Awakening of the 1730s and 1740s, liberated the conscience of women and men to follow and support ministers of their own choosing, men who possessed the experience of true religion and not merely an education and a contract with a town to preach. Even those who stayed loyal to long-term ministers and parishes began to do so with an awareness that they were making a choice while others were making a contrary choice.

Throughout the second half of the eighteenth century, there were constant reminders that the English colonies were, individually and in aggregate, more religiously complex than the inherited one-to-one relationship between church and state could comprehend. Boston, Massachusetts, alone featured Anglicans, New-Light Congregationalists, Standing Order orthodox churches (i.e., New England's traditional Congregationalists), early Unitarians, Baptists, and more. In Virginia, Baptists and Presbyterians, and later Methodists, were extending the frontiers of the Christian religion and competing for adherents in Anglican parishes, and they were financing their activities without assistance from Virginia's Assembly. These practices of differentiation would figure prominently in the 1785 debates in Virginia over whether to continue the long custom of state support, but also extend that support to "teachers of Christianity" beyond the Episcopal fold. When the bill for the support of religion was carried over from one Assembly session to the next, the Assembly printed copies of the bill and sent them out to the counties of Virginia, seeking comment. The citizens of Pittsylvania County were quick to petition the Assembly. Fifty-eight petitioners found the bill to be "based on principles so liberal and impartial, as to preclude the remotest jealousy of preference to any denomination of Christians" and urged its passage. More than four times that many Pittsylvania men signed an opposing petition stating, "With candor may we say the bill appears to be very unequal and unjust—for as the hearts of men alone can be benefited by preaching, it would be unequal to assess people in proportion to their annual tax—in that case individuals in many instances would have as much or more to pay than many numerous familys." Those opposing the bill worried about the way the bill might prove "subversive to all true religion," and they were concerned about their taxes, believing that "it would be distressing to have the money extorted from us and collected by a publick officer as we daily experience the consequences of a hand arm'd with authority."[3]

In the middle colonies, some taxing of the town to support the local church continued, but the exceptions and disputes between townspeople increased. The theory that a civil polity had but one ecclesial counterpart was stretched beyond both recognition and utility. The Bill of Rights (1791) ratified the existing state of affairs; there was no one church for all states and people. Many rejoiced in the legalization of this liberty of conscience, clergy included, for they would never be forced to support another religion chosen by Congress. They were slower to notice that the foundations of their own support had been eroded by the same guarantee. With the new principle of the "consent of the governed" came also a new principle of ecclesiastical support, one we might call the "consent of the gathered and willing." Citizens were still subject to local levies; state establishments in Massachusetts and Connecticut continued in pale versions of their earlier forms; state constitutions recognized God as the source of virtuous government; but religion as a publicly financed good was on the wane. What of public religion? The practice of religion in public persisted as clergy addressed legislative assemblies, led prayers on civic occasions, and carried on a ministry to the public as though little had changed. The Protestant clergy continued much as they had before the Revolution, but their status as officers of the state was for all intents and purposes gone. By 1800, religion was a private good, far more so than any colonial clergyman of 1750 could have predicted, much less desired.

CHAPTER ONE

Paying for God: The Genesis of an

American Institution,

1800–1860

In the early 1830s, Lyman Beecher—once a pillar of the Standing Order in New England and now president of a fledgling Lane Seminary in Cincinnati—traveled back to the East to look for money in its cities. The lectures given during Beecher's successful "agency" were collected and published in 1835 under the title *A Plea for the West.*[1] The lectures embody millennial rhetoric, high claims for the power of evangelical religion, education, and voluntary institutions to shape souls, and an ambivalence toward Roman Catholicism. Beecher claimed it was plain that "the religious and political destiny of our nation is to be decided in the West."[2] At root, however, *A Plea for the West* is a fund-raising tract that locates God's work in the Ohio and Mississippi river valleys and argues that eastern seaboard Christians ought to help pay for that work: "The thing required for the civil and religious prosperity of the West, is universal education, and moral culture, by institutions commensurate to that result—the all-pervading influence of schools, and colleges, and seminaries, and pastors, and churches. When the West is well supplied in this respect, though there may be great relative defects, there will be, as we believe, the stamina and the vitality of a perpetual civil and religious prosperity."³ All of these things required money and effort, of course. And so Beecher asked his prospective donors, "By whom shall the work of rearing the literary and religious institutions of the West be done?" His reply was this:

> Not by the West alone.
>
> Whence, then, shall the aid come, but from those portions of the Union where the work of rearing these institutions has been most nearly accomplished, and their blessings most eminently enjoyed? And by whom, but by those who in their infancy were aided; and who, having freely received, are now called upon freely to give, and who, by a hard toil and habits of industry and economy, and by experience are qualified to endure hardness as good soldiers and pioneers in this great work? And be assured that those who go to the West with unostentatious benevolence, to identify themselves with the people and interests of that vast community, will be adopted with a warm heart and an unwavering right hand of fellowship.⁴

In *A Plea for the West* we see Lyman Beecher engaged in cultural production at a furious pace. From the westwardly extensible myth of the American West to a polite form of nativist suspicions about the church of Rome, Beecher helped craft the nineteenth-century American mind. Still, his most lasting contribution came when he helped elevate fund-raising to an art form by imbuing it with a religious soul.

PAYING FOR GOD

At the heart of American religion lies a deep irony. Most religious accounts of why people should support their churches posit a relationship between human beings and a being beyond the human community. The only way to give money to God is to give it to a mediating human institution like a church, or perhaps to engage in direct charity on behalf of God, to provide a dollar or a meal to a beggar because that's what God might do if God were here and worked with the material at hand. Thus religious people pay for God in the sense of paying to be in relation with God through religious institutions they support, and they sometimes pay for God as one might pay for lunch for a friend who is a bit short of money. This chapter is mostly about religious people paying for God in the first use of that term. But it is worth noting that paying on behalf of God has also been an enduring feature of the American religious mind. Knowing what

God would want done is often answered in contemporary America by "What Would Jesus Do?" The power of the "WWJD?" question for contemporary Americans one century after it was posed by novelist Charles Shelton is that it deals with this discomfort of being called to act in response to the divine with only corporeal substance to work with. It also offers an easy-to-grasp incarnational theology based on the earthly work of Christ that fits nicely with the individualism of the American mind in both Shelton's time and our own. Jesus is, first of all, the model for how to act as a Christian in every situation. Second, if everyone would simply follow the model of the human Jesus, everything would work out just fine. Thus human salvation—or a pretty good earthly American substitute for it—lies within the power of the individual.

The perspective of this chapter is that of finance. The leading question, therefore, is how have the ways and means for collective religious activity been secured over time? Beneath the question of fund-raising technique, however, lie two other, more interesting questions: How have Americans dealt with the basic discomfort of paying for God? And how do the rhetorical, institutional, and theological choices they have employed reflect changing conceptions of what the religious enterprise is all about?

THE GREAT PRIVATIZATION

The disestablishment of the church in the United States is one of the most common themes with which historians of American religion have worked. Most European observers of the eighteenth and nineteen centuries were quick to comment on the fact that religion in America was free from government interference and that American churches were remarkably vital and tolerant of one another as a result. This is as the architects of the separation of church and state, James Madison and Thomas Jefferson, and others like the Baptist leader John Leland would have wished it to be, for they too thought primarily in terms of political philosophy and categories of freedom of belief, conscience, and expression, limited government, and the dangers of factions. Religion was to be free of government so that it might not undermine a multichurch nation's prospects. Viewed from another perspective, however, religious disestablishment was the largest instance of privatization in all of American history; it moved a large part of the traditional public sector into the private marketplace in a relatively short period of years.[5] For those portions of the ecclesiastical world accustomed to state finance—the Anglican, Reformed, and Congregational churches in the South, the mid-Atlantic states, New York, and New England—disestablishment was not a godsend delivered by political philosophy but a frontal challenge to their understanding of who ought to pay for religion and why.

To be sure, the growing toleration of dissenters in the years before nationhood had shown Americans that some churches could obtain voluntary support. But the private church system was in many respects an add-on to the basic religious service that each colony's towns and cities provided its people. Remnants of this outlook, even among dissenters, are visible in contemporary Western Europe and the United Kingdom. An American parallel is the system of public primary and secondary education for which everyone pays, though some also pay extra to send children to religious and private schools. The truly free-market-supported church was without parallel in the experience of the Europeans who colonized North America. Given the overwhelming political logic for disestablishment in the new nation, it fell to the religious bodies themselves to accommodate their thought and practices to the new economic realities. As the Revolution began, ten of the original thirteen states had some form of tax-supported religion. In 1833, with the final elimination of commonwealth support for the Congregational Church in Massachusetts, every religious group was left to its own resources.

During the nearly two centuries while religion was understood by early Euro-Americans as a public good deserving public support, a variety of means to finance religion evolved, much as a hodgepodge of user fees, licenses, and taxes is used to this day to pay for public goods. Many of these devices were carried over in some form into the postestablishment era. In the case of religion, there were poll and property taxes, which could be quite high. As late as 1838, Connecticut congregations were taxing their own members 0.26 percent of their property value each year, nearly double what they had been charged when the tax was levied more broadly in the state in 1810, before disestablishment. Such "taxes" amounted to a levy of approximately 5 percent of the income produced or producible from property.[6] Annual poll, or head taxes, were also common and ranged between forty cents and a dollar in the early national period, a time when the prevailing laborer's wage was just under a dollar a day. Connecticut churches rented their pews by auction, often with minimum bids set in advance. Massachusetts churches, which had sold their pews at the time of building (like a condominium), typically taxed the pewholders anyway on the value of the pew. Annual and special subscriptions were also used. The subscription book or list was a piece of paper on which households and individuals were asked to pledge a contribution to the church. The subscription was passed along to the next member of the community until the goal set by the church's leaders was subscribed or surpassed. The subscription only became binding on donors when the goal—be it for annual support, a missionary project, or a new building or organ—was achieved.[7] The permanent fund was another technique commonly employed by churches both before and after disestablishment. People made a pledge to a fund that would generate interest income to support the work of the church. In the South, it was not uncommon for churches to hold glebe lands that were rented out to farmers, or to hold human slaves and their offspring who were rented out on a similar basis.[8]

The dominant and established groups had enjoyed public support for their churches as public goods long enough that the values represented by the way such support was raised were disconnected from their religious messages. The churches were good for the public, and thus any means the public accepted for their perpetuation was as good as any other means. Those churches outside particular state establishments but who possessed European state church roots (Anglicans in New England and Presbyterians everywhere) tended to think like public churches and "tax" their members and pay their clergy regular salaries. Outsider and dissenting groups possessed a different view of the means of finance. Quakers, Baptists, Universalists, and early Methodists tended to stress the value of voluntary contributions as an concomitant expression of their ecclesiological preference for the gathered and separate congregation. One of the four founding pillars of the Free Methodists was the free pew, the idea that membership could not be conditioned on being able or willing to rent a pew. None of these groups was served by a clergy that expected to be paid like gentlemen officers of the state. Baptist ministers most often worked without set expectations as to pay at all, receiving the "free-will offerings" of their hearers instead. Nevertheless, these groups' dissenter and independent statuses prepared them well to hold the affections and necessary support of their memberships in the postestablishment era. Indeed, voluntary contributions and the rhetoric that cultivated them would become the norm in the American churches after the earliest years of the nineteenth century.[9]

The speed of the change from public support of religion, or at least its expectation, to total voluntary support was stunningly fast. As Rhys Isaac has shown with reference to Virginia, the attempt to accommodate the evangelical denominations by expanding the form of establishment failed to win any support. The plan had been to widen the establishment of religion to one in which every freeman paid a tax but got to specify to which church it went (much as was the case in late eighteenth-century states to the north). The Anglican gentry and even the Presbyterians recoiled in horror at the notion that "any layman, or mechanic, if he finds a motion within him from the spirit, may leap from the anvil or the plough, and in a few minutes go forth a preacher of the word of God" and be supported by publicly collected funds in pursuit of wild doctrines and disorderly gatherings of the faithful. The evangelical dissenters, meanwhile, believed that the real waste of public funds was their expenditure on the gentlemen clergy. For Methodists and Baptists, the gentry's clerics were "hirelings whose Chief motive and Design would be Temporary Interest." From the dissenters' perspective, if the establishment were removed, then the clergy who mistook learning for piety would have to compete in an arena where the true servants of the Church (the truly pious) would be rewarded by their congregations according to the measure of their service to the gospel.[10]

The early nineteenth century thus created a unique economic situation for all the churches of the United States. Even in New England, the formerly publicly financed churches were forced back on the resources of their memberships. Lay-led, itinerating, or poorly paid dissenter and outsider groups simultaneously evolved a model of ministry involving more paid leaders, as they were freed by law and circumstance to seek followers to their view of God and the gospel—a process that favored full-time, hired ministers free to pursue their calling in the extension of their flocks.

As they moved from the public sector into the private sphere, American churches had available two broad models for support: the private club and the voluntary member–supported institution. These support and financing models are familiar. In a private club, such as a country club, one cannot take advantage of the benefits of the club and its services without paying the assessed dues or apportionments. Religious groups that charged pew rents and ostracized those who used the "free" pews in the back of the church were employing a version of the private club financing. Another feature of private club–style financing is that the organization sets the price. If you want a place in the club, you pay the fixed price. In actual practice, pew-renting congregations often had "tithing men" or vestrymen who would periodically set the prices and assign and reassign the pews as families became more affluent, prominent, and able and willing to pay for more expensive seats closer to the front. In any case, the church set the prices for the pew.

In contrast to private clubs, public radio stations today raise their funds through the voluntary contributions of members from among their far more numerous listeners. The listeners, meanwhile, know that they do not need to pay the recommended membership fee in order to obtain the service. The stations, for their part, are aware that listeners might choose to go elsewhere and so do not press the issue of contributions too far. Most churches in the first half of the nineteenth century chose to go with the second financing route: to offer themselves as privately supported public goods (much as public radio does today). They did so partly out of conviction and partly out of the need to deal with evangelical competition. True religion had no price, and no man or woman should stand in the way of a believer meeting the Creator in any congregation where that Creator was worshiped. On the other hand, the presence of more than one Protestant church in most communities by midcentury also meant that clergy and congregations lived with the knowledge the members could go elsewhere. Yet the fact remained that someone had to pay for God and most especially for God's representatives; the priests and pastors had to be paid. So the die was cast: the American churches were to be dependent on the voluntary contributions of their members.

The decline of the pew rental system in the first half of the nineteenth century owed much to the struggle between democratization and gentility. Throughout the 1800s, Americans, who entered the century calling only their social betters "Mister" and "Missus," aspired to an ideal of generalized gentility while dismantling the institutions that gave social rank special privileges in church and society. They strove to affect the clothing and manner of refined persons while holding to a democratic rhetoric that suggested that social class counted for naught. Abandoned were practices involving formal class distinctions carried over from the eighteenth century, like the dunning of the pews, in which a lay leader assigned pews based on both bids received and the distinction of the pew holders. But the custom of dressing in one's best clothes for Sunday worship intensified throughout the century (as did the American taste for fashion in dress).

Social distinctions lacked for many defenders among evangelical leaders. The wealthy Tappan brothers, Arthur and Lewis, were instrumental in dismantling the practice of pew rents as a form of acceptable church finance. When they helped build Broadway Tabernacle in New York City as a venue for Charles Grandison Finney's preaching in 1836, they built it as a free church; no one was allowed reserved or preferred seats at any price. In this they were complying with the wishes of Finney that the gospel and a seat be offered on an equal footing to all who came, in accordance with his reading of James 2:2–4: "For if there come into your assembly a man with a gold ring, in fine apparel, and there come in also a poor man in vile raiment, and ye have respect to him that weareth the fine clothing and say unto him, Sit thou here in a good place; and say unto the poor, Stand thou there, or sit here under my footstool, are ye not then partial in yourselves, and are become judges with evil thoughts?"[11]

In his desire for "free" churches, as in his push for so many other innovations in the American way of religion, Finney was to have his way. By 1850, the practice of renting pews had been largely abandoned. The cost of that abandonment could be quite great. The $26.05 that Charles N. Bancker paid in 1833 to the vestry of St. James Church in New York City for his pew is equivalent to $457.82 in 1999 currency. The passing of the pew rent system left a substantial financial void for voluntary financing to fill.[12]

Just because Charles Finney despised pew rents did not mean that he had no expectation of financial support from Christians. On the contrary, he maintained in his *Lectures on Revivals* that "young converts should be taught that they have renounced the ownership of all their possessions and of themselves, or if they have not done this they are not Christians. They should not be left to think that any thing is their own, their time, property, influence, faculties, bodies or souls." God was now to be acknowledged as the rightful owner of all persons, and this evangelical understanding of total ownership and utter dependence on God was to drive a new way of looking at stewardship. The church would never overcome backsliding and move forward, Finney argued, "until Christians, and the churches generally, take the ground, and hold to it, that it is just as much a matter of discipline for a church member practically to deny his stewardship as to deny the divinity of Christ, and that covetousness fairly proved shall just as certainly exclude a man from communion as adultery."[13] A fine religious state was being created in which individuals were set free for voluntary action and convicted by conscience to perfect submission lest in their freedom they rob their God.

By 1850, voluntary support had been experimented with for over half a century and had acquired to itself a literature of advocacy and technique. Still throughout the early national era, this trend in church finance was a wonderment. Just how remarkable a feature voluntary religious support appeared to be in the context of recent Western history could be seen in the writings of Alexis de Tocqueville and Hector St. Jean de Crèvecoeur and most especially in John Carroll's correspondence with ecclesiastical superiors in Europe.[14] For the first century and a half of the national experience, American Roman Catholic history can be seen as the struggle between two groups in the church—one that believed the European Catholics did not appreciate the virtues of religious freedom and voluntary support experienced in the United States, and another group that believed American Catholics failed to appreciate what was lost in giving up on the goal of a unitary church supported by a unitary state. Meanwhile, American Protestants, given their own needs, developed a set of practices and rhetorics designed to sell people on paying for God that set the tone for religious fund-raising more generally. Catholics struggling in the antebellum years to maintain the loyalty of the faithful and to incorporate Irish immigrants in a rapidly expanding country embraced the voluntary support methods of the Protestant churches. Perhaps no Catholic leader grasped the opportunities inherent in the American system of voluntary support as well as Archbishop John Hughes of New York. Whether founding Fordham University on a purchased estate in the Bronx in 1841 or building St. Patrick's Cathedral in Manhattan, the native-born Hughes demonstrated a flair for fund-raising, raising new church buildings, and appealing to the pride of Roman Catholics to support their institutions in a manner commensurate with that employed by their Protestant neighbors. Hughes became the paradigm for the "bricks and mortar" churchman for the next century of Roman Catholic growth. Both groups—the Protestants in creating the rhetoric of voluntary support of the churches and (later on) the Americanist Catholics in justifying themselves to European questioners of going native—reveal discomforts, worries, and hopes concerning the ways these churches were developing in the American context. Indeed, both trusteeism and the Americanist controversy, the most vexing polity problems for the nineteenth-century Catholic Church, had their roots in voluntary modes of religious finance.

This was not the only time since the conversion of Constantine when churches had sought funding from private sources, to be sure. For centuries, cathedrals and parish churches were built in Europe, Ireland, and the British Isles on the gifts of the nobility and the pennies of the poor. Clergy had been supported through benefices (much like an endowed chair) and members of religious orders were often dependent on family members outside the order for support.[15] Still, the experience of most members of churches in making contributions was that small sums were voluntarily given toward specific charitable goals, or in the form of alms for the poor. The mental construct for this giving was thus that of charity, often called benevolence. When the American churches were, in Beecher's phrase, "thrown upon God and ourselves," their instinct for thinking about raising money for the church was to talk in terms of charity and benevolence. Given the demand for more money and more reliable flows of money in the antebellum years, the watchword quickly became "systematic benevolence."

Lyman Beecher, one of the most influential churchmen of his day, is often cited as a herald of the surprisingly good fortune of voluntarism. After spending the better part of his ministry defending establishment, he was to discover that being cut off from state largesse meant that the church in New England was on its own, which "created that moral coercion which makes men work. Before we had been standing on what our fathers had done, but now we were obliged to develop all our own energy."[16] Thus the requirement that churches be supported by their members served, in part, as a revitalization strategy. However, those who had to raise money were aware of the darker side of voluntarism. They called the practice of raising salaries for themselves and funds for their institutions "begging." From the founding of Harvard onward, the colonial colleges had been funded by "begging missions" back to England.[17] And the Anglican commissary James Blair had raised money for the development of new churches in Virginia and elsewhere by begging for it from English sources (including, we might add, from the public treasury). What disestablishment did was, in effect, to turn every pastor, however willing or able, into a development officer among his own people. The voluntary societies, modeled on British reform societies, as pan-denominational entities also helped set the tone of church fund-raising, even as they became congregations' chief competitors for funds.

THE TROUBLE WITH AGENTS

The antebellum eastern seaboard of the United States was filled with "agents" crisscrossing the land asking for funds for worthy causes and asking for a time in the meeting of particular congregations to place before their people a case for support. Contemporary accounts of these agents' testimonies suggest that the best fund-raisers also put on the best shows, with heroic and troubling accounts of missionaries in hot and exotic places, seamen given but rare chances to forego drink, gaming, and sexual vice for the pleasures of goodness, and slaves freed from vicious reprobate masters. Local church finance doubtlessly appeared a pedestrian cause after these tales were told. Nevertheless, priests and ministers often found themselves with the unenviable task of making an appeal for support alongside the agents for their own less exotic ministries. Out of this trouble with agents came a move on the part of ordained church leaders to push voluntary giving in a systematic and more controllable direction.

Pharcellus Church was a Baptist pastor and theologian. An 1824 graduate of Hamilton Seminary in upstate New York (now Colgate University), he had moved his moved his family to Rochester in 1835 to take up a career in teaching; a year later, he published one of the first books on the financing issues surrounding American church life. Often covering such issues as publisher of the religious weekly the *New York Chronicle*, Church observed the situation of agents of his day:

> The agent, conscious that his reputation, and perhaps his living, depend to a great extent upon the amount which he brings into the treasury of his employers; and finding an almost universal reluctance on the part of the

people to meet the demand, one having this and another that excuse, sets himself at work to make out as glowing a story concerning his object as possible; and to make it appropriate to the various classes upon whom he has to operate, he now touches the pride,—now the sympathy,—now the emulation,—now the fear of a coming judgment,—now the vanity,—and now the self-respect of his auditors; and watching his opportunity, when the crisis comes, he causes the boxes or cards to fly through the house, lest a moment's reflection should dispel the magic of his wand, and thus diminish the amount of the contribution. At such an appeal for money infidelity sits in the pulpit, and the devil laughs in the gallery.[18]

In writing *The Philosophy of Benevolence* (1836), Church embraced many of the same themes as his contemporary Finney, the chief of these being that becoming a Christian ought to make a difference in one's use of money. "There has always appeared to me something singular in the conduct of professors of religion, in reference to the use of their worldly substance," Church wrote. "If I mistake not, the cases are rare, in which the adoption of the Christian faith leads to any new modes of procedure, in regard to the use of money. It is not so with time, the gift of speech, or any other earthly blessing." Covetousness, the label current for unholy money lust in the 1820s and 1830s, was also a concern that Finney and Church shared. Church linked covetousness to the missing practices of Christian giving in this way:

> But do they ever confess that they have robbed in tithes and offerings, that they have not given as much money as they ought, that covetousness has taken a strong hold upon their feelings, and that this has caused their spiritual decline? No, never did I hear such a confession. And is it because they are innocent in this respect and never withhold from the cause of humanity and of money which they ought to bestow? Oh, that such a plea were founded in truth! It cannot be; for the great majority of those who are connected with our churches, either never give at all to religious objects, or at least, have no fixed principle in doing it.

Church believed, by contrast, that if a Christian should work on the Sabbath in the same manner as any other day, he would not be likewise regarded as having committed a trivial sin, but the voice of the church would be raised against him in "tones of reprobation that he could not mistake." The great difference was, of course, that so many more people were sinners of this particular variety and committed the sin of covetousness in private.

Pharcellus Church also believed that the rise of the benevolent empire was a salutary development in the life of the republic and deserved greater support. He recognized some might read his complaints to suggest that immense sums were not being annually contributed to the "different plans of human improvement." On the contrary, he maintained, "when we say that the number who act on a system of liberal beneficence, in the use of their money is small, we mean that it is so, in comparison with what it ought to be, not with what it has been." He recognized that he was living in a remarkably charitable era compared to other times, but he insisted that contemporary benevolence was only the beginning of what should be. His greatest complaint was that "among those who make it a point to give, . . . there is no fixed principle of action, as there is in supporting their families, [which] is evident from the inequality of their benefactions." Some were clearly doing more than their share, and some, possessing great means, were doing less than theirs. By contrast, truth and duty in the Christian life were uniform, "speaking the same language in every heart and producing the same results upon every life."

It is from Church, and particularly from a fictional account he provides in the *The Philosophy of Benevolence,* that we learn much about the climate of religious philanthropy in the 1830s. The religious causes of the benevolent empire were sometimes seen to be in direct competition for the support people gave to their local churches. Indeed both institutional types were young and in constant need of funding. In his story, "A Visit with Deacon Brooks," two agents visit a lay leader of a Baptist church who wishes to claim that he gave at the church and who wants to turn them away. Their lively ensuing disputations articulate both the common views Church wished to refute and an enduring cry for more money, more regularly given to solve the endemic need for special appeals.

The canvassers who visited Pharcellus Church's deacon Brooks were at pains to draw a distinction between the benevolence represented by their cause and the self-service involved in the wealthy man's contribution to his congregation:

> "Allow me to inquire, deacon B.," said the lawyer, "have you any plan of serving God and your generation, in the use of that estate of which you are made the steward? Do you render it productive of the greatest possible amount of good? From how many hearts have you extracted with it, the thorn of anguish? How many wanderers has it enabled you to direct into the way of truth and eternal life? Do you as regularly serve Christ with your money, as with your time, your voice, and with other earthly blessings? Have you yet yielded to the claims which he makes upon your worldly substance?" "As to that matter," said deacon B., "I have always

done my part to support my minister, and I take pleasure in doing so, for he is a learned and celebrated man, and I am instructed by his sermons. I have not been backward in paying my money, to repair and embellish our meeting-house, and to keep the parsonage in good condition. These things I have done as regularly, as I have provided for my own family. Why is not that serving God with my property?"

The canvassers, for their part, argue that in supporting public worship for his own benefit, and that of his family, deacon Brooks was "better than those who take no interest at all in matters of this kind" but had not made a charitable gift, for they asked: "Is not the instruction you receive from your minister, as well worth the money you pay him, as the labors of your school teacher are of what you pay him?" The author, in the guise of the deacon's visitors, was arguing for liberal benevolence extended beyond the church. He asked in summary, "What a numerous class of church members are in the habit, like deacon B., of reducing every religious enterprise to the same carnal rules of calculation? They will give, it is true, to buy a reputation for liberality, in behalf of themselves or their churches, but are totally blind to those secret influences which the scriptures represent as operating in the spiritual world."

Again, like Finney, Church wished to make Christians anxious in their duty. "If the church were to require at least so much as the adoption of a liberal system of beneficence in the use of earthly substance as a condition of membership," he wrote, "it would naturally lead to frequent exhibitions of the reasons of the duty. In this way a public conscience on the subject will be created in the church, which her members would be as fearful of violating, as they now are to break the Sabbath, or to be guilty of other misdemeanors." Without a discipline of giving that produced more money, ministers—but especially the agents of the causes—were prone to do whatever was necessary to keep their causes afloat. In Church's view, this left "those pious men" serving two masters: "They have been forced to divide their exertions between the two objects of creating the means, and appropriating them to the work of human improvement. And of the two, it may be hard to say which has proved the more difficult task."

Perhaps nowhere did Pharcellus Church write as honestly on behalf of the antebellum clergy as when he broke into open laments about how difficult it was to raise money. He thus introduced a line that became a recurrent theme throughout American religious history: the recurrent "if only" line. If only people would give generously without being prodded. If only people would understand their duty. If only the people in the church valued the godly life the way their pastors did. In Church's case, the lament of the clergy against the people on whom their support depended read this way: "Still, if the same men who have been chiefly concerned in our benevolent operations for the last half century, could have had the money which they have actually received, poured into their hands by the spontaneous outburstings of a charitable principle in the churches, so that they should have been left free from the care and expense of collecting it, how much more good might they have done!" Church compared the way money ought to be raised to a system for bringing underground water to the surface by means of obstructions and pathways. "Such is our work," he wrote hopefully, "in regard to the origination of benevolent funds. There is money enough in the hands of pious men for all our objects, that is now left to flow through the subterranean channels of this world. All we have to do is to afford them such instruction in the duty or giving upon system, and to effect such a change in the organization of the churches, that these funds shall be spontaneously poured into the treasuries of mercy and good will." Pharcellus Church knew that there was enough money in Jacksonian America to take on any vice and advance any pious cause. All that was yet needed was a system to get the money.

SYSTEMATIC BENEVOLENCE

By midcentury the move toward a rhetoric of systematic benevolence had inspired a generation of clergy in the directions Pharcellus Church had sought to move them. Not only that, but the American Tract Society, founded in 1825 to "make [Jesus Christ] known in His redeeming grace and to promote the interests of vital godliness and sound morality, by the circulation of Religious Tracts, calculated to receive the approbation of all Evangelical Christians," had taken on systematic benevolence as one of its central issues. In 1855 the society had 659 colporteurs—traveling Christian literature salesmen—on its rolls. Three of the popular titles they sold had been issued at the beginning of that decade. Parsons Cooke's *The Divine Law of Beneficence*, Edward Lawrence's *The Mission of the Church; or, Systematic Beneficence*, and Samuel Harris's *Zaccheus; or, The Scriptural Plan of Benevolence* became such popular tracts that they were being reprinted and sold thirty-five years later.

The author of the first of the tracts, Parsons Cooke (1800–1864), was a pastor from Lynn, Massachusetts.[19] Cooke's method in *The Divine Law of Beneficence* was largely biblical exposition of an older sort, wherein the writer searched the scriptures for laws and then closely argued the text when its revealed laws seemed strange to modern ears. Cooke, like many expositors, also did not hesitate to dismiss those worries that enlightened moderns brought to the text that would, on at least one reading of the text, undermine the text's authority for nineteenth-century Anglo-American readers. Thus Cooke went to extreme lengths to argue that the holding of property in common in Acts 4 and 5 was anything but a challenge to private property. "It is not asserted," he wrote, "that all gave up all their property, but that all subjected their property to a free use, so far as the existing occasions required. In a like sense, the disciples were said to have left all and followed Christ. Yet they neither alienated their estates, nor dissolved their families."[20] Already we can see that Cooke, like the other representatives of the Tract Society, was at pains to craft a middle way between the communitarian and utopian Christians of the early national period, who took their biblical insights to radical extremes, and the larger group of church-going people who already gave biblical precedents very little serious thought. He went on to read the Bible's account of the early church to be in perfect harmony with the structures of the American republic: "You will next observe, that these gifts were all freewill offerings. Each one's right of property was respected; no law imposed a fixed rate of contribution, and none required the whole of any one's property. Here operated that principle which we have already noticed, leaving individual hearts to spontaneous action, and yet securing a generous action. So much for the Christian law of alms, as it appears on the first page of Christian history."[21]

Having disposed of the fear that being Christian might compel the alienation of private property, Cooke went on to find in 1 Corinthians 16:1–2 a New Testament "Law of Beneficence" that was binding on all. Clearly, Christians were not to be so free as one might have supposed from Cooke's initial defense of property. The verses from Paul on which Cooke built his financing scheme read as follows: "Now concerning the collection for the saints, as I have given order to the churches of Galatia, even so do ye. Upon the first day of the week, let every one of you lay by him in store, as God has prospered him, that there be no gatherings when I come." From this followed the Law of Beneficence: "We have here, as we propose to show, a rule which binds all to the principle of setting apart, every Sabbath, or at least statedly, a portion of their income or their means of living, as God shall prosper them, for charitable uses."[22]

Cooke was no communalist, but he was a Calvinist, as became clear when he gave his view of why it was that human beings were commanded to be beneficent. "God is not dependent on us for the support of his poor," Cooke argued. "He could have so diffused the gifts of his providence as to have had no poor. Or he could so have fitted our frames to the world, and the world to them, that all the elements of human life and comfort would have been as abundant and free as air and water, so that, like the lilies of the field, the whole human race might meet every want without toil or spinning; and he might have published his gospel to every creature without our aid."[23] But the fact was that the gospel had not reached every ear and the poor and wretched were abundant. God had, instead, left the creation incomplete so as to call forth "co-workers" who would be blessed by becoming benevolent:

> The fact that he could have published the gospel and fed his poor without us, while he could not, without our concurrence in giving, secure to us the blessedness which attaches to those that give, indicates that his main design in laying on us the necessity of giving, was to give scope to our benevolent affections. For this end he has ordained that we shall have the poor with us always, in so many forms of human distress besetting our path, pleading at the bar of our conscience for the forth-puttings of that charity which is the high excellence of our nature.[24]

For Cooke, then, the work of redemption was summed up in one's becoming benevolent, "for all the ends of redemption accomplished upon man are comprehended in his renovation from a state of supreme selfishness to that of perfect benevolence." In Cooke's view, there were but two great purposes that God had placed before humanity: to take care of the poor and to spread the gospel. Both, of course, took money, and both were there for the purpose of enriching those who gave of their money. Or, as Cooke preferred to say, "the sum of the matter thus far is this, that God throws on us his poor, for the purpose of enriching us."[25]

With such a highly charged account of why Christians were called to benevolence, it is not surprising that Cooke would be critical of the forms of fund-raising that he saw about him in the 1840s. Throughout Cooke's tract there was an undercurrent of criticism of the way he saw the charitable causes of his day raise their funds based on dire depictions of need. He often retrojected this criticism into his exposition of the better way things had worked in biblical times: "When the poor Christians at Jerusalem were in great suffering, and the apostles went round to solicit relief of Gentile churches, their inspired letters, sent here and there, contained no rhetorical painting of the distresses to be relieved. In all that they said, there appears next to nothing adapted to draw upon the natural sympathies."[26] A proper solicitation, for Cooke, did not play on the emotions, but rather only appealed to reason. God was to be glorified and the "hearts of men" sanctified. That was reason enough to give to any cause. Not that Cooke wanted just a little for the work of the church. Indeed, in pointing to the lessons of "Old Testament Law" he found that "a conscientious Hebrew could hardly have spent less than one-third of his income in religious and charitable gifts."[27] Lest his readers worry that they could not afford so grand a sum, he pointed out that charity paid: "Nor did this generous charity hinder the secular thrift of the people. It was so adapted to their welfare, spiritual and temporal, and so sustained in the providence of God, that the people were prosperous or straitened in proportion as they obeyed or disobeyed this law. When they honored the Lord with their substance, and the first fruits of all their increase, their barns were filled with plenty. When they robbed God in tithes and offerings, they soon found that they had robbed themselves."[28]

Cooke's plan was for people to set aside large sums (as they had prospered) and have them ready for systematic distribution when need was at hand. He believed the great virtue of the plan was that "so many and great ends" were achieved by a method he believed universally applicable to rich and poor alike. Better yet, it was economical: "Most systems of finance consume a large percentage of the funds in the expense of collecting and the same is true of our benevolent agencies. But the universal adoption of this rule will, as we have seen, save what is now a great loss, which we suffer as the penalty of our neglect of the heaven taught plan."[29] And best yet, it did away with the annoying agents, for as Cooke saw his plan, it saved the expenses of itinerant agents "by establishing a local agency in every man's mind, and so commanding the gratuitous services of a thousand agents where it dismisses one."[30] The settled clergyman in Cooke clearly preferred the agent of the conscientious mind to the real-life ones with whom he was asked to share his pulpit.

A Congregationalist minister born in 1808 and living until 1883, Edward Lawrence of Marblehead, Massachusetts, made his case for systematic beneficence in a midcentury tract titled *The Mission of the Church; or, Systematic Beneficence.*[31] Lawrence's method was to argue more in the style common to moral philosophers of the era, relying on propositions introduced and proved (at least to his satisfaction) to carry the argument for what turned out to be a system. Unlike Parsons Cooke, Lawrence relied less on the Bible than on knowing comparisons to historical and mythic figures from classical antiquity. Despite these differences in method and style, Lawrence believed as strongly in systematic beneficence. Both the propositions Lawrence employed and the fruits he attributed to his system are revealing.

Lawrence's first proposition was that "a man's charitable contributions should be proportionate to the vastness and and importance of the objects sought in beneficence."[32] His second proposition was that "every man's charitable contributions should be proportionate to the adequacy of the instrumentality to be applied."[33] His third proposition was that "every man's charitable contributions should be proportionate to his pecuniary means and facilities for applying the instrumentality."[34] These three propositions meant, in effect, that since Christian beneficence proposed to secure "the recovery of the human race from sin to holiness," every person's charitable contributions should be vast because the job to be done was vast. To those who supposed that there was adequate remedy to be found in the church and in Protestant civilization more generally, Lawrence pointed to the decadence of Protestant-dominated lands whose civil law seemed powerless against amusements, avarice, or vice. As for the Roman Catholic Church, it thrived on what he saw as ignorance. "Let it but give an open Bible to the people," Lawrence wrote, "with liberty to read and think for themselves, and it bites the dust."[35] Lawrence believed that worldwide Roman Catholicism was not up to the job, for it displayed the full "defects of knowledge denied" and the effects of a "famine of the words of the Lord." If Protestants and Roman Catholics were lacking, he reserved even greater disapprobation for Muslims, whom he termed, "followers of the false prophet." He faulted Mohammed for having taken the Bible unto himself and thus "strangled the traveling lamp" of truth.[36]

Beyond Christian and Muslim lands, Lawrence saw lands shrouded in paganism (under which he grouped Hinduism and Buddhism, together with other Eastern religions) with even worse morality. Clearly, given paganism's use of "parricide," "infanticide," "sutteeism," "self-torture," "laborious pilgrimages," and "obscene rites," it could not be trusted to bring about the reconciliation of God to the world. And so the work set before the church was vast, and only the gospel was up to the job. The gospel, moreover, could only be extended to all benighted places if the faithful embraced a giving system equal to the immensity of the church's mission. Lawrence thus linked two great causes of evangelical Protestantism. The missionary crusade and a systematic way of financing the church were but opposite sides of the same coin. So ended the philosophical argument for systematic benevolence.

Lawrence was not content to rest having made a moral case for systematic benevolence, but rather went on to use most of the tract to demonstrate its superior efficiency and theological legitimacy. Lawrence believed that too many clergy had presumed too much about the knowledge of Christians respecting what God required of them and their property. "From motives of delicacy," he wrote, "religious teachers who receive their support from the voluntary subscriptions of their people, may have shrunk from the same degree of explicitness upon this subject which they felt to be necessary in respect to other Christian duties." He added, knowingly, that the difficulty many pastors had in obtaining their full promised salaries doubtlessly contributed to their reluctance to broach issues of giving. Nevertheless, he maintained that "the specific for a pastor to starve himself away from his people, is to decline instructing them in the duty of beneficence, and to withhold from them the knowledge of the wants of the perishing world."[37]

Lawrence would have ministers instruct their people in his plan, of course. This plan he presented as biblical and given for the ages. Less worried than Cooke about the implied threat to private property of the early Christian church, Lawrence neatly disposed of that worry by saying that what was important about the early Christians was their "entire devotion" and their selflessness.[38] The plan itself hinged on Paul's description of the Macedonian Christians, who, despite their poverty, on the first day of each week "laid by in store as God had prospered them" (1 Corinthians 16 and 2 Corinthians 8; Lawrence tends to quote from memory and combine texts).

As was predictable for attempts to argue that the Bible provided a sound blueprint for contemporary life, Lawrence started out arguing that there was no difference between the times when the scriptures were recorded and his own time. Fairly soon, however, he found it necessary to suggest ways in which the biblical system had to be adapted to current realities. In the midst of these compromises, one can see Lawrence struggling with an awareness that nineteenth-century America was more economically complicated than the first-century Greco-Roman world. Lawrence noted that to the casual observer the matter of how to be beneficent might appear to be a matter of income. He preferred, instead, that what a person gives be in proportion to the "sum total of his property," his annual income, and how much he could "earn by industry," "save by economy," and "spare by self-denial."[39] Each of these forms of proportionate giving were illustrated at length by reference to examples ordinary and heroic. Of the latter type, John Wesley, William Cary, and Mrs. Judson should serve to urge Christians on to self-denial, "the great law of our religion."[40]

The further Lawrence got into his plan, the less oratorical it sounded and the more it resembled a cross between a nineteenth-century business plan and the promises of a traveling medicine man. There were four basic ways to be proportionate in one's giving, reflecting economic differences in the standing of contemporary Americans. Wage workers and laborers could be expected to use the weekly period. The monthly period of determining one's giving was suited to small-business owners and shopkeepers. The annual period was best suited to manufacturers, men of great wealth, and to farmers whose incomes had such great seasonal variation. Finally, for capitalists of various sorts, Lawrence recommended setting apart "a portion of each gain in every enterprise."[41] The rewards for following this plan, which increasingly sounded like the rough draft for the Internal Revenue Code, accrued to individuals, the church, and society in general. Lawrence claimed that the "tendencies and advantages" of employing his system were as follows:

1. To diminish the expenditure of benevolent societies
2. To secure a larger number of contributors
3. To secure from each contributor an amount more proportionate to his ability
4. To give to charitable contributions the more scriptural form of free-will offerings
5. To make these free-will offerings the fruit of a more cheerful spirit
6. To give consistency and efficiency to the character of Christians, by bringing their life into harmony with their doctrines and professions
7. To raise the church in its charitable contributions to a more elevated Christian devotion
8. To promote union among Christians of different denominations, and thus increase the power of the whole church for the good of the world[42]

The last of the American Tract Society authors was Samuel Harris (1814–99). Harris wrote *Zaccheus; or, The Scriptural Plan of Benevolence* while he was a pastor in Conway, Massachusetts.[43] He later became a professor of theology at Bangor Seminary and was selected to be the fifth president of Bowdoin College in 1867 at the suggestion of his predecessor Leonard Woods. Harris, a graduate of the class of 1833, was the first alumnus to occupy the presidency. Said to have been uncomfortable with his roles as fund-raiser and disciplinarian, he resigned in 1871 and went on to teach at Yale University. Harris's later difficulties with fund-raising were foreshadowed in *Zaccheus*. The pains to which Harris goes to overcome objections to his plan convey a poignant portrait of the minister as a man hoping for an easier way to raise necessary funds.

Remarkably for a tract whose scriptural superscription was from Luke 19:8, "And Zaccheus stood and said unto the Lord, 'Behold, Lord, the half of my goods I give to the poor,'" one of the great claims made for scriptural benevolence was that it was not a response to the emotions. Scriptural benevolence, Harris wrote, "forbids giving merely from impulse, as under the excitement of an eloquent charity sermon, or the accidental sight of distress."[44] One of Harris's obvious worries was that people would be swayed too much in their giving by the emotions. Perhaps, too, he was afraid that the rhetorically superior appeals would win out against the Christian's duty to be systematic (read "rational") in his or her giving. Like Cooke and Lawrence, Harris derived his system from Paul's writings to the Corinthian church. In Harris's case, everything hung on the admonition "upon the first day of the week, let every one of you lay by him in store, as God hath prospered him." From this flowed a requirement that "charitable appropriations be systematic. It requires some plan, deliberately and prayerfully adopted, assessing on the income a determinate proportion for charitable purposes."[45]

Looking about him, Harris saw that the world of business was efficient while the church's affairs were a mess. He asked, "What shall we say of those professors of Christ's religion who show so thorough an understanding of the necessity of system in worldly business, so utter a neglect of it in their contributions to benevolence: who are full of forethought and anxious calculation to realize the utmost of worldly acquisition; deliberate and farsighted in planning, cautious in executing, lynx-eyed to discern an opportunity of gain, exact to the last fraction in their accounts, but heedless and planless in all they do for charity?" One can sense Harris's despair as a pastor and promoter of pious causes when he writes, "And Verily, 'the children of this world are wiser in their generation than the children of light;' but 'the children of light' show no lack of that wisdom, till they come to use property for the benefit of others than themselves."[46] Throughout Harris's book there are subtle and not-so-subtle hints of a ministry done in competition with a nascent consumer culture. The failure to set aside a store of money for the Lord made men and women prey to "vicious or luxurious desires" and waste money on needless "dress, delicacies, equipage, and show."[47] Harris believed that the "well-appointed fortifications of selfishness" required not the "light troops" of desultory giving, but a regular systematic program such as he proposed. Only a system would remove the excuses for selfishness he found so annoying: "I have lately given to another cause," "I give as much as convenient," "I have so many expenses," "I give as much as others." Only a system would "put Christ on an equal footing."[48]

Harris knew the cause of systematic benevolence was a hard one to sell. Compared to Lawrence and Cooke, Harris was less confident that a purely biblical case would convince his readers. Thus he spent a great many pages touting the side benefits of scriptural benevolence. He claimed that, among other things, systematic benevolence would dispose the giver to increase his contributions; be more convenient; promote savings as a barrier against the temptations of selfishness; prevent yielding to second thoughts; make giving more pleasant; and form habits of benevolence that would accrue to one's children.[49]

Harris also knew that what he had to offer was a lifestyle and not just a moral obligation. So it further bolstered his plan that benevolence had become one of the habits of highly effective antebellum people:

Beneficence tends to promote prosperity. It promotes industry, energy, and enterprise. The man has placed before himself a lofty object, suited to draw out all his energies. Henceforth he is no trifler, but an earnest man, sharing in the very sentiments of earth's purest and greatest ones. The grand idea of toiling to rescue the world from sin never mastered a man's soul without enlarging it, without stimulating all his faculties to unprecedented vigor, unfolding resources not imagined to be in him, and producing a concentration and perseverance of action, which cannot fail of realizing great results.[50]

Not only did beneficence concentrate the active life, it promoted the inward dispositions of sobriety and economy. These qualities also paid dividends, for as Harris wrote:

Such a course attracts the favor of the good, wins their confidence, and if the man be poor, or a youthful beginner, their friendship gains him employment and otherwise promotes his interests. Besides, being thrown into company with such, he avoids the temptations of evil associates. The habits of fidelity to his trust, of watchfulness, system, and exactness, which systematic benevolence forms, are the very habits to win for a young man respect, employment, and friends, and to lead to a judicious management of business through life.[51]

Systematic benevolence tended to restrain investors from making poor choices, in Harris's opinion, since they would have their eyes trained on things that truly mattered. The fascinating truth about Harris's book and so many others that would follow it is that the authors always end up offering their readers a "free lunch." They set out to get people of faith to do the right thing for theological reasons, but in the end they cannot resist winning their case by appeal to this-worldly utility. Perhaps Harris, more than most, was aware of what he was doing. As it turned out, he never wrote another book of practical advice; he turned his writing and teaching, instead, to purer problems, most notably the nature of God.

By the middle of the nineteenth century, the growth of the American economy and with it individual wealth and incomes gave some clergy reason for pause. The people whom they served were becoming more affluent, while they were merely scraping by or abandoning their charges with pleas of poverty. The causes they stood for—missions, education, the spread of the gospel through tracts, and Bible reading at home and abroad—received a mere pittance of the newfound wealth. One of the earliest full-length books proposing a solution to the problem of church finances combines a critique of the late antebellum economic system with a long technical explanation of how churches might assess their members to meet ecclesiastical needs. Its title, *A Practical Treatise on Church Finance with an Analysis of the Financial Plan of the General Conference of the Methodist Episcopal Church, South,* accurately conveys the second purpose, but it is in the critique where the Reverend W. M. Prottsman's passion most clearly appears.[52] Written in 1856, *A Practical Treatise* argues against the economic lifestyle embraced by most churchgoing Americans and especially Methodists, who especially ought, Prottsman believed, to know better. Christians in the South were becoming wealthy, but wealth represented ambiguous power—"to do evil as well as to do good."[53] Meanwhile, church life appeared to be full of opportunities to confuse personal pleasure with godly charity: "Giving money to 'consecrate amusements,' as it is frequently called, is in truth [giving to] our duties. Such are charity dinners, charity bowls, charity performances at theaters, &c. Those who *enjoy* this kind of almsgiving may well consider the poverty, distress and misery which they give their money to relieve, a great blessing indeed. Eating, drinking and dancing are strange sorts of self-denial!"[54] Prottsman also thought that his contemporaries tended to twist the meaning of charity when they repeated the classic excuse for not giving, that charity begins at home. "When charity begins at home," he observed, "it always ends where it begins." A man acting on this principle furnished "for himself and his family the necessaries, comforts, and even the luxuries of life," all of which he would term charity at home.[55]

Prottsman did not like a lot of the businesses he saw around him. While he endorsed John Wesley's view that every man had a duty to get all the money he could, he also suggested that there were limitations imposed by God as to the means of getting that money. In his view every occupation that produced evil, misery, or distress was a violation of God's law:

> Getting money by the manufacture or sale of spirituous licquors [*sic*], either by wholesale or retail, where reason indicates that it will produce evil, is forbidden by the moral law, and every dollar thus received is the price of misery somewhere. Getting money without rendering a fair equivalent in some manner; by gambling; by flooding the country with a demoralizing trash, called light literature; by desecrating the Sabbath; and by all and every means productive of evil, is contrary to the will of God.[56]

Prottsman was notably silent on the morality of money obtained by the labor of slaves. Still, as a pastor, he saw many common business practices that he could not condone, such as "taking advantage of the ignorance of others," buying cheap and selling dear, and "putting double prices on goods" (that is, placing a higher price on something than what one will accept after bargaining with a buyer). Even more bothersome for Prottsman was the magical way money could reproduce itself, "turning money over" in the parlance of the day, through financing inventories of goods to be sold. "One thousand dollars at twenty per cent. profit, *turned over* every four months, will amount in six years to $26,623.33. This is indeed a loving figure to many. And one which many religious duties would likely be neglected to obtain."[57] Everyone, it seemed, was getting rich by these means except ministers, widows, and other true Christians.

Prottsman believed that if the proper use of money was to satisfy wants, as his contemporary political economists insisted, then any use of money to beget wants was improper. Alas, all he saw about him were wants multiplying themselves. The purchase of a fashionable chair created a want for new parlor furniture to match it and before long "the old house, that was good enough with the old furniture, must come down to give place to a far more costly one."[58] After that it was time to upgrade the carriage, horses, and tack. But money spent the least bit extravagantly was money not spent in the church for holy purposes. Prottsman multiplied the census figures for Methodist real and personal property by 1 percent and found it to be equal to sixteen times as much as the same people had paid for missions the previous year. Where was the waste to be found? In useless jewelry, liquor, and clothing replaced for fashion's sake. To those who argued that fashion was harmless, and fitted humanity with a sense of art, Prottsman replied that it "costs more in one year than all the agencies of the gospel." To these wastes of money, he added spending on fashionable grave sites and reading the "sentimental trash" called light literature. Did some say that readers could be morally improved by novels? Nonsense—"if they teach a moral lesson, they stole it from the Bible." Worse yet, Prottsman had visited enough parishioners to know that such literature was increasingly prevalent in Methodist homes and bore "all the evidence of more general use than the Bible."[59]

When people did turn their attention away from consuming the goods of this world for promoting the values of the next, they too often raised support for those purposes by means of fairs, lotteries, and suppers. But money given for the pleasure of such frolics could not be virtuous. A church steeple might be erected by such means, but, to Prottsman's way of thinking, "every such fair is a loss by just the amount it supposes to gain." Christians could not be led to a life of self-denial by these means, and for Prottsman and other clergy, self-denial was the heart of the Christian life. Or at least the heart of *their* Christian lives. Take any Methodist Annual Conference, Prottsman argued, and the monies owed to their preachers would rarely amount to as much as one dollar per member.[60] Moreover, the same records showed that less than 75 percent of the owed claims (approved salaries) were actually paid. This caused many in the 1850s to leave their itinerancies in despair. Others, like Prottsman, remained in the ministry but noticed the growing disparity between themselves and the people to whom they preached:

> It is sad for ministers, whose business is of a higher kind, that the covetousness or dishonesty of their people should make it just and necessary for them to attend, with any anxiety to lower affairs. And it is a sad misfortune for the poor covetous souls who cannot be considered respectable unless they are in the church, that the ministers are not some sort of ghosts who neither eat nor drink, wear nothing material, and have no bills or toll to pay. How can the preacher give himself up to the word and to prayer, when he is constrained to serve tables? And how can he minister without distraction, when poverty and care, and want haunt and worry him all the day long?[61]

If things were bad for ministers and their families in the parish, they were even less stable for church dependents outside the parish. Prottsman reported that in one conference of some 18,000 members the validated claims of the superannuated ministers and widows and orphans of clergy amounted to $3,000. The monies raised by voluntary subscriptions for this cause beyond the local church amounted to only $600. These needy church dependents therefore received twenty cents toward every dollar they had been promised.[62] The only hope, in his view, was that Methodists would adopt the financing scheme adopted by the 1850 General Conference and recommended to the various annual conferences for their implementation. Though Prottsman's desperation comes through on nearly every page of his book, his cause was eventually triumphant not only in Methodism, North and South, but also in most of the other larger American denominations. These churches called their means of supracongregational finance different things—"assessments," "apportionments," or "*per capita*"—but each practice helped pay the core expenses of being connectional churches. How large these expenses could legitimately be and precisely what counted as a taxable cost versus a missionary activity that should be supported by voluntary contributions would vex church leaders for the next 150 years. Yet even in the Congregational and Baptist churches with polities of strong local independence, the idea that belonging to a state or regional conference or association conferred financial responsibilities on local fellowships was gaining acceptance.

Throughout the nineteenth century, the ways in which religious groups, and especially Protestants, raised the funds to pay for their activities became more and more steeped in religious rationale, biblical precedent, and the language of sacred obligation. Indeed, it is fair to see the history of gathering funds for church support in the years between the Revolution and the Civil War as a progressive sacralization of finance. Not only had the causes and benevolent interests of American religious life multiplied during these years; so too had the requirements for resources to fund them. The response of religious leaders to the financing challenge, as we have seen, was first to call for systematic benevolence. Increasingly, after the war, the rewards and sanctions of the total religious system were added to augment the moral case for systematic beneficence. These later appeals to the sacred came in several forms, as will become clear in chapter 3. By 1860, however, five basic ideas had become part of the fabric of American Protestant church life with respect to its finances. The first, of course, was that the church really was dependent on the voluntary gifts of its members. The next was that, left to their own devices, people tended toward selfishness. The third was that giving needed to be systematic, lest results be disappointing and unpredictable. A closely related fourth notion was that, appropriately for People of the Book, the Bible had something to do with the way Christians ought to give. And finally, resisting the other firm conclusions, was the idea—based in demonstrable fact—that the clergy were uncomfortable in their role as money beggars for the ministry.

In the years to come, these basic ideas about what the Protestant churches needed to survive and what prevented them from thriving would grow, change in emphasis, and reappear with new favorite terms attached to them. Older terms like systematic beneficence would decline in usage amid the cultural and churchly fashions of later eras. Yet at least one perennial problem was there to stay, that of how to support a growing religious enterprise in a voluntary society. And make no mistake, the Protestant enterprise was growing rapidly in the very period, from 1800 to 1860, when its financing schemes were established, tested, and revised. Not only the effects of the privatization of religion but also tremendous geographical expansion, population growth, and the religious changes wrought by the Second Great Awakening were altering the nature of the enterprise that was being financed. Perhaps nowhere is that more easily seen than in the choices American Protestants made in the religious built environment, for in America supporting the church was closely tied to supporting a church in a particular building at a particular location.

CHAPTER TWO

Capital Ideas: Building
American Churches,
1750–1860

For hundreds of years Protestants have raised money in God's name. From the beginnings of Protestant church life in America to the present, that money has been spent largely to operate churches. Next to clerical compensation, sheltering congregations has consumed more of the resources of religious groups in America than any other activity. These capital investments in conducting religious enterprise in particular places at particular times reveal the nature of the enterprise as few literary artifacts can. What they reveal in a few short words is the competitive dimension of American Protestantism and the concomitant contrary impulses toward assimilation (to be like other groups) and differentiation (to be different from and superior to other groups).

The history presented in this book begins in 1750. That year is not so much a watershed as it is a vantage point from which the future could be glimpsed, for already the division of a town's or village's community into several competing churches had begun in the aftermath of the Great Awakening. The fact of competition among congregations would come to characterize Protestant Americans' concept of the church so firmly over the next century that it is difficult to imagine the physical and cultural landscape of contemporary American society without the idea of competing churches. Indeed, it is to this critical period of 1750 to 1860 that we owe the prevailing American conception of the church. In the United States, a church means simultaneously a building and a body of people that gather for worship and fellowship. Despite theologians' and ministers' efforts, the word *church* rarely connotes something translocal, as in the Church universal, or even the United Methodist Church. Though the translocal definition is important to religious elites, the common meaning of *church* has steadfastly remained the place where one goes to church, or the places where others go to church. This highly localized understanding of the church also suggests the importance of attending to the capital expenditure choices that congregations made over time, since, in the Protestant context, these churches were not merely outlets of a larger enterprise, but rather expressions of a people personally and directly involved in the worship of God.

How do we approach the religious built environment if we wish to know the motivating values, ideas, and functions behind the capital investments of Protestants in their churches? I suggest that these capital investments provide significant clues as to how people dispersed over time and space have viewed the role of the church, seen themselves in relation to their neighbors, and indeed even formulated their conception of God and what God requires in a church. To examine these clues we will need to view the built environment like a series of skeletons left behind that disclose both function and evolving conceptions of what should be the function of religious architecture.

LOCATING THE SECOND CHURCH: THE CRISIS OF COMPETITION

The earliest Christian churches in America were built as the place for all the people of a given locality to worship. The early American church, no matter of what ecclesiastical tradition, was the early American town at prayer. Initially each church and community was premised on the belief that there was a single correct religious tradition, and colonial settlements through the seventeenth century were small enough to require no more than one physical instance of that tradition per village. The introduction of a second church in subsequent years was traumatic because it represented a breakdown in a prior and cherished communal form of life. It introduced the market and choice to a place (religious life) where most would have thought it undesirable, even unnatural.

The ability to choose one's church, one's denomination, and even one's particular fellowship and house of worship within a denomination is so fundamental to modern Americans that it is difficult for us to discern what a second church in town meant to seventeenth- and eighteenth-century Americans. Contemporary scholarship has also valorized choice as a liberating principle in American religious life. Roger Finke and Rodney Stark depict the rise of religious competition to be a positive good not only for the individual but also for organized Christianity as a collective enterprise, since more choices in how to be a church member resulted in more church members. For his part, Nathan Hatch views the voluntaristic religion coming out of the Second Great Awakening, with its high reliance on the power of individuals to choose to be saved and to choose the institutional means of their salvation, as nothing less than the democratization of American religion. Ministerial defenders of the prior social arrangement like Lyman Beecher, of course, had a much different view. Beecher's ministry in Connecticut and Massachusetts spanned the years 1810 to 1832, the very years when the Standing Order—or established Congregational Church—first faced substantial competition from Baptists and Methodists and finally had to compete on an equal footing for members and financial support. For Beecher, neither the rise of competition nor choice in religion was an unalloyed good. Later in life, he would come to comment favorably on the possibilities presented by voluntary associations of religious believers, which were, by then, an accomplished fact. Earlier, however, the rise of competition appeared to Beecher and his class of church leaders as undermining the leadership of the wise and thus the beginning of chaos. A Unitarian minister writing in 1837 lamented that "within a few years, a vast change has taken place in the ecclesiastical conditions of New England. The Traveller as he passes through our towns and villages beholds in every direction altar erected against altar. Societies competent only to the appropriate support of one temple have hastened to erect two, three, four, perhaps more."[1] Religious competition brought social transformation that was fraught with peril for the well established and promising but uncertain to those of lesser status.[2] Not just clerical self-interest in the absence of in-town competition, but also a communal value in the absence of competition—of being Dedham, or Litchfield, or Williamsburg at prayer—led communities to oppose the introduction of more churches.

Despite communal resistance, second churches were built in towns and cities throughout the late colonial period and these additional fellowships fell into two distinct types. The first type was the additional church built at some remove from the original center of the town near where the second and third generation of town inhabitants had been settled. Thus with local prosperity, population growth, and geographical dispersion, a new generation would establish a church of the same denomination three to four or more miles away from the old church. New church starts of this variety were painful to the community and to the remnant church members and adherents for two reasons. The preexisting congregation was somewhat depleted of its members. More important, from the perspective of the community, familiar and communal relationships of long standing were somewhat severed. This occurred as the sons and daughters of the old town's inhabitants stopped making the long trek each Sunday to the morning service followed by an extended period of time with family and friends for shared meals, conversation, and Bible reading prior to the Sunday evening worship service.

The pattern of introducing a form of religious and community competition through growth and dispersion was repeated in countless small towns up and down the eastern seaboard. The phenomenon has left its trace in the names of towns and the churches identified by their names. Towns with names like Barnett Center are linked to outlying places with names like North Barnett and South Barnett. The church at Guilford lies a scant few miles from another town with a New Guilford church. And places with names like "Midway," denoting a settlement grown up between two places the inhabitants thought more significant than their own, remind us of how the country was populated by Europeans and their churches. The institution of a large Sunday early afternoon dinner also serves as a lived memory of the way religious life set off time and experience for Americans, even as that material dimension of American religiosity and culture is largely transmuted into Sunday brunch or drive-thru hamburgers on the way to the children's soccer game.[3]

While a new church of the same tradition in an outlying settlement could be troubling, a new church of a competing sect within town limits tended to be much more communally disruptive. Quakers, Baptists, Universalists, and others who held to the importance of a gathered fellowship of believers posed an obvious challenge to the first churches of American villages and towns, whether they were established churches of the North or South, or simply the preferred European state church transplant of a Scots-Irish, German, Dutch, or English settlement in the middle colonies. Yet so did European transplants outside their normal "feeding ranges." Episcopalians were a threat to Congregationalists in New England, and Congregationalists and Presbyterians were perceived as threats to the Anglican churches of Virginia and the Carolinas. In each case, the core challenge was to the legitimacy of the form of belief and church life of the church that was already in place. Only in the six major American cities of the eighteenth century—Boston, Newport, New York, Philadelphia, Baltimore, and Charleston—did colonials ever achieve anything resembling modern denominational pluralism. Not coincidentally, these were also the first places where

Jewish synagogues were established.[4] In nearly every case, the more religiously cosmopolitan cities had first negotiated the challenge of expansion-driven growth within their primary religious tradition before they were forced to adapt to the challenge of a group of Christians who believed differently or indeed to a group of non-Christians.

If a new congregation from the same denomination up the river or down the road could be somewhat compared to an additional franchise of the same kind of fast food, then the introduction of a religious competitor within town is more comparable to an outlet for a truly competing brand with its different but substitutable good in the place of the one currently being purveyed. Thus Quakers and even Anglicans in seventeenth-century Massachusetts towns or Baptists and Presbyterians in mid-eighteenth-century Virginia were regarded with genuine dismay. The nature of the competition went beyond any possible analogy to modern consumer markets, for these competing forms of Protestantism inscribed differences in doctrine and practice, and until the twentieth century these doctrines and practices were widely viewed as systems of eternal sanctions and rewards. Given this insight, the truly surprising thing is not that American theological battles have been vociferous or that attempts at differentiating one denomination or faith group from others have been historically so strong. Rather, it is astonishing that a large measure of toleration between religious groups was achieved so early in American history. While most Americans by the late twentieth century came to see association with a particular Protestant—or even Catholic—tradition as little more significant than the choice of a brand of automobile to drive, earlier generations competed for souls with the conviction that doctrines and practices mattered.

Institutionally the churches and other religious bodies in America use the same processes that other human enterprises employ to structure their collective life and appeal to adherents. These processes are the twin techniques of assimilation and differentiation. In *assimilation*, the enterprise, be it a business or a fraternal club, or a church, adopts features that are popular with persons whom it wishes to attract. The way in which salad bars were introduced into every imaginable restaurant in the 1970s and 1980s or airbags into passenger vehicles of the 1990s would be a good case in point of assimilation. So too, as we shall see, would be the ways that Christian congregations borrowed from classic and vernacular architecture and from one another as they constructed the built environment in religious life. *Differentiation*, by contrast, consists of making oneself, or at least presenting oneself as different from and usually superior to other similar entities. Thus in the contemporary marketplace the slogan "Best of all it's a Cadillac" is used to differentiate an automobile that in purely functional terms (how much it can carry and how fast it can go) is strikingly similar to competitors selling for half as much. Religious groups have also made wide use of differentiation to communicate their values and preferability to people. While the tale of religious assimilation and differentiation could be told in the familiar terms of secularization, theological accommodation, doctrinal disputes, and intradenominational schisms and reunions, the built environment of American religious life has also served to physically articulate the feelings, aspirations, and practices of Americans living out their faith in concrete terms. Architectural style proves to be an especially important means of articulating similarities and differences.

FURNISHING GOD'S HOUSE IN A STYLE
TO WHICH WE HAVE BECOME ACCUSTOMED

Early Protestant Americans worked with two basic received forms of European church architecture. On the Atlantic seaboard, colonists either built "auditory" churches (geared toward hearing the preached Word) of the kind they had experienced in England, France, or the Netherlands, or meetinghouses suitable to their understanding of the church as a gathered body. Those groups with pre-Reformation roots tended to think in terms of the former, while English Calvinists and Continental Pietists tended to erect meetinghouses. All of the earliest churches were fairly crude in their furnishings and structure, but the material culture of early American religious life paralleled that of the domestic sphere. As with colonial cabinets and chairs, so with church buildings. Churches of either basic type quickly took on a new finery, and innovations in detail proliferated as more churches were built and as artisanship advanced beyond the stage of necessity.

Long before the Puritan period had fully passed, New Englanders and Virginians incorporated fine aesthetic details into their new churches. Indeed Calvinism's long shadow worked to encourage the sublimation of personal aesthetic tastes for fine things into church buildings.[5] That is, by building a beautiful church one could indulge one's taste for beauty and even a modicum of luxury without committing the sin of personal indulgence or ostentation, since the house of worship was at the very least a community house, part of a common-wealth and not part of one's individual wealth. On a higher view of things, the church was God's house and therefore worthy of any luxury or expense. Still, copying the features of contemporary homes when building God's house was becoming the dominant trend that would drive future changes in church architecture.

The impulse to model a church on venerable and therefore presumably sacred models of church architecture was continually at war against the impulse to adapt religious buildings to the contemporary uses and conceptions of the built environment. Thus debates about heating churches went on long after the general population had added stoves to their dwellings and places of work. Moreover, these debates were often clothed and complicated by religious arguments about comfort as a form of sin, discomfort as a form of virtue, and human ingenuity as God-given grace or creaturely hubris.

One theoretical dictum that fits most instances of church building is that congregations build when they must *and* when they can. They must build when they reach a certain size and have no other place to meet, such as the time of first settlement or when a building burns to the ground. More remarkably, people appear to construct or structurally modify their buildings whenever they can. A systematic reading of Robert C. Broderick's *Historic Churches of the United States* is bound to disappoint the antiquarian, for virtually no unmodified examples of American church buildings are to be found.[6] No sooner did the paint or mortar dry, than someone in a growing congregation began to think about the next building project. Thus countless churches built in the meeting-house style soon added bell towers, even in the South, where churches set at crossroads were too far from farms and plantations for bells to have any utility. Assimilation to a cultural ideal of "what a church should look like" was a powerful force from at least the eighteenth century onward. Two of the oldest remaining churches are good cases in point. The Old Ship Meetinghouse (illustration 1) was the second building to be occupied by the church in Hingham, Massachusetts, and was built just three years after John Norton, a graduate of Harvard College, succeeded the founding pastor, Peter Hobart, who had served the town since 1635. The actual building's frame was raised in three days in July 1681, and the structure was opened for worship on January 8, 1682. Roughly every thirty years thereafter, some major renovation was undertaken. A west gallery was added in 1730; the next year a ceiling was built below the beams and trusses that helped create the appearance of the interior of a ship, from which the church derives its nickname. In 1755, an additional gallery was added on the east side of the building together with a more fashionable high pulpit, and the older more utilitarian pews were replaced with substantial box pews with finely turned spindles and exquisite mortise-work cabinetry. A generation later, in 1791, the town voted to tear the church down and replace it with a new building, but the plan never reached fruition. In 1869, the pulpit and box pews from the 1750s were removed, having fallen out of fashion, and the church was redone in the auditorial style popular in the day. Finally, in 1930, a descendent of the

1. Old Ship Meetinghouse, Hingham, Massachusetts, Historic American Buildings Survey, National Park Service (Dorothy Abbe, 1959). Library of Congress, Prints and Photographs Division, HABS MASS, 12-HING, 5–17.

church's third pastor, Ebenezer Gay, paid to have the church restored to its early eighteenth-century state (see illustrations 2 and 3). The ceiling was removed, exposing the original timbers. The discarded pulpit was brought back, together with the doors that closed off the old box pews. Of the original eighty pew doors, thirty-two were found, many in the possession of the descendants of the original pewholders.[7]

The oldest house of worship still standing in the original colonies is the Old Brick Church erected in 1632 in Isle of Wight County, Virginia (illustration 4). The building is unusual in the sense that it is only one of three medieval Gothic brick-buttressed churches built in colonial America. It took more than twenty-five years to complete its construction. Yet it was much like the frame meetinghouses and churches more characteristic of the period in another respect. Throughout its history, it was often "improved" by succeeding generations, the most substantial modification being the large tower on its western entrance. Once again ceilings were changed; furnishings were replaced with woodwork-

2. Old Ship Meetinghouse, pews and gallery, Hingham, Massachusetts, Historic American Buildings Survey, National Park Service (photographer: Dorothy Abbe, 1959). Library of Congress, Prints and Photographs Division, HABS MASS, 12-HING, 5–25.

ing of greater refinement; and new windows were periodically installed, the last time being in the 1890s, when Tiffany glass was put in.[8] If one wishes to find examples of old churches that were not brought into conformity with later fashions, one must look to either the surviving meetinghouses of the Quakers or places of worship like the Anglican church built in 1728 in Saponey, Virginia. The Saponey church survived virtually unchanged deep in the woods of Dinwiddie County in part because subsequent parish divisions and population growth passed it by.[9] As one moves through the colonial period, newer churches —whether Congregationalist, Anglican, Presbyterian, or Baptist—become more and more assimilated to the Christopher Wren ideal introduced to America by James Gibbs in his *Book of Architecture, Designs, and Ornaments* (1728). One of

3. Old Ship Meetinghouse, pulpit, Hingham, Massachusetts, Historic American Buildings Survey, National Park Service (photographer: Dorothy Abbe, 1959). Library of Congress, Prints and Photographs Division, HABS, MASS, 12-HING, 5–26.

the most stunning examples of this assimilation is the First Baptist Meeting-house of Providence, Rhode Island, built in 1774.[10] Though utilizing the meet-inghouse form, resembling an enlarged family dwelling[11] in its main body, the building as a whole shared more in common with the Episcopalians' St. Michael's Church (1752) in Charleston, South Carolina (illustration 5).[12] The comparison is telling, for while Quakers throughout the seaboard colonies continued to build relatively small meetinghouses consistent with their status as oppressed or barely tolerated dissenters, the Baptists of Rhode Island had, after a century and a quarter, come into their own. The architecture of St. Martin-in-the-Fields in London or Old South Meeting House in Boston was increasingly available to all faith groups who could claim dominance—or at least a strong

4. St. Luke Church (Old Brick), Isle of Wight, Virginia, c. 1632–65. Photographed by Mary Ann Sullivan, Bluffton University 2002.

minority following—in particular communities.[13] Soon even Quakers and the African Americans who founded Mother Bethel African Methodist Episcopal Church in Philadelphia would find themselves building churches that assimilated in form to the emerging churchly ideal.

Not only did few churches escape "improvements" out of the drive toward architectural assimilation; some even were completely cast off. The Federal period Congregational church on the Litchfield, Connecticut, village green appears to have been unchanged over two centuries. It offers a silent witness to the apparent good sense of Connecticut River valley Yankees who built once in good taste and then left well enough alone. In fact, this church, built in 1829, had gone out of fashion less than fifty years later and been replaced by a wooden Carpenter's Gothic structure erected to match the Episcopal and Catholic churches of the town in that up-to-the-minute Victorian style. Henry Ward Beecher helped lead the fashion critics who arranged to have the old church moved off the green to a new location where it could serve as a public hall; he wrote of the church of his youth, "There was not a single line suggesting taste or beauty." The new Gothic structure was brightly painted inside and out. Right above the pulpit, worshipers were greeted by the painted invitation "Worship the Lord in the Beauty of Holiness." *Harper's New Monthly Magazine* reported glowingly on the structure in its March 1877 issue, but by 1929 that kind of

5. *Left*: First Baptist Meetinghouse, Providence, Rhode Island, Historic American Buildings Survey, National Park Service (photographer: Frank Farley, 1939). Library of Congress, Prints and Photographs Division, HABS RI, 4-PROV, 1–2. *Right*: St. Michael's Episcopal Church, Charleston, South Carolina, Historic American Buildings Survey, National Park Service (photographer: Charles Bayless, 1977). Library of Congress, Prints and Photographs Division, HABS SC, 10-CHAR, 8–15.

beauty of holiness had itself gone out of style. The Victorian Gothic was razed, and the 1829 church was brought back to its original location, with its former purpose restored.[14]

No sooner had a colonial mode become the established way to build than Americans were no longer colonials, but rather citizens of their own country. As befitted the new republic, it turned to classical Greek and Roman forms for inspiration. Of the two, Greek Revival architecture left the most lasting impact on the religious landscape. To this day, Doric and Ionic columns and capitals grace substantial entrances to churches that are otherwise of Wren/Gibbs derivation. The pioneering generation that moved west of the Alleghenies and the Appalachian Mountains at the end of the Revolutionary War built the same crude meetinghouses of rough-hewn logs that their ancestors erected back east. One of the most famous of these is the still extant Cane Ridge Meeting House (illustration 6).[15] But these churches did not last long in Ohio, Kentucky, Tennessee, or the territories even farther west. The idea of a "proper church" was already planted in the minds of settlers, and congregations were almost as quick to build new houses of worship as they were to found colleges and name their towns after the great cities of antiquity and obscure biblical locations. For many of the settlements, a proper church was more than a place of worship. It was a much prized mark of civilization. A fine church building (better yet two or three) was a sign that the community had arrived, a help in making the town a candidate for official county seat, and evidence that the Ohioan was the equal of his Yankee or Virginian cousin.[16] It is less surprising then to find that people of different denominations, particularly if they were wealthy, might well make a substantial subscription to the raising of a new church. They were investing not only in the private good of religion but also in the public good of their community. Thus, in town and county histories for the first half of the nineteenth century, accounts are given of prominent Protestant manufacturers, lawyers, and merchants making gifts for Catholic churches. This signaled the changing meaning of multiple churches. Some lay persons were clearly seeing churches as community assets, and they were sufficiently secure in their own faith that they could provide funds for a Catholic church for their workers or neighbors without worrying that they were strengthening a genuine competitor.[17]

By the time the old Northwestern Territory communities were on their second or third generation of church buildings, they had a few new choices about what style they would assimilate to. The Gothic form developed in the Middle Ages was beginning to be celebrated as the only proper and holy form for church architecture. The revival of Gothic led to great artistic statements like St. Patrick's Cathedral in New York City and to simply beautiful board-and-

6. Cane Ridge Meeting House, Kentucky, Historic American Buildings Survey, National Park Service (photographer: Theodore Webb, 1934). Library of Congress, Prints and Photographs Division, HABS KY, 9-CANRI, 1–2.

batten white wooden Carpenter's Gothic churches in thousands of small towns throughout the United States. (See illustration 7.) But more than any other legacy, the revival of Gothic church architecture, often mixed with Romanesque details, produced the neomedieval castlelike churches of late nineteenth-century urban America, a type most closely associated with the so-called institutional church, a development that would itself change the nature of the Protestant religious enterprise (the topic of chapter 6).

I n the years leading up to the Civil War, a lasting pattern was established for American Protestants and their churches. They built churches as needed, and they rebuilt churches and improved them as acts of devotion and self-expression. Each generation of pastors and people made the church building its own, bringing the fashions of the day from their homes into the house of God. All the while, they closely watched what other churches were building in terms of style and features. Mimicking one another, Protestant congregations assured themselves that no one church would pull too far ahead when it came to being attractive and offering the finest work of human hands to God. Yet in paying such close attention to competing churches, American Protestants es-

7. Minneapolis New-Church Society (Norwegian), Historic American Buildings Survey, National Park Service (photographer: F. W. Brown). Library of Congress, Prints and Photographs Division, HABS MINN, 27-MINAP, 5–1.

tablished a long-term pattern of nearly constant investment in local churches' capital stocks. Voluntaristic competition in American Protestant church life meant that keeping up with the Joneses' church would constitute a regular drain on church finances and a regular incentive to give more money.

CHAPTER THREE

Reinventing the Tithe

and Discovering Stewardship,

1870–1920

The years during the Civil War produced almost no literature concerning the finance of the Protestant churches in the United States. This is to be expected insofar as the nation's attention was clearly fixed on a colossal and bloody domestic conflict. By the time clergy began producing church-finance literature again in the 1870s, the United States was a different country with other concerns and revised modes of communication and travel. The next half century, through the end of World War I, was emphatically the age of steam locomotives, ships, manufacturing, the telegraph, the telephone, and electricity. The church fund-raising literature of these years bespeaks a great confidence in modernity, which is reflected in two overriding concerns. One was to deduce the correct biblical mode of supporting the church by reading the Bible more correctly than any readers had done before. The other preoccupation of fund-raising writers was creating the right modern system for attracting and collecting support. Along the way, nearly all church leaders would come to adopt the word *stewardship* to describe their aims and practice.

Edward P. Gray, an Episcopal priest, wrote *The Apostolic Treasury* in 1870 out of somewhat different concerns from those that motivated antebellum authors.[1] They had been concerned about convincing others to give. Gray was more interested in the details of the church's finances. Presupposing a churchman who was convinced of his duty to give, then how ought he to bestow his tithes and offerings? Gray noted that, given this presupposition, the usual answer was that people ought to disburse their gifts themselves. He then made an interesting list of the claimants on those funds, which provides a sense of all the causes he as a priest in Reconstruction era Minnesota was expected to promote: "Bishop's Salary; Clergyman's Salary; Parish Expenses; Parish School; Parish Charities; Diocesan Missions; Convention Expenses; Aged and Infirm Clergy; Orphan Asylum; Hospital; Divinity School; Diocesan Schools (Boys and Girls); Domestic Missions; Foreign Missions; Freedmen's Commission; Indian Missions; Prayer Book Society; Tract Society; Church Book Society, and Increase of the Ministry." Gray's list also demonstrates how much of a larger culture of organized Protestantism had already been established by 1870. Gray himself took these Episcopal Church causes as given. Yet how the conscientious churchman might respond to all the causes worried him. Gray painted a dire account of what might happen. The churchman "finds himself sorely puzzled, because he is supposed to know the proportionate demands and necessities of all these claimants." The giver hesitates, hoping for more information, but in the end does nothing or gives only to what seems to the most urgent cause. The result? "A good resolution is lost to the church for want of the ready means and encouragement to fix it into a habit."[2] Thus begins one of the earliest pleas for unified giving in the church, paralleling the development of "systematic benevolence" in secular philanthropy, which sought in these same years to gather all community resources into a single fund so that the truly needy might be most efficiently served.[3] Whereas most writers before and after Gray were concerned with enlarging the amount brought into the storehouse, Gray was mainly interested in the distribution principle modeled in Acts 2, by which goods were held in common after Pentecost and distributed "as any one had need."

A common fund, filled by voluntary offerings and distributed according to needs considered beyond the purview of the local vestry, was to be favored, and above all the pew rental system had to go. "The Church in England," Gray wrote, "is the poor man's church, by law and right, as well as the rich man's; but in America, the pew system has made it the church of the so-called respectable and well-to-do, and the poor have no common inheritance or recognized right in it."[4] As with pew rents, so too fairs, lotteries, entertainments, dances and the like needed to end lest the grotesque "parody on Christian liberality" continue.

All church finance, Gray believed, ought to be underwritten by freewill offerings, paid by rich and poor alike according to their ability. This might also, Gray hoped, improve the position of the clergy who were made to depend "on making themselves 'acceptable' to those who have paid for their pews, rather than to those 'who have the charge and government over them' in the Lord."[5] Better the bishops order ministry than it be the province of the rich.

When one such bishop, William Crosswell Doane, the Episcopal bishop of Albany, New York, reflected on the way patterns of finance disordered the church he oversaw, he pointed first and foremost to its effects upon the clergy. With eighty-four priests in his care, he had made thirty-four changes in appointment his first eight months in office. "Such a state of things," he lamented, "destroys the stability of parishes, breaks up and mars the efficiency of clergymen, and washes out all characteristic color and tone from the Diocese." The principal cause for these moves was low salaries. No clergyman's salary ought to be below $1,000, Doane thought, and "no parish ought to be without a parsonage. And bad as I think the compulsory celibacy of Rome is and I think it is *very* bad, I think that it is surpassed by the meanness that sets a premium on an unmarried priest because he is cheap, or looks out for a clergyman who has inherited or married a pittance of property, wherewith he can eke out the dolings of a stinted support."[6] An Otsego County farmer had asked for not too expensive a pastor, claiming that "we are content to be a place to *break colts in.*'" Doane knew all too well that they did break them, "in spirit and in energy." As a bishop, he was seeing the worst in humanity at work in the church. For Doane, the whole system of proprietary parishes was less than Christian. He reported his experience that "it has come to pass that, the 'I like, or I do not like a clergyman,' is the signal for his dismissal, or for such withdrawal of support, pecuniary and personal, as involves his resignation."[7] The worst tendencies of the fee-for-service arrangement were those that usurped the authority of the clergy.

For Doane and other Episcopalians (and Catholics, we might add), the American experiment had gone awry in the notion that a lay people aggregated themselves into a parish and called a pastor; then parishes aggregated into a diocese and elected a bishop. He complained, "It so happens that neither priest nor Bishop is so created; that the Church does not begin at this end. The power does not *originate* in the people. There are not people till there are clergy first."[8] Thus Doane was among the strongest advocates of a clerical view of the church's constitution. It is interesting to contrast him with his evangelical counterparts who had as their principle that the church was constituted by the presence of two or three gathered in Christ's name and by the idea that leadership emanated out of the gathered church.

Seminary leaders also voiced their view that the present plan of church finance was unwise. Dr. William Adams, one of the founders of Nashotah House, added his support to the idea of a common fund to support the clergy and linked its need to the evils of churches being sold and moved at the whim of their richest members. Writing in the *American Churchman*, he urged his mostly clergy readers:

> Look at St. — Church, New York, which the fashionables sold, used the proceeds for their up-town church, and a large congregation of baptized men, women and children were turned out into the howling religious wilderness of lower New York—a region desolated by Mammon. And the church was sold over their heads to be torn down, and stores built upon its consecrated ground. Every dollar of these funds had been given for GOD's service—every stone of the building had been consecrated, by Bishop and people solemnly praying and vowing it to GOD forever.[9]

Adams hoped that soon would come the day when all church property would be vested in the diocese, for clearly, unless that came about, the horrors of the past would be repeated. Churches would continue to be sold for stores, for manufacturing "Mexican Mustang Liniment, and worst of all, churches would be sold to Unitarians, Univeralists, Roman Catholics and Jews for their places of worship" unless the property rights were transferred to the diocese to prevent such sales. As for the clergy, they too needed to be insulated from the whims of the rich if they were to minister unmolested. And so a common fund was needed to assure no man on account of station received more or less the attentions of a priest than he deserved. If the church would take on these ideas, Adams believed, then it could "cast out many devils, and make room for much progress."[10]

REINVENTING THE TITHE

The search for acceptable ways to finance churches in a competitive environment was a transatlantic phenomenon. British churches, indeed, were looked to as models for "scriptural laws" and plans for church finance as much as they were looked to as reliable guides in practical divinity and ministry to the industrial masses. The nineteenth century had produced in the British Isles more ministries than apparent means of support, even in its established churches. Thus Protestant churchmen in Ireland, Scotland, Wales, and England preached the necessity of voluntary giving as part of a vast missionary enterprise that began with a recognition of one's duty to God. The Ulster Prize was given for the best essays advocating voluntary plans of support. These essays then were printed in Great Britain and reprinted in the United States by the independent tract societies and by denominational agencies such as the Methodist Episcopal Church's own tract society. Such tracts became popular resources among clergy and found their way into seminary libraries in multiple copies. One such collection was *Gold and the Gospel,* which contained an essay titled "The Measure of Christian Liberty [one-tenth]" by Henry Constable, curate of Athnowen, in the Diocese of Cork, and an anonymous essay titled "The Scripture Rule of Religious Contribution" that likewise proved to be a rule requiring a tithe of one-tenth of one's income and possessions.[11] The prizes offered for winning essays in the Ulster competition were as much as $600, or roughly half a year's wages for an average minister and well more than a month's wages for even the most princely compensated clergy of the time. On both sides of the Atlantic, evangelical Protestantism's aspirations for mission and ministry were outstripping its resources.

Tithing was attractive as a source of funding to the degree that clergy could convince themselves and others that it was a spiritual law, as unappealable as the laws of motion, force, and gravity. It was also obvious to these advocates of tithing that their churches had been getting by on a good bit less than a tenth of their members' money. Anything would be an improvement on the piddling sums they sometimes received from people of wealth and means. But the advocates of tithing were not prepared to accept less than a tenth any more than advocates of grape juice were willing to accept wine in the Lord's Supper. At various points in time, different biblical texts were key. Sometimes it was texts from Leviticus, sometimes ones from Deuteronomy, Genesis, or Malachi.

A short 1878 book from C. P. Jennings titled *The Christian Treasury; or, The Church's Sources of Income* made things utterly clear that had only been hinted at earlier.[12] Jennings was dean of St. Andrew's Cathedral in Syracuse, New York, and wrote to argue that the "tythe" was the only acceptable form of sustenance for the church and its ministers. A voluntary Old Testament tithe was biblical, still binding on all the people and in keeping with the needs of the church. Moreover, it was just the beginning of what church members were to bring forward, for according to the New Testament (again the precedent was Paul's Corinthian correspondence) Christians were expected to give freewill offerings according to how they had prospered. It was on the authority of Paul that church members were to support charitable causes beyond the local parish. Much as the Ecclesiologists, having rediscovered Gothic architecture, claimed that Gothic was the *only* way to build a church, Jennings asserted throughout his booklet that there was but one way to finance churches. What had been a better, more biblical means of church finance for midcentury writers was becoming, at least in the view of the Protestant clergy, obligatory: "Every one owes the tythe to Jesus Christ. Not less than one-tenth of a man's income will discharge the debt. It is to be paid before any other debt. Jesus Christ should be the preferred creditor; nay, more—no man has a right to pay his debts to another man with the property Jesus Christ personally challenges as his own. Furthermore, it is a debt to be paid before anything else can be called a gift, or free-will offering to Christ."[13] What earlier writers could have only hoped for, Jennings made bold to proclaim. "The sustentation of the Clergy is a question of honouring Jesus Christ as Lord," he wrote. "It is one of His appointed methods of rendering homage to Himself. The Clergy are the Christian official Priesthood. The Sovereign would feed them at his own table. He expects His people to furnish that table."[14] For Jennings, theological and practical considerations ruled out all methods for "furnishing that table" except the tithe and offerings. Among the practices he deemed unworthy, even "humiliating" and exceedingly questionable" were assessments, subscriptions, pew rents, fairs, festivals, and state support.[15] The primary methods of church finance employed at the beginning of the century were now, in its last quarter, largely being pushed aside for the methods bearing more fruit (even if still not as much as the clerics wished) and sustained by a rhetoric of righteousness.

In *One-Tenth for All; or, Proportionate Giving God's Rule*, an anonymous tract dating from the 1870s, the theme of proportionate giving and the amount of one-tenth are linked. Biblical arguments from Leviticus and Deuteronomy are advanced that one-tenth is the amount God has always expected. This is, therefore, a transitional moment in thinking about financing between the proportionate giving and tithing eras. More remarkable than the goal itself, however, is the anonymous author's excitement over what great things systematic giving of any form will do compared to what the church is used to experiencing:

> "*The first thing* to be secured," said a distinguished financier, in the late rebellion, "*is periodicity.*" "Periodicity" is the bed-rock of great national financial operations. Payments made at definite times and "appointed seasons," are the foundations upon which extensive business interests are conducted. As reliability in regular payments at definite times enhances the credit of any kind of commercial paper, so proportionate giving at "appointed seasons" is one of the means by which a more benevolent spirit can be developed and cultivated in the Christian Church."[16]

Gathering resources "little by little" promised to raise vast amounts without the pain that a large gift at one time might cause. Just as the federal government taxed lucifer matches one at a time, and railroads financed their stock by quarterly subscriptions, so churches might raise the money that needed to be raised. And, if another example might better strike home, the author noted, "by a small tax on their weekly wages, the sewing-machine companies have induced thousands of poor women to buy machines who would not have dared attempt the entire payment at one time."[17] Surely, when it came to improving giving to the churches, periodicity was the first thing to be secured.

In 1873, two southern Presbyterians, Alexander L. Hogshead of Abingdon, Virginia, and John W. Pratt of Lexington, Virginia, produced a set of scholastic treatises on tithing. The title for their treatises bound in one volume was *On the Gospel Self-Supporting*.[18] For his part, Hogshead argued that God as sovereign and redeemer claimed the worship of his people and that the acts of worship appropriate to their relationship with God were not arbitrary, but rather rooted in the nature of the relationship. Therefore, he ranked prayer, praise, and material offerings as chief among the creature's acts of prescribed worship. While prayer was an acknowledgment of dependence and praise a recognition and adoration of God's perfection, offerings were of two sorts. The first were sin offerings, or sacrifices, which had been obviated by Christ's atonement. But the second type continued to this day; they involved "the acknowledgment of God's ownership in us and our property, and hence of dependence and obligation, and the expression of faith, love and gratitude for material as well as spiritual blessings." Thus was laid the foundation for a pair of theological questions: If God required offerings as an act of worship and acknowledgment of God's ownership of all, how much of an offering was enough? And when one knew how much to offer God out of honor and respect, how was God supposed to spend the offering? To these questions Hogshead had ready replies. A tithe, or 10 percent, was God's everlasting minimum expectation. As to where God's money should go, Hogshead wrote that God "also finds a place in the practical work of the church, for the consumption of the substance his worship produces. Thus in his wisdom securing from this service a two-fold benefit—after paying honor to him and securing blessing to the worshiper, the product of his worship supplies the need for material means in the work of the church."[19] That Hogshead was attempting to gain the theological high ground there can be no doubt, for he went on to savage a pamphlet being circulated in the northern Presbyterian Church USA on the topic of ministerial relief for presenting the case for giving based on an "unscriptural" premise. The northern Presbyterians had sought to begin an actuarially based pension and benefits system and argued in their promotional pamphlet that "in that stage of the science of applied Christianity, there is not a single branch of the church that has taken hold of this matter in a scientific way, or put in operation a system worthy of the object or worthy of the age."[20] These claims struck Hogshead as offensive, since they were coming from men who had supposedly bound themselves to God's holy scripture as the only rule of faith and life. Did the church or its ministry need to be supported by modern business schemes? No, Hogshead thought, for God had already provided a perfectly adequate means for supporting the gospel ministry if only his people would attend to the scriptures. What follows Hogshead's critique of unscriptural means of church finance is, quite naturally, an extended explication of virtually every conceivable New Testament text having to do with support of the church believers' obligations to God; the aim was to show that these texts point back to the Old Testament, such that Christ and Paul endorsed Moses insofar as Moses represented the moral law that was not abrogated when Christ replaced the ceremonial rites and observances of the law.

In Hogshead's hands, therefore, 1 Corinthians 9:7–14, became Christ's plan for the support of his ministers. When the apostle wrote, "Who planteth a vineyard and eat not of the fruit thereof?" for Hogshead the meaning was clear. The church and her ministers were to receive a tenth part of the proceeds. For Paul "did not regard the law of Moses that provided for the maintenance of God's ministers as obsolete."[21] Maintaining such a strong place for the law in the ongoing life of the Christian church was characteristic for Calvinists. It's not surprising, therefore, that Presbyterians were among the first to rediscover the perpetual obligation of the tithe. Nevertheless, in another respect, in the way they exegeted the body of scripture with inconvenient omissions, they were like other evangelical interpreters of the Bible in the late nineteenth century. If a skeptical objector should note that most discussions of giving in the New Testament appear to be about voluntary offerings, the interpreters would handle it much as Hogshead did, by saying, "the increased privileges and the enlarged work of the new dispensation demanded a standard of free-will offerings, supplemental to the fixed law beyond the ordinary measure of the Jewish free-will offerings. The old fixed law of tithes, embracing first-fruits adapted to all times and obligatory under all circumstances, as the minimum standard, was unchanged. No converted Jew would think of falling below that measure."[22] The fixed measure then was a minimum. This idea would prove enormously resilient, offering as it did the hope of a great increase of church support without having to beg for it except as an obligation to God.

Alexander Hogshead also strenuously objected to the term most in vogue among ministers of the 1870s: *systematic benevolence.* Offerings to God could not be systematic benevolence, for they were Christian worship. Benevolence was not a feeling directed properly to God, but an expression of one's kindly disposition toward fellow human beings. While other pastors were promoting giving to and for the work of the church with terms like *benevolence, liberality, bounty,* and *charity,* Hogshead preferred "Christian oblations" or, simply, "religious offerings." "If they do not see Christ, and do not give it to him, then there is not faith connected with their giving, even when on system, and because of habit, it is practiced."[23] What Hogshead witnessed—instead of people freely giving offerings to Christ—was very few churches' taking up a regular offering as part of weekly worship and as a means of grace to be found alongside hymns, prayers, scripture readings, and sermons. Where collections were made, they were usually in his experience aimed at a particular cause—foreign missions, home missions, or for the printing of Bibles—and in those instances offerings were an on-the-spot response to the pitch made for a particular cause. This is important, for we see just how late it was before the weekly offering was introduced, in at least one region of the country, as the major means of obtaining a church's regular operating support.

If the Bible provided authority for an enhanced flow of compulsory tithes and voluntary gifts to the churches, it was ritual practice that sealed giving. During the closing years of the nineteenth century, the institution of the offering was recovered and enlarged in the life of American churches and afforded a central place in the liturgical practice of most Christian bodies. The collection itself was not a new practice; it was closely tied to the Eucharist in Latin Christianity. There it served as a collection for the poor of the congregation prior to the receipt of God's good gifts in the communion service. In American Protestant and Catholic congregations alike, therefore, the collection was not where the ordinary finances of the church were supplied. An 1875 liturgy order from the Brick Presbyterian Church in New York City reads, "At the close of the sermon the collection for the poor of the church shall be taken up. After the collection shall have been received, the minister shall announce in substance that, 'this church is now about to celebrate the Sacrament of the Lord's Supper.' "[24] This congregation was, like many other wealthy churches, still renting its pews, and the distinction between the collection for the poor and either rents or tithes was clear. Yet in other precincts, where ministers itinerated or preached only for the freewill offerings of those who gathered to hear them, the collection was becoming the ordinary means of church finance.

By the 1890s, the offering was everywhere becoming a weekly ritual whereby parishioners would "present their tithes and offerings" to the Lord, which would be followed by the singing of the doxology in recognition that it was God from whom all blessings flowed. A systematic approach had triumphed to the extent that the offerings themselves were often placed in specially printed envelopes with two pockets—one for church support and one for mission or benevolences.[25] The envelopes themselves helped add mystery to the ritual. Everyone participated, but, as the Methodist minister W. W. W. Wilson gleefully noted, no one but the pastor need know how much each gave upon "hearing of the voice of Conscience within him."[26] The offering ritual itself was usually bracketed by an admonition to "freely give as ye have freely received" and a dedicatory prayer following the doxology in which the gifts were dedicated to God. Indeed, the 1886 revision of the Presbyterian Church USA's *Directory for Worship* signaled the extent of the change. The word *collection* from the chapter called "The Preaching of the Word," and an entirely new chapter, "Of the Worship of God by Offerings," was introduced. The 1893 *Directory* from the southern Presbyterian Church US likewise added a chapter called "The Worship of God by Offerings."[27] What the magisterial Reformers had tried to purge—the idea that human beings independently possessed anything they could offer God—was restored to a central place of significance. The ritual of voluntarily offering up money to support the church and its benevolent activities was now accompanied by prayer, parade, presentation, and singing. The liturgical orders of the 1890s manifested the acceptance of this new essential element in American worship.[28]

ROBBING GOD

John W. Pratt's long essay on tithing moved significantly beyond Hogshead's in two ways. The first was in his determination to push the institution of the tithe back beyond the giving of the law through Moses to the time of Abraham; as reported in Genesis 15, Abraham made an offering to Melchizedek of a tenth of the booty he had recovered from the kings who had been robbing Lot and the king of Sodom. The name Melchizedek literally means "king of the priests," and in the Genesis account Melchizedek figures principally as a connection to the one true God. But for Pratt, since Melchizedek was a king and therefore probably richer than Abraham and had done nothing reported in the text to deserve such tribute, the payment of a tenth could only be the result of compliance with a preexisting divine ordinance. For Pratt the inference from these reflections was inescapable: "Tithes to God were ordained by God himself, and had become a law for every worshiper of the Most High before the time of Abraham."[29] Pratt furthered his case by quoting Genesis 28:22: "of all that thou shalt give me, I will surely give the tenth to thee." Clearly, Pratt thought, Jacob was observing the same divine ordinance that his grandfather Abraham had. And because Jacob was not even a Jew, much less a Christian, the case was clinched. The tithe was not caught up in the morass of Mosaic legislation, but belonged to the ur-religion of the first true followers of the one true God.[30] Pratt deals with this eternal obligation in a characteristically American way by assuring his readers that the claim for a tenth could not be enforced by any constraint of law. "The faithful performance of this duty depended solely on the enlightened and faithful consciences of the people," he wrote. Thus it was proven that "the law of tithes belongs to the domain of morals and not to that of ceremonials."[31]

The other significant development in Pratt's essay was the use of a new phrase that would be used extensively in the tithing literature for the next half century. The title of his essay was "Will a Christian Rob God?" Long after long subtitles like Pratt's ("Or the Tithe the Minimum of the Christian's Oblations") went out of fashion, there would appear again and again in the Christian stewardship literature the idea that the failure to give at least a tithe to the church was tantamount to "robbing God." Malachi, a Hebrew prophet writing in the fifth century B.C.E., became the model for the advocates of tithing, and not surprisingly, for he in his time had also argued the position of the priests against the withholding practices of the people. The key text from his prophecy appeared in the third chapter in the book named for him: "Will anyone rob God? Yet you are robbing me! But you say, 'How are we robbing you?' In your tithes and offerings! You are cursed with a curse, for you are robbing me—the whole nation of you! Bring the full tithe into the storehouse, so that there may be food in my house, and thus put me to the test, says the LORD of hosts; see if I will not open the windows of heaven for you and pour down for you an overflowing blessing" (3:8–10). From this seminal text flowed three ideas. First, not paying one's tithes and offerings to the church was not merely holding something back from a human fellowship, or expressing disapproval for the minister with one's pocketbook; it was robbing God, the Almighty. Second, the whole of the tithe needed to be given to the church, or storehouse, and thence distributed. This contrasted with the emerging practice of systematic benevolence in which individuals gave to a variety of philanthropic causes directly. Finally, the reward for trusting enough to tithe was the individual prosperity of "an overflowing blessing." Tithing businessmen who were asked how did they afford to tithe, could be expected to reply, "How could I afford not to tithe?" These three ideas, rooted in Malachi 3:8–10 and liberally applied to the American church, became the basis for the recurrent stewardship catchwords "robbing God," "storehouse giving," and "overflowing blessing."

Not all the church finance literature at the close of the nineteenth century was theological in flavor or took the tithe on as its subject. A Methodist minister from Freeport, Long Island, W. W. W. Wilson, commercially published a much read plan for dealing with annoyance of raising funds for so many different denominational causes. His booklet, *The Model Benevolent System*, offers insight into what the Methodist pastor was being asked to do each year.[32] In his church there had been separate collections for colleges, Freedmen's Aid and Southern Education, the Bible society, the tract society, church extension, Women's Sunday School Union, Conference Claimants, Women's Home Missions, Women's Foreign Missions, orphanages, general benevolence, and Pastoral and Church Aid. The problem for Wilson and other pastors was that each group had its literature, its story, its claim to lay before the congregation, and conference superiors and denominational board managers tended to view ministers as field agents for their causes, a role that cut into the pastors' sense of themselves as "spiritual leaders." Wilson also thought it made for poor fundraising since "usually collections are taken, when no one but the pastor knows they are to be, and the people often resent surprise that is given them and the want of confidence reposed in them by withholding their money."[33] Wilson's answer was to introduce a system that, remarkably, prefigures a late twentieth-century United Way workplace campaign. Each September the church would hold a Good Tithings Day. On the preceding Sunday, the pastor would present the causes in the morning and evening services at the times normally set aside for preaching. During the week, each member, friend, or child of the church received a set of literature from the causes themselves and an envelope in which to put his or her offering. On Good Tithing Day, a great deal was made of presenting the envelopes during "a long service," and the causes subsequently received a pro rata share of the proceeds. Wilson advised those who would embrace his system: "The Sunday School should be out in force though we do not think it well to reserve seats for them to sit in a body, lest the older people, who are to do the principal amount of giving, should be crowded out."[34]

Wilson offered other advice and incentives to enable pastors to survive this necessary evil. "The more attractive [Good Tithings] day is made," he wrote, the larger the crowd would be and, consequently, "the greater the return of envelopes." For pastors and churches that were still in need of help, Wilson would provide "the entire outfit" of cards, envelopes, and other materials for exceedingly low rates that would be quoted for a mere fifteen cents in return postage.[35] Wilson thus reflected his times, an era when there was a sure-fire system for everything. He also reflected his church—a church that was uncomfortable with seeking the resources to support all of the benevolent causes into which it had entered.

Not every guide as to how to support churches was an earnest treatise or even as serious as Wilson's plan. One example from England, which sold well in the United States, went to the other extreme. It was a book by the Reverend Gilbert Monk, a popular church literature author of such helpful volumes as *The Young Preacher's Guide*, *Where There's a Will, There's a Way* (which promoted the use of bequests), and *Manual of Short Liturgies*. Despite the book's pretentious title, *Pastor in Ecclesia*, it lived up to its promise to be a practical guide to "the art of money-raising."[36] Instead of appeals to what was scriptural, Monk condemned contemporary clergy for having too little interest in money and the business affairs of the world and urged them to demonstrate "initiative, vital interest, and concentration" on their labors in a businesslike fashion. The greater part of the book itself was taken up with the many exciting and vital ways a young curate-in-charge had raised money in his parish. Readers learned in successive chapters of the power of determination in dealing with church councils, and the gains possible through instituting a flower service, a rummage sale, a campaign for a new organ, a harvest festival, a tea, a concert, and the sale of Christmas trees. For Monk, it was not so much that people needed to be conned out of their money as that religious leaders needed to make new and great things happen among people who expected no change at all. Thus Monk represents another school of thought as to what was wrong with the turn-of-the-century church. For the tithers, the problem was that the church had lost its moorings in tradition; it was not biblical enough. But for Monk and many other church writers after 1890, the problem was that the church was too old fashioned, refusing to do something new, to offer amusements to elevate men and women, to meet the spirit of the age. Though few other stewardship books in the coming century would be quite as glib as *Pastor in Ecclesia*, the underlying dispute about church finance would prove lasting. This basic disagreement of purposes and means—whether money raising was necessary, but fun, or a deadly serious business—would continue to erupt throughout the twentieth century.

Nor did an emphasis on tithing completely displace older systems of finance where they were still found reliable. Pew rents continued into the next century to provide substantial income to some, usually upper-class, congregations. As late as the 1920s, H. Paul Douglass, surveying sixteen churches in American cities, discovered six still receiving some income from pew rentals. These included First Presbyterian Church in Detroit (50 percent of current income), Fourth Presbyterian Church in Chicago (34 percent), and St. John's Protestant Episcopal Church in Detroit (15 percent). One Methodist church in Brooklyn still rented pews, but only received a minimal amount of income from the practice.[37] Up through the 1930s, Manhattan churches in wealthy neighborhoods continued to have visitors wait outside before services until all pewholders were seated. More common in Methodist and Baptist churches, and in rural churches more generally at the turn of the century, was the subscription book method remembered by William Leach from his childhood spent in a Methodist parsonage in Western Pennsylvania:

> The Church stewards at the beginning of the year passed around the paper for pledges to the preacher's salary. This was the large item. Other papers paid for the coal and the hymn books. The big one was for the preacher. There was a treasurer, but most pledgers preferred to pay to the preacher direct. There was reason in this. They wanted him to know that they were faithful. So the preacher always kept a book to record payments which came to him.

> Sometimes instead of money it would come in the form of half a hog, or a leg of beef. Or he might trade out a pledge at the village grocery store. The preacher learned to watch his prices pretty well.[38]

Leach also remembered that his father's wages were never paid in full until right before the annual conference. The congregation would be in jeopardy of not retaining their pastor were they to fail to pay their agreed upon support, and so suddenly perhaps as much as three months back wages would come into the minister's household. Leach remembered this as the time each year when the pastor's children would get new clothes. Given these memories, it is little wonder that William Leach would go on to become the editor of *Church Administration*, the leading journal for those who would bring greater business discipline to church affairs.

STEWARDSHIP DISCOVERED

"Stewardship is a school for raising men rather than a scheme for raising money," wrote Josiah Strong, one of the leading Social Gospel advocates of his day. Strong spoke of stewardship for yet another serious group of church leaders who thought about how best to support the church and the work of the Kingdom of God. Although they were as serious as the tithing advocates, they located Christian obligation not in legal formulae but rather in the whole of life. Not just in their tone, but also in their orientation toward the use of material abundance, the stewardship writers were different. On the one hand, their work reflected a strong concern with the teachings of Jesus. On the other hand, their writings evinced a new understanding of economics. Wealth did not just happen. It was not purely the result of industry or good fortune. Nor was it shrouded in the mysteries of Adam Smith's "unseen hand." Instead, with the help of such figures as Richard Ely, himself a Social Gospel proponent and founder of the American Economics Association, they found that wealth came from capital invested in ideas and machines. This too was an age in which newspapers and periodicals were full of stories about the great men of wealth— John D. Rockefeller, Andrew Carnegie, Cornelius Vanderbilt, and J. Pierpont Morgan. Each of these fabulously wealthy figures had lived long enough to be no longer regarded as upstarts and crooks. Rather, most people saw them as men who had built something lasting. The American industrial dynamo they had wrought was generally considered a singular achievement. Though labor leaders and some muckraking journalists like Ida Tarbell would question the human costs and the business ethics of the magnates' ascent, there was virtually no thought of rejecting the steel, iron, rail, and machine age for a simpler, more rural life. Religious writers from 1890 onward gave their attention mostly to harnessing wealth and humanizing industrialization, not to questioning capitalism at its base. Thus two early figures of the Social Gospel, Washington Gladden and Josiah Strong, nicely reflect the spirit of the age that lasted from approximately 1885 to the end of World War I. One of the chapters of Josiah Strong's best-selling *Our Country* was titled "Money and the Kingdom."[39] After having depicted the many possible bad things that could happen to America if left untended to and all the terrific opportunities awaiting Christians at home and abroad for promoting the Kingdom of Christ, Strong turned to money and property as the keys to solving the problems and realizing the opportunities:

> Money is power in the concrete. It commands learning, skill, experience, wisdom, talent, influence, numbers. It represents the school, the college, the church, the printing press and all evangelizing machinery. It confers on the wise man a sort of omnipresence. By means of it, the same man may at the same moment, be founding an academy among the Mormons, teaching the New Mexicans, building a home missionary church in Dakota, translating the Scriptures in Africa, preaching the gospel in China, and uttering the precepts of ten thousand Bibles in India. It is the modern miracle worker; it has a wonderful multiplying and transforming power.[40]

After a while, Strong perhaps thought he had warmed too much to his topic, as he allowed, "God forbid that I should attribute to money power which belongs only to faith, love and the Holy Spirit." But still, he believed that money could multiply many times the value and effectiveness of other factors working toward the Kingdom. In his view the powers and principalities of this world would become "the kingdom of our Lord" once money power had become Christianized. As for other domains, politics, architecture, the schools and learning, and the arts had all largely been Christianized already. What remained was for "money power" to be Christianized. Were this to happen, a change no less revolutionary than the Reformation would befall the church. What was needed, Strong maintained, was not what leaders up to his time had argued for, more giving corresponding to "an enlarged estimate of the 'Lord's share,'" but a whole new conception of possessions. "Most Christian men need to discover that they are not proprietors, apportioning their own, but simply trustees or managers of God's property," Strong wrote. He hastened to point out that he did not mean that God owned everything in some easy-to-accept "poetical" sense that was "wholly unpractical and practically unreal." Instead, he wished to assert the right of God over not one-tenth of an individual's possessions but ten-tenths. The end result yielded a universal principle: "that of our entire possessions every dollar, every cent, is to be employed in the way that will best honor God." One who really accepted the stewardship outlook, Strong believed, could never think that he had discharged his obligation by consecrating a tenth to the Lord. "One who talks about the 'Lord's tenth,'" Strong observed, "probably thinks about 'his own' nine-tenths." Stewardship was about denying oneself, taking up a cross, and following Christ. As for wealth, there was not lack of wealth in the churches, even in hard times. Let the "rod of conviction and consecration" strike the "rock of selfishness," Strong predicted, "and abundant waters of benefaction would pour forth."[41]

Later church leaders have tended to picture the era of the great missionary advance as one in which church members gave generously to their boards of foreign mission. That was hardly the experience of contemporaries. In 1887, Margaret Woods Lawrence noted that the Congregational churches were probably the greatest supporters of the American Board of Commissioners for Foreign Missions. Yet, she said, if that denomination's members were to each pay but half a penny a day, that would more than double the largest amount the board had ever received in any year. She drew two other comparisons to reinforce her case. The amount spent by church members annually on tobacco could fund more than ten American Boards at their present level of activity. Change the vice to consumption of intoxicating drinks, and the expenditure would cover the expenses of fifteen hundred such mission societies.[42] The comparison says much about the self-image of late nineteenth-century Protestant leaders. At times, they saw themselves in charge of highly self-indulgent churches of people making ungodly choices with their lives, choosing smoking and drinking over spreading the gospel to foreign lands.

Lawrence, in particular, believed that the problem lay in the belief that giving to the church was "charity." As long as people categorized the church as an optional spending priority, they would fail to fund it according to its true worth in their lives. She quoted approvingly another writer who held that Jesus did not "solicit subscriptions" but, instead, commanded the work of his church:

> Putting all questions of religious culture aside, the church is a financial and social necessity. Tear down the sanctuaries of the city and suspend public worship, and what would follow? On the ruins of the churches would rise the grog-shop and the brothel. All classes of business, except those that minister to vicious indulgence, would languish. Men would fortify their houses like castles. Real estate would depreciate. Insurance companies would decline risks in such a godless community, not from piety but from policy. Unthrift would flourish, life be insecure, wealth a hazardous possession.[43]

Even if church leaders were to continue to request benevolent contributions, some believed that the churches needed to do a far more effective job in forming their members. John H. Vincent, one of the great figures in the Sunday school movement believed that what the church ought to do, the "Sunday-school ought to train its members to do." The Sunday school was naturally the place in which pity for "man's sufferings" and "honest, indefatigable, Christian effort for his good" should be kept before Christians. This entailed training in true benevolence, but instead Vincent saw mixed and questionable motives at work in Sunday schools: "We do take up collections for the cause of foreign missions, and in emergencies for churches or towns that have been burned down, blown down, or shaken down, or for sufferers from plagues, savages, or dynamite. Pathetic appeals are made, money is raised, the amount reported amidst applause from the crowd that gave it, and a record made on the secretary's book for future reference. And children are taught to believe that this is 'benevolence!' "[44] Children needed to learn about the world and to develop sympathy for all its parts and all the ways they might increase their love of neighbor, Vincent believed. He also alluded to the near monopoly the foreign mission boards had on collections among children.

Perhaps the apotheosis of the Progressive Era stewardship tract was John

Wesley Duncan's 1910 book, *Our Christian Stewardship*.[45] From the very beginning, readers encountered an author determined to be masculine and modern in his advocacy of the both the tithe and the concept of Christian stewardship. A prefatory note from William A. Quayle promised readers that this author was on the level: "He is sane. He has not a drop of the fanatic in his blood. He is wholesome and is talking about a business which must concern those who want to do a man's part in a manly business. To give, not as children, but as grown women and men, is fitting those who are to do the world's work for the *tomorrow*." For this sane man, nevertheless, the church of Christ had reached a crisis. The new battleground for the Lord was at home in the United States, just as much as it was on the foreign mission field. Doors were opening to teaching Christ in formerly closed lands. Millions of "foreign-born subjects" were teeming to "our shores." The question was put to Christians and the hour was now: "Shall we continue to play at missions, or rise to our opportunity, meet the great problem and solve it in the name and strength of our conquering Lord?"[46] Money was needed to help this war effort, and money and wealth were Duncan's subjects. Wealth was like dynamite, a great tool if used properly and destructive in the hands of an anarchist. Money was like electricity; it was stored power, and the question was whether the battery in which it was stored would do wonders, such as curing a severe pain, or cause death in an electric chair.[47] A clerk with a week's wages in his pocket had a week of stored effort to return. Would he invest by improving himself at the YMCA, send the money home to his mother ("Blessed be that boy who gives so much of himself to the best friend he has on earth!"), send the money to India for missionaries, or drink and gamble those wages to his own destruction in a saloon? The questions of stewardship were that personal and that globally monumental.[48]

Duncan soon turned to the tithe as the effective instrument to give what God needed, but not too much. Some said that to give all was the only true rule of Christ, he reported. This was nonsense he replied, for God commanded sensible, conservative, sustainable giving, not utopian schemes.[49] But the tithe was commanded nonetheless. Duncan knew he was up against doubters, but he was undeterred in his own conviction: "MEN ask almost sneeringly, How does it happen that we are just finding out that tithing is taught in the Bible? How does it happen that this question should be suddenly raised when it has been buried since the days of the Son of man? No one who has read history will speak in this way. It was not buried at the time of our Lord. It was born before history was born, and practiced by the peoples of this world for centuries before the Christian era, and during the Christian era until the time of Henry VIII."[50] It remained for Henry VIII, "this adulterous and covetous ruler," to remove the tithe from the civilized world. But ignorance did not excuse the debt, and the tithe was still due. Moreover, since Christ was due the tithe and was inseparable from the church, the church was to receive the whole of the individual's giving. And why not? "Is not the church less liable to make a mistake [in the use of funds] than the individual?"[51] The church might also have more dynamic influence in its community if its members would pay into the treasury their tenth and not fritter their charity away a bit at a time.[52]

Duncan's view of stewardship was both the old and new religion, combining biblical precepts and great collective mission programs on the part of well-organized modern denominations. But beneath all his aspirations for the acceptance of a robust stewardship was a hope that modern Christianity would finally move beyond being an activity in which only clergy and their female supporters had interest: "The ministers of Christ have led the great revivals of the past, but we verily believe that the next great revival is going to come from the pew, led and sustained by a devoted ministry, in connection with the bringing in of our substance to God, in the tithes and offerings prescribed in His Word, and from God's safes will come freely the money which shall send the consecrated missionary to the waiting harvest fields."[53] The alternative to a great lay awakening was too difficult for Duncan to bear, for "too often God's people have relied upon teas and suppers and socials, harmless in themselves, but to be despised whenever thought of as the support of the kingdom of Christ." God's church was not to be a beggar; it must exercise the first claim upon men's lives, talents, and money or all allegiance to the "King of kings" was hollow.[54]

STEWARDSHIP REVISED

Harvey Reeves Calkins's *A Man and His Money*, published in 1914, was a new kind of book in the field of stewardship studies. Calkins broke with a generation of stewardship writers who tried to make their case solely on biblical grounds. Instead, his book began with a short story and a long digression on the "pagan law of ownership." In the story, two boys fight over a piece of tinted feldspar found in a creek on their father's farm. The issue for the boys is whether the finder is to be the keeper, or whether current possession is, after all, nine-tenths of the law. Calkins's conclusion concerning these questions serves as an effective summary of his view of stewardship. Both boys are wrong to have argued for possession, for after all the fool's gold was always the property of their father and their father alone. The attack on the pagan law of ownership argued from history that most antique and contemporary views of property ownership were pagan—that is non-Judeo-Christian—however sophisticated they might appear to be. Great captains of industry and finance, together with poor laborers, were just as blind as the two boys in the opening story in believing that wealth was theirs to possess or covet. God was not only owner of all but also present in all: "God imminent is the wonder of the world. Nor does he indwell nature and mind alone. He is present in the world of trade and industry. The tragedy of commerce is the violence that is done to his indwelling Presence, for property and wealth, wages and income, are marks of his peculiar grace."[55]

Calkins was a former missionary to India, an effective storyteller, and previously the author of books on missionary experiences and an introduction to Methodism. His account of stewardship differed in tone from the stern and stuffy theological tomes of the preceding half century. It was modern in another sense as well, for in his attack on private ownership and wealth he parted company with a long series of writers who were afraid of sounding like socialists. Not that Calkins wished to identify stewardship and socialism. Still, he believed that the churches had "failed at an opportune moment to gear themselves to a changing social order."[56] He believed that secular socialism was a means of property appropriation with an incomplete goal that was properly only fulfilled by the stewardship of God's possessions. Stewardship played Isaac to socialism's Ishmael; they were blood brothers, but only one of them was fit to inherit. Calkins wrote, "Stewardship is the commanding social message that shall reach and shape the coming generation. That message, recognized and acknowledged, shall itself name a social program that will be inevitably Christian."[57] Calkins was thoroughly a Social Gospel man in his conception of the aims and purposes of the gospel. He was consequently critical of the roots of stewardship thought a half century earlier, writing, "The revival of stewardship did not come merely that church organization itself might be strengthened. The church is, or certainly should be, the bearer of the divine word to society."[58]

Stewardship in the hands of Calkins was becoming the organizing lifestyle of the people of God whether they knew it or not. Stewardship meant soil conservation in the cotton belt. Stewardship meant the support of the local church and missionaries abroad. Stewardship meant the choices made about what factories would produce and how the men within them should be treated.

At the time when Harvey Reeves Calkins wrote *A Man and His Money*, he was the stewardship secretary of the Methodist Episcopal Church. Calkins shared in the thinking of a generation of leaders in other denominations including E. B. Stewart, Robert E. Speer, John R. Mott, J. Campbell Light, Ralph S. Cushman, A. A. Hyde, William E. Lampe, F. A. Agar, and John Timothy Stone. These men were determined to place stewardship at the center of religious life; it was the outward manifestation of the life of praise and prayer, and every bit as important as the conventional forms of piety. Their's was an active Christianity, shaped by a renewed sense of human capabilities for social improvement to parallel the fantastic new technical achievements of the age. Transatlantic telephone calls had just become possible; the Panama Canal was open for business; motorized winged flight was moving beyond the experimental stage; and no section of the globe, it seemed, had not been reached by some brave gentleman explorer. It is hard to convey how muscular, hopeful, and grand the church writing of the Progressive Era was. It is, perhaps, enough to note that the stewardship men were among the leading figures in their denominations, not mere bureaucrats.

For more than a generation, Calkins's *A Man and His Money* was the big book in American Protestant stewardship. While maintaining the value of tithing and proportionate giving, Calkins also paid far greater attention to the idea that God was the owner of all things. To this end, he introduced a distinction between ownership and possession. Human beings were said to possess things, and ownership in the worldly sense of the term was just that—possession of a thing for the time being, but not to be mistaken for permanent control. This ownership/possession distinction shows up again and again in later stewardship materials for the first half of the century, including the 1922 book of women's Bible studies written by Mary Askew. Her *Christian Stewardship: Six Bible Studies for the Women of the Southern Presbyterian Church* was published by that Southern Presbyterian General Assembly's Stewardship Committee.[59] In an introduction, M. E. Melvin, the committee's general secretary, wrote that biblical stewardship was not only being rediscovered but was also the sole foundation for individuals' ordering their lives according to God's plan. As such, stewardship needed to command a greater share of women's attention: "A sense of Stewardship must come before personal evangelism, the Family Altar, or interest in missions."[60] In placing stewardship ahead of the family altar, Melvin was making a very strong claim, for the family altar was, particularly in southern evangelical culture, the center of women's piety. If a woman's domain was the home and her secular role was understood to be principally that of wife and mother, then her spiritual role was to see to it that her husband and children observed the worship of God in the home and attended to the reading of the scriptures and prayer in that setting. Melvin thus was pushing women to an enlarged sense of their vocation while also critiquing the boundaries that pious womanhood had heretofore observed. Indeed he believed that stewardship and women had a natural affinity for one another. "As the guardian of child life, the dispenser of the home income, the conserver of finer ideals," he wrote, "the stewardship message has a peculiar appeal to women."[61]

Mary Askew met her assignment of providing women with six Bible studies on stewardship by preparing extensive lesson plans packed with far too many scripture readings and verses taken out of context to support much in the way of discussion; but her method, not unusual for its time, was to produce a mountain of evidence supporting the basic theological position that she believed to be the biblical one. The general flow of her studies led to the conclusion that God was the owner and man the possessor and that there existed a partnership between the two. Human beings, though accountable for their stewardship, were inevitably liable to the sin of covetousness, for which only the gift of thankfulness could provide an antidote. Much as with other affirmations of stewardship of the period, Askew's biblical explications often gave way to self-affirmations and proclamations of the superiority of Christian civilization. Why some might ask were Christians in possession of a large portion of the material wealth of this world? The answer was clear, Askew thought: "There is a deep, underlying cause for such prosperity and material things by the so-called Christian nations, which we shall look into somewhat further on in these studies. Here and now let us see how often and how freely God the owner has given to man, even to those who neither know nor recognize Him as such, the full possession of the earth and the fullness thereof."[62]

It was in discussing women's opportunities as Christian stewards and their methods of meeting responsibilities as stewards in which Askew distinguished herself from the male writers of the period. Here she turned from the affairs of nations and the concerns of prosperous businessmen back to the domestic context that Melvin hoped that she and other women would rise above, writing: "We will all agree that the place in which we live constitutes one of the broadest of these [opportunities], whether that place be our own home or only our boarding place, a mansion or a bungalow of the simplest sort, one "hall bedroom" or a "place" for each season of the year. For every woman dominates (not domineers!) the place she calls "home" and may make it an opportunity for stewardship; or, shutting her eyes to this it becomes her largest opportunity for self-gratification."[63] Comparing modern times to those of the great woman of Shunem who opened her home to the prophet Elisha, Askew argued that today's women, in a time of "widespread luxury and household comforts," were holding back from offering true hospitality. Her contemporaries might complain that they had only one bath or no guest room or no maid any longer to serve the meals, but women must learn that it is not "what we share but how we share it and why we share it that determines our use of our homes as His stewards."[64] As with hospitality so with furnishings, "said a Christian woman, lately become queenly alive to her stewardship, 'I cannot let that picture remain

in my living room—I am sure it would not please Jesus were He my guest.'"
Nothing that would wound or displease Jesus, whether in material furnishings
or habits or customs, should be found in a home. Next in place to a woman's
use of her home as a steward, Askew believed, were her uses of the many
possessions that could not be bought or sold. A woman's true riches consisted
of such things as health, beauty, skill in athletics, "the blessed freedom of
American birth and rearing," education, cultivated tastes, good birth and a
godly heritage, dear family ties, memories of a Christian home, and "a full
knowledge of salvation through Jesus Christ." "How rich we are" Askew wrote,
"American women of the church of Jesus Christ!"[65] With all of these possessions, women must choose to throw them on the scale of the world for their
own advancement and success, or to put them into service of the King, for every
one of these gifts of womanhood could be used for the service of the Lord. "Is
your beauty leading men and women away from or nearer to their Father, who
gave it to you?" Askew asked. Of all of a woman's possessions, Askew believed,
the dearest were her children. There was no keener test of stewardship than her
willingness to give them back to God. Thus Hannah's dedication of Samuel
became the model of Christian devotion. Askew was also aware of the powers
that some women exercised outside the home. Nursing and teaching offered
opportunities for stewardship with women's lives. The newest form of such
power was women's full citizenship represented by the right to vote. Askew
asked, "Are we exercising our 'balance of power' in every community on the
side of His righteous?" It was women's duty now to use their power to change
things by the ballot as well as "by the ages-old influence women have possessed
since the beginning of time."[66] When she turned to other methods by which a
woman might meet her responsibilities as a steward, most of Askew's advice was
the by now conventional stuff of stewardship literature. But in two respects
Askew rang new changes on familiar bells. She argued that a woman who was
finding that her church, her auxiliary, or her circle or Sunday school class was
stingy in comparison with the ability of its members to give was probably
detecting a sign that the gifts given had not been prayed over. For no one who
prayed over a paltry gift could in good conscience feel at ease giving that gift to
God. Askew also spoke with a real depth of feeling about curbing personal
spending on luxuries. Was the fur coat really needed, or would a good service-
able cloth coat do as well? Askew sought to reinforce the traditional values of
Protestant thrift, not for their own sake, but for the sake of the stewardship of
the Kingdom.

The other great voice of stewardship in the 1910s and into the 1920s was Ralph
Spaulding Cushman. Cushman's appeal rested partly on his passion for the

subject and partly on his personal skills of persuasion. Like many princes of the pulpit between Henry Ward Beecher in the nineteenth century and Peter Marshall in the twentieth, Cushman was skilled at blending multiple short biblical quotations with snatches of poetry—Whittier, Wordsworth, Elizabeth Barrett Browning—religious prose—William DeWitt Hyde, John Ruskin—and sentimental hymns to achieve the emotional effect of ascent in his preaching. Cushman, born in 1879, began his ministry in 1903 and became a popular speaker well beyond the confines of his own Methodist Episcopal church, where he eventually became a bishop. He published five stewardship books, all between 1918 and 1927, and was a legend within church circles for the turnaround his ideas had wrought in his Geneva, New York, parish in the 1910s.[67] For Cushman, stewardship was not exclusively or principally about the use of material possessions. Instead, in Cushman's theology, stewardship summarized the gospel, much as for others of his generation the words "the fatherhood of God and the brotherhood of man" described the Social Gospel. Indeed many of the themes of the Social Gospel were interwoven with Cushman's theology of stewardship. So key was stewardship to his theology that he described it as "Jesus' philosophy of life" and "the very essence of the character of God."[68] Like other turn-of-the-century liberal Protestants, Cushman created for himself a canon within the canon that was nearly exclusively composed of the teachings of Jesus. The central message that Cushman found in the teachings was this: "when Jesus began to teach his philosophy of life he was compelled to seek for words with which to portray the true relationship of a man to God and his kingdom. It is an interesting study to list the words that he used to this end: 'servant,' 'husband,' 'child,' 'sons,' 'friends,' 'stewards,' are some of them. . . . Each has also the limitation of being unable to suggest the whole truth. Accordingly, no word is altogether satisfactory, but among these words the one that Jesus emphasizes most broadly covering the whole scope of human relationships to God is 'steward.' "[69]

For Cushman, being a steward was an all-embracing religious vocation. Jesus did not teach that the stewardship of money was the highest stewardship, only the "first necessary step into the larger and richer stewardship of all of life."[70] According to Cushman, the highest stewardship was that of personality. "Personality," of course was not a word that appeared in the Greek New Testament, but it was an important word to Cushman. For his readings of the teaching of Jesus had convinced him that Jesus' great innovation was to make the person supreme to all else but God. Therefore, stewardship of persons could take place when stewardship of things, including money, with their attendant covetousness had been overcome. All human beings were stewards; the question was just "What kind of steward?" People could test their Christianity and stewardship by asking the biblical questions "Am I my brother's keeper?" and "Who is my neighbor?"[71]

Although Cushman held to the centrality of the teachings of Jesus, he read the history of the Christian church as being rooted in the first Pentecost, wherein the spirit of God was accepted and expressed in the stewardship of holding all things material and human in common by the early Christians. Clearly, the church had fallen away at times—had fallen victim to its ancient enemy, covetousness. Yet Pentecostal awareness of God required, today as then, the consecration of property to God, and the appropriate amount now as always was 10 percent of one's material resources.[72]

As the years went by, the stewardship movement turned less and less on a God the owner/man the possessor philosophy and more on a conviction that the tithe was stewardship's bottom line. In 1926, a southern Methodist named Julius Earl Crawford published *The Call to Christian Stewardship*, a book designed to bring Christians to the tithe by any means possible. The book offered four different pathways by which Christians might reach the goal of becoming tithers. For Crawford, stewardship was nothing less than a synonym for holiness. It was "the life of sanctification." Therefore, he asked his readers, "if you had the power to make the Church, in one night, what you would like for it to be, what kind of Church would you make it? A praying Church? A working Church? An orthodox Church? A soul-winning Church? Or what? I would make it all these in one: *a Church of one hundred per cent Christian stewards.*"[73]

Since a church of stewards necessarily was a church of tithers for Crawford, the means toward tithing was less important than the fact that people became tithers. "Have you faced the tithing issues fairly and squarely?" he asked. Either tithing was a good thing, or it was not. His first route toward coming to the tithe was the legal route, and here he rehearsed the familiar "eternal Law of God" biblical arguments for tithing, with an additional nod to William Blackstone to the effect that a law remains in force unless repealed. Clearly, however, these arguments had failed to persuade two generations of American Christians who were becoming increasingly resistant to "the Bible says" commands from their leaders. Crawford next moved on to the "Efficiency Road." The cause of an empty church treasury, he believed, was also summons enough to become a tither. Once one realized that the church needed money for its great work, the remaining question was "How should that work be funded?" There could be only one answer to this query, for "the only financial system that God has ever given to his Church is the tithing system."[74] All other human-devised plans were inadequate, for, as the Methodist bishop Joseph S. Key had argued, "the Church can no more be supported by volunteer gifts than the State." Meanwhile Satan, making a rare appearance in stewardship literature, was said to be safeguarding his own cause by inducing Christians to temptation in money matters, and causing them "to rob God, to neglect their needy world neighbors, to insult Christ with beggarly pittances, and even to sell their souls, like Judas, for a few paltry dollars." All this sin could be easily avoided just by observing God's efficient plan for church finance.[75]

The third reason for tithing Crawford called the "Prosperity Path." Here he broke away from other writers of the Social Gospel era. It was fine for Christians to want to be financially successful; there was no shame in prosperity. But if one wanted the blessings of God, then one needed to deal fairly with God by giving him his due, the first fruits of prosperity. Crawford piled up story upon story of the near magical reversals of fortune that attended the simple commitment to put God first. He concluded with the simple admonition that people who wanted to be successful could not afford not to tithe. Finally, the highway to tithing was grace. Though Crawford put it last in order, it was decidedly his preferred path, observing, "It is the gospel highway. Pilgrims who come this way are Christian indeed in the amount, spirit, and design of their giving. They have washed their robes and made them white in the blood of the Lamb, and across their frontlets and upon their breasts is inscribed 'Holiness unto the Lord.' They have responded to the entreaty of love." Liberality, not law, was grace's measure of giving, but, asked Crawford, "can we truthfully say that a man who doesn't tithe is liberal?" Crawford's offering to the stewardship literature demonstrated not only a shift away from a single focus on biblical mandate toward efficiency arguments that were characteristic of the twenties, but also a turn toward gratitude as the motivation for giving that would grow as the century progressed.[76]

DID PREACHING STEWARDSHIP AND TITHING WORK?

Did all the efforts to preach the righteousness of tithing in its various forms work? To what extent did preaching stewardship find success as measured by behavior? Contemporary reports indicate that even instances recounted as the great successes of tithing revivals accomplished only partially their intended results. The *Indianapolis News* reported on a turn-of-the-century meeting of the North Indiana Conference of the Methodist Episcopal Church:

> Tithe-giving as prescribed by Scriptural law requires that we shall give one-tenth of our income to the Church. It is not very extensively prac- ticed, but according to Bishop Warren and other Church authorities at-

tending the Conference there is increasing evidence of a revival in the spirit of tithe-giving in this country. In one Indiana Church it has grown so rapidly that when its pastor read the report of his Church's finances before the Conference today, it fairly startled the other ministers, less fortunate in their pastorates. A large number of the members of the Redkey Church have agreed to practice Scriptural tithing and are conscientiously giving one-tenth of what they earn to God's service. The result has been that this Church has prospered greatly.[77]

The newspaper went on to describe the stunned reaction of ministers with larger churches that had not prospered in terms of giving to anything like the extent of modest Redkey Methodist Church. Many of the clergy "declared they were going back to their Churches to preach the glory of tithing," and the conference's bishop said that he had never seen the report "of this little Church duplicated in world-wide Methodism."[78]

What had little Redkey Methodist Church actually accomplished? An initial tithing band of eleven members had added to their number until they were sixty men, women and children, in all. This was an impressive number until one saw that the church's total membership was 367 individuals. Thus, in this congregational model of success, less than 17 percent of the members of the church were actually tithing.

Similar results were achieved in a larger church in Riverside, California. The Reverend F. P. Sigler, who felt a call from God to preach the glory of tithing tried to "secure a hearing" in Riverside's First Methodist Episcopal Church and finally got a platform for his views at a Wednesday night prayer meeting. He offered a "tithing covenant" patterned both on religious covenants and, particularly relevant in the case of Methodists, on the covenants and pledges of the temperance movement. Seventy-four of the members of Riverside Church initially signed the tithe covenant, and others later committed to tithing their incomes, so that 172 members—93 women, 68 men, and 11 children subscribed. This constituted 9.9 percent of the church's total membership of 1,022.[79] In cases reported by other writers, Memorial Presbyterian Church in Indianapolis eventually recruited 75 tithers out of a membership of 600, or 12.5 percent, and at the Third United Presbyterian Church of Chicago, led by one of that denomination's leading advocates for tithing, E. B. Stewart, about one-quarter of the membership, or 46 individuals, had agreed to tithe.[80] Even the redoubtable Ralph S. Cushman had to settle for a maximum 256 tithers at the Geneva Methodist Episcopal Church in his 1915 stewardship miracle.

Why were these instances of increased, but by no means universal, tithing considered such successes? The answer probably lies in the fact that the increases in congregational revenue achieved by even partial successes were dramatic and led to further hopefulness on the part of highly committed clergy and lay people in what might yet be accomplished for the Kingdom of God in their local settings. The results also caused pastors and treasurers to regard their congregations from a different frame of reference. In the Riverside, California, church, for example, 172 tithers paid in eight months $6,260, or an average of $36.40 each. The remaining members of the church, 850 in number, contributed during the same eight months $6.02 per member. From these striking differences, clergy were quick to extrapolate:

> If the entire membership of this Church should tithe instead of the 172, the average per member would be $51.06 per year, and this multiplied by one thousand, would give us the startling sum of $51,060, and from this could be supported
> 100 native preachers in India,
> 100 native preachers in Africa,
> 100 native preachers in Japan,
> 100 native preachers in China,
> 100 native preachers in Korea,
> 100 day schools maintained in China,
> and still have $27,060 left for the work of home missions in our own land.[81]

For the extrapolating clergy, there was a natural human desire to estimate the profit potential in a new undertaking. And, taken at face value, instituting tithing appeared to be a panacea. But its heralded effects proved to be less than they seemed, since separating out tithers from nontithers provided a frame of reference that made it appear that the tithing emphasis itself caused a sixfold increase in particular individuals's giving. To put it another way, the comparison of tithers with other church members assumed that, absent the tithe, all givers would be making the same low contributions to the work of the church as those made by the nontithers. In fact, tithing has, in most cases, simply moved highly committed and generous church members to become marginally more generous. In the Riverside example, the 16.8 percent of members who tithed were providing 55 percent of the church's support, which was actually less than the historic 80/20 pattern for Protestant churches, in which 80 percent of the support comes from 20 percent of the members. Average giving in the Methodist Episcopal Church for this same period hovered around $12.50 per member.[82] Annualizing Riverside's total giving produces a per capita contribution of

$14.84—something less than the windfall church leaders touted. Yet this 20 percent higher level of giving over the national average for the denomination was psychologically gratifying and often provided the financial breathing room for congregations to pay their pastors somewhat more, pay their bills, increase mission giving, and even begin dreaming about adding to their buildings. In the places where it was perceived to work, tithing was more important for boosting the mood of the congregation than it was for improving the bottom line in the short term. A congregation in which some were willing to sign a tithing covenant and actually give a tenth of their incomes to the church was bound to be a congregation in which a critical mass of parishioners had a stake in the success of the mission.

It was common for ministers, in order to figure out whether they were getting their fair share of church members' incomes, to calculate what a tenth of average per capita income would generate for their enterprise. Using 1920 census figures, Julius Earl Crawford found that per capita income was $586 and that there were 25 million Protestant church members in the country; thus the minimum for the "Lord's share" ought to be $1,465,000,000. In reality, total Protestant giving for 1922 was, at most, $445,626,545. For Crawford, the unpaid Protestant tithe was over a billion dollars. On the other hand, these same figures suggest that American Protestants as a group were allocating 3 percent of their pretax gross incomes to their churches.[83] A half century of preaching and teaching the tithe, and of framing Christian attitudes toward possessions under the rubric of stewardship, had not produced a nation of Protestant tithers. Nor had that half century of effort dimmed the clergy's hopes that their people might yet be more generous.

CHAPTER FOUR

Paying the Clergy:
Officials, Professionals,
or Servants?

L
eadership by a paid professional class constitutes the rule in
American Protestantism. As dangerous as a "hireling ministry"
may have seemed to Protestants like Roger Williams and early
American Quakers, most have preferred to have a paid leader. Whenever anyone employs someone, a labor relations situation is automat-
ically created. That applies to organized Protestantism in America, but
while clergy are clearly labor, determining who constitutes management is more difficult than in most business enterprises. The economic
fortunes of organized Protestantism have been so linked to those of the
clergy that the clergy may be forgiven for gauging the health of their
faith communities by their own economic success and job satisfaction.
This chapter is a brief inquiry into the patterns of paying American
ministers and the historical meaning of those patterns.

THE DIGNITY OF HIS OFFICE

The ministry began the eighteenth century in the English colonies at the top of
the professional pyramid. Ministers were gentlemen, and only gentlemen were

fit to be ministers. They were in the classics and the liberal arts. Entry into the clergy was tightly controlled through unwritten patterns of authority. Lawyers and physicians, though also the beneficiaries of liberal educations, ranked socially below the colonial clergy in the seventeenth century. During the course of the eighteenth century, clerical social standing declined relative to the increasingly successful Atlantic merchant families. The revolution and its aftermath raised the status of the lawyers, such that John Adams would confide to his diary with evident delight, "How greatly elevated above the Common People and above the Divines is this lawyer."[1] Still, clergy remained classed without question as gentlemen, and the ministry was an office that, like military leadership, could confer a genteel status not tied to wealth or family origins.

Learned discernment of the scriptures was at the heart of colonial ministerial authority. In a society of people more interested than most before or after them in religious questions, the clergy were schooled in the ancient languages, theology, and moral philosophy through which such questions were approached.

The Great Awakening undermined the authority of the profession because a second religious principle—that of the direct experience of the reality of God— entered into the North American scene as an expectation placed on religious leaders. Clergy had always been expected to be of high moral character and exemplary, but this was a standard applied to any true gentleman. Thus a clergyman was assumed to be knowledgeable about his subject matter and to practice what he preached. The new expectation that ministers should display personal passion, reflective of their own saving experience of God, was a requirement no amount of education, wealth, or good breeding could guarantee. Moreover, the fact that itinerating revivalists might equal or outdo settled ministers as regenerate preachers would prove with time to be just as damaging to the public office of ministry as revival opponents predicted.[2]

Even before Adams had noted the relative decline of the clergy, ministers themselves were paying attention to what they were paid and how their pay compared with that of other callings. Indeed, every generation of American clergy has closely monitored its income levels as signs of worth and status. Of course, the worries of those supported by churches go back further, at least as far back as the New Testament church, in which the right of ministers to honor and support was asserted with the reminder that "the laborer is worthy of his wages" (Luke 10:7; 1 Timothy 5:18). In the American context, clerical support was a topic of interest in the English colonies from the earliest days. Both Increase Mather and his son Cotton wrote pamphlets urging that people of churches and towns do justice to the ministers who have performed the duties of their office and communal service. In 1700 Cotton Mather argued that contracts and not voluntary offerings were commanded by Christ, and he added, "It is beneath the Dignity of [the minister's] Office to be maintained by Alms: the Office of the minister is honourable; if we consider whose ministers they are; They are Ministers of Christ, I Cor. 4.1."[3] Among the writings about the theological subjects for which he became famous, Jonathan Edwards confided his pleasure that he was the highest paid clergyman outside Boston.[4] Before him, his father, Timothy Edwards, was conscious of the fact that many other ministers in the Connecticut River valley were making more.[5] Indeed, alongside the theologically oriented religious literature in American history, one can find a growing business-oriented religious literature, composed of facts, charts, figures, and interpretation of those figures. At least two-thirds of this business-of-religion literature involves in one way or another paying the laborers in the churches' vineyards. Not a small amount of this literature is plaintive or exculpatory in tone. Yet among all the allegations of mistreatment at the hands of an employing congregation that they led are pieces of historical evidence, and the historian must separate facts from the meanings that the original interpreters—most of whom were clergy—gave to those facts. Historians of the economics of American religion will want to consider the following questions: What were clergy paid and how did that change over time? How did what ministers received compare to what other professionals and individuals in the economy made? How did that relationship between the economic standings of the professions change over time? And then, of course, since the meaning of money goes far deeper than even these relevant comparisons and trends would suggest, we will want to examine the comments about ministerial income paid or received as indicators of the social meaning of money for the clergy.

The clergy of New England and Virginia sometimes had difficulty collecting their salaries. Disputes between ministers and their towns during the colonial era over the payment of salaries is well documented. These disputes involved a wide variety of causes. Towns also had trouble dividing land, paying for roads, and obtaining promised amounts of service from freeholders. In this regard, the dysfunction of towns in early political-economic development or at generational succession times became, derivatively, a problem for the churches and their ministers. At other times, particularly in the South, a minister's income was promised in commodities, whose value might decline in relation to unmarketable surpluses or be hard for planters to actually deliver in times of better prices due to their own obligations to creditors for debts incurred in prior seasons. Of course, sometimes a slow payment of ministerial wages reflected problems between the pastor and his fold.[6] On the other hand, from the perspective of later history, the clergy were still in a position to assert the highest claims on their society. As John Tufts put it for his fellow clergy as officers of society:

> "They [the people] fail of their Duty, when they give him but just enough to Maintain a Middling Tradesman's or Farmer's Family decently & honourably for Men in their Station. That which is Honourable for the one, is not so for the other. In Men's living there ought to be a regard had to their Place & Station in the World as well as to their Estates. As 'tis dishonourable for a man to live above his Estate & Station [in] the World, so it is for a Man to live beneath his. For any in a publick Post of Honour to live beneath it, upon a Level with common private Men, is a Disparagement to themselves and the Post they sustain, tends to bring their Office into Contempt, and will render them less capable of doing that good which otherwise they might do, and is a Reproach to all of their Order. The more Honourable any Office is, the more Reasonable & Necessary is it that the Officer should live Honourably.[7]

And what could be more honorable than the office of the ministry? The clergy of the eighteenth century had a lot at stake in being public officials. In any case, from the perspective of either the people or pastor, everyone agreed on the way the system of finance was to work in theory—the community was to have a good religious officer of its choosing and support him out of funds collected by the community. As a public good, religion was financed from a public purse funded by taxes and levies, collected and spent locally. Then matters changed.

THE UNIQUE PROFESSION

The ministry, from the American Revolution onward, was uniquely at an economic disadvantage as a profession. The principal way in which it differed from the learned professions of law and medicine was that in those professions, practitioners were able to set their own fees, while clergy served at the sufferance of their clients and relied on those clients' more or less voluntary gifts.[8]

Like other professions, the ministry regulated admission to its practice. While anyone could preach in the early republic, not everyone could be an Episcopal priest or a Methodist minister. In the same way, from 1830 to 1880, most anyone could style himself a doctor, but only some could join the American Medical Association or a state medical society. State bar associations also regulated market entry for lawyers. The profession of ministry also was limited (to a greater or lesser degree) to those possessing a definite body of knowledge, and sometimes having training or experience. But where medical and legal services might be withheld from particular individuals if the client was unable or unwilling to pay, the ministry, in keeping with its mission, often gave of itself freely to those who could not or would not pay. Ministerial services were poured out for free in anticipation of other returns-conversions and righteous living. Since God's grace could not, in the post-Reformation scheme of things, be premised on fee payment, the Protestant minister was in a poor position to press the issue of payment too hard.

Other professions evolved fee schedules in given geographic areas. The ministry, when it helped its members set economic expectations at all, usually did so on an annual basis without definite goals regarding the number or kind of procedures required to earn the congregation's recompense beyond regular preaching. Moreover, any minister's wages were paid by a group and not by individuals who received services in proportion to their level of payments. Though some members of the laity might wish their gifts to bring more notice, the clergy were in the vanguard of those arguing on evangelical principle that no man of the cloth should be a respecter of persons, by which they meant toadying to the wealthy and generous.[9] The difficulty, of course, with the clergy's evangelical position was that it created the space for a classic free-rider problem. In this new understanding of the ministry, people did not have to pay for their access to religion. Indeed, there was always someone waiting to provide religious access for free. The clergy, for their part, noticed the problem, but they were unwilling to adopt any sanctions to encourage payment for services. They even helped dismantle the practice of renting pews over the course of the nineteenth century, the one method that brought in steady supplies of funds without clerical prompting. This left the clergy in a weak position. Faced with the task of raising support on gratitude and guilt alone, it is not surprising most found securing their livings a task they resented.

The ministry was decidedly a profession (with respect to possessing specialized knowledge and limiting entry to its practice), but it lacked the capacity for economic leverage that characterized law and medicine. Even the public professions of teaching and military officership were better insulated from consumer pressures. In these two professions, one might face a collective audience in the form of pupils or soldiers, but the pupils and soldiers did not set and pay one's wages. Teachers and military officers were commissioned by hierarchical entities that represented the public, but also provided a buffer against the whims of the mob. Preachers, by contrast, found themselves addressing the very people who had employed them and would make subsequent decisions about their employment and wages.

Ministers in the early republic could be acutely aware of being caught between their obligations to the gospel and their hearers. In 1825, an eighteen-year-old frontier preacher named Elijah Goodwin wrote, "I did not think it was right to preach for money; still, I thought a little money was very convenient when it came to paying ferriage at the rivers. In traveling and holding protracted meetings with others, I learned that preachers who said the most against paying preachers received the most money for their labors. Perhaps this was because, in preaching this way, the attention of the brethren was directed to the subject. I never took any part in this kind of preaching, and therefore got but little money." The life of a Protestant minister in the early republic, when the ministry was no longer regarded as a community office, could be full of the practical and ethical problems that faced Goodwin. On the other hand, Goodwin's own life demonstrated that the new paradigm provided unparalleled opportunities to begin ministries in new places and to obtain support from them. Before he died in 1889, he had founded Disciples of Christ churches in Illinois and Kentucky and was regarded as the father of the churches in three central Indiana counties, he had married well, and he had become a published author.[10] Indeed, through most of the nineteenth century, though increasing numbers of men came to the ministry from families of little means, the ministry was held in such high esteem that not a few found themselves marrying well and conveying wealth to their heirs.[11]

EVIDENCE FROM THE HISTORICAL RECORD: FOUR SOURCES

In a chapter of this length, it is impossible to narrate the history of paying the American Protestant clergy by presenting a series of Elijah Goodwins. It would also be difficult to know whether those clergy were truly representative of their cohorts and times or whether they were exceptional in some respect. To obtain more representative perspectives, therefore, we turn to the historical record in search of what is known and knowable about the ways ministers were compensated. Annual records and minutes of meetings from the mid-nineteenth century onward provide excellent evidence of what ministers in some traditions were actually paid. Two denominations, the Presbyterian Church in the the United States of America and the Methodist Episcopal (later United Methodist) Church, kept excellent records, from which one can gain some insight into class differences between the solidly middle-class Methodists and the somewhat more elite Presbyterians. For the years 1906 to 1936, these denominational sources are confirmed and extended to other traditions by data collected on churches and their ministers by the federal Bureau of the Census. Finally, the minutes of denominations' periodic gatherings also yield literary evidence of clerical debate about the contemporary significance of ministerial pay, and we will consequently use one such set of minutes from the United Lutherans to "listen in" on internal debates within the ministry in the 1940s.

THE PRESBYTERIANS

Of all the denominations studied in the preparation of this book, Presbyterians tracked the progress of their home missionaries' salaries most closely. Evidence from the mid- to late nineteenth century is particularly interesting insofar as even fledgling missionaries made decent salaries, while settled pastors could do quite well by the standards of the time. In 1853, the Board of Missions at the Presbyterian Church in the United States of America supported 290 missionaries. Salaries for these missionaries went as high as $1,000 and as low as $215 (the latter salary being paid in Alabama). The average salary was $372.00 per year, with fledgling congregations paying on average an additional $240 to their missionary pastor.[12] By 1856, there were 561 missionaries in the field, and the average salary had increased to $462.41.[13] The Board of Missions report for that year, however, lamented that "if the people whom they served had increased the amount paid by them to their ministers, as much in proportion as the Board had increased their average appropriation, our missionaries would now be much more comfortably sustained. And this must be done, or many of them must continue to suffer from the want of an adequate support."[14] This sets up the basic refrain in these denominational reports: "If only the people were more faithful, then the ministers would not have to suffer so." A few years later, when this generosity actually occurred in 1859, as average additional contributions by congregations on mission posts increased four times as fast as board contributions, the board secretary was simply happy to note that salaries had increased over $100 in the last six years, which coincidentally were years of negligible price inflation.[15]

In aggregate, Presbyterian missionary salaries closely tracked what other clergy in the denomination made. In 1872, for example, the first year in which the salary of every minister in the denomination was to have been recorded (though only half actually were) aggregate ministerial salaries of $2,597,342 paid to 4,441 ministers averaged $584.85 per minister, not including the value of church-provided housing. Averages obscure extremes, however. For example, the 656-member Albany Fourth Church paid its pastor, Henry Dawling, D.D., $6,000 in 1872. The pastor of Fifth Avenue Presbyterian Church in New York City, John Hall, received a salary of $10,000, which would equate to $145,000 in dollars adjusted to year-2000 price levels, but in its time it was an even higher annual salary relative to the prevailing incomes of Americans in the 1870s.[16] Merely converting wages in one year to their value in a later year adjusted for inflation tells us only part of the story. The conversion does not convey all of what a salary represented in its own time, for one would have either to factor out subsequent real increases to prevailing wages based on productivity or compare a known wage with other known wages in the original time frame. To do this in a shorthand way with the current example, we would note that in that same year, 1872, when Hall made $10,000, a teamster, the most highly paid of those who worked for wages on the Erie Canal, made $4 a day, or, at most, $1,000 for the year. Carpenters' daily wages on the same project were $2.50 a day, or roughly $600 a year. A common laborer could expect $1.50 a day, or $375 a year, assuming full employment throughout the year.[17] A highly skilled set of workers in Ohio in another 1872 wage survey likewise made slightly less than $20 a week and, missing about two weeks of work on average during the year, earned less than $1,000 for the year. In the next seven years, they would see their real wages fall by a third while earnings of clergy held fast.[18] Women's earnings were even lower. Of 500 women working in Indianapolis in 1893, fully 75 percent reported weekly earnings of less than $6, and most of them worked six days a week, including more than five hours on Saturdays.[19] Dr. John Hall was making a fine wage indeed.

Region made a great difference in nineteenth-century clergy salaries. In the Presbyterian strongholds of New Jersey and Philadelphia, pastors did quite well. Philadelphia clergy in the 1870s typically recorded salaries, exclusive of manses, ranging between $2,500 and $5,000. Further south, Dr. John Backus of Baltimore received a salary of $8,358 from a congregation of just 157 members. Clergy in the plains states earned less than their eastern counterparts. A typical range for the Midwest was between $900 and $1,500 for the year. Even pastors making considerably less in their younger years could claim a respectable living. Typical in several respects was the Reverend Victor M. King, who oversaw three Sunday Schools (congregations in formation) in Kansas. From the largest (Baldwin City, 44 members), he received $200; from the smallest (Vineland, 24 members), he received $75; Jack City contributed $125 to his support. King did not receive as much as the $2,000 received by his peers in Leavenworth and Lawrence, Kansas, but still earned an adequate plains-state salary.[20] Part of these lower rates of compensation undoubtedly had to do with the lower cost of subsistence in the interior of the United States relative to the coasts.[21] In cities like St. Paul, Chicago, Cincinnati, Columbus, and Kansas City, clergy made a very decent living relative to the prevailing annual nonfarm earnings of $486.[22]

A decade later, an 1887 survey of 347 Iowa schoolteachers discovered that the monthly earnings for schoolteachers hovered just above $30, but the small sums received were usually more than adequate to cover the annual cost of living reported by the overwhelming majority of teachers of less than $300 per year. Just over half of the Iowa teachers were men, and about half reported supporting other dependents.[23]

About a third of the Presbyterian clergy carried on their synod's rolls for the year 1872 did not report a salary or church assignment. Indeed, to this day, there have always been clergy employed as teachers, professors, and leaders of charitable enterprises whose incomes have not been reported, alongside others who are retired, and a very few who are unemployed. In the nineteenth century, there was also the problem with churches failing to make proper reports, along with the very real possibility that the clergy were earning additional money by means of teaching or directing school. In some other denominations, notably the Baptists, there was an equal likelihood of the clergy pursuing farming on the side of their gospel labors. What is clear from the Presbyterian case two-thirds of the way through the nineteenth century is that a colonial-era denomination had perpetuated itself, even with an insistence on a learned clergy, in an environment of denominational competition without pauperizing its ministers. Though the clergy received higher salaries in more established regions, and especially cities, they did well relative to prevailing wages wherever their denomination had churches.

MINISTERS' SALARIES IN THE RELIGIOUS CENSUSES

The Presbyterian case prompts the question, how did other denominations compare in their payment of ministers? The Bureau of the Census conducted four censuses of religious bodies in the early part of the twentieth century. These censuses were ultimately abandoned because of a combination of funding issues and questions raised about why the government was collecting information concerning numbers of members, church property, and the payment of ministers. The 1906, 1916, 1926, and 1936 surveys changed their basic scope and collection methodologies enough between surveys to render decade-to-decade comparisons difficult. Nevertheless, these studies gathered business and institutional data about American religious bodies never equaled in subsequent history for comprehensiveness. For the purpose of this book, the information gathered about clergy salaries confirms and deepens our understanding of the ministerial support derived from the Methodist data series that follows, from

TABLE 1. Annual Salaries of Ministers in Selected Denominations (Nominal Dollars)

Denomination	1906	1916	1926	1936
National Baptist Convention	$ 247	$ 572	$ 350	$ 308
African Methodist Episcopal	347	478	573	350
African Methodist Episcopal Zion	350	502	730	407
Southern Baptist Convention	367	1,072	906	475
Methodist Episcopal Church, South	714	1,037	1,041	617
Methodist Episcopal Church	812	1,223	1,459	863
Northern Baptist Convention	833	1,166	1,589	1,038
Presbyterian Church in the United States	956	1,351	1,401	937
Congregational Churches	1,042	1,343	1,511	1,079
Protestant Episcopal Church	1,242	1,632	1,714	1,283
Presbyterian Church in United States of America	1,177	1,474	2,150	1,336

Source: United States, Bureau of the Census, *Census of Religious Bodies,* 1906, 1916, 1926, 1936 (Washington, D.C.: U.S. Government Printing Office).

Note: The 1926 Religious Census did not tabulate information about the number of pastors or their salaries, so the salaries can only be estimated using the historical labor expense ratios applied to known 1926 expenditures, with further adjustments for a difference base count. The 1936 Religious Census only counted 188,766 churches, whereas the 1926 had counted the expenditures of 216,042 congregations.

fragmentary records from other groups, and from the evaluations of early labor historians and sociologists who commented on church finance and spending patterns in the interwar period.

Out of several hundred possible data points, we have abstracted a table that charts the ministerial salaries of eleven large Protestant churches, chosen because these bodies (in merged and combined forms in some cases) are still large and visible on the American scene today.[24]

The data in table 1 are presented in terms of average support in nominal (then current) dollars. The decade-to-decade comparisons reveal some surprises insofar as salaries actually appear to go down sometimes. Some of this has to do with the aforementioned changes in data collection methodology, since the earliest survey asked denominational offices what their churches paid

TABLE 2. Annual Salaries of Ministers in Selected Denominations (1906 Dollars)

Denomination	1906	1916	1926	1936
National Baptist Convention	$ 247	$ 472	$ 179	$ 200
African Methodist Episcopal	347	394	293	228
African Methodist Episcopal Zion	350	414	374	265
Southern Baptist Convention	367	884	464	309
Methodist Episcopal Church, South	714	855	533	401
Methodist Episcopal Church	812	1,008	747	562
Northern Baptist Convention	833	961	814	675
Presbyterian Church in the United States	956	1,114	717	610
Congregational Churches	1,042	1,107	774	702
Protestant Episcopal Church	1,242	1,345	877	835
Presbyterian Church in United States of America	1,177	1,215	1,100	869

Source: United States, Bureau of the Census, *Census of Religious Bodies*, 1906, 1916, 1926, 1936 (Washington, D.C.: U.S. Government Printing Office).

their clergy, while the later censuses relied on self-reported compensation figures. More significantly, the data jumps demonstrate the wage and price instability of the early twentieth century. This thirty-year period contained years of extreme inflation and deflation that have no parallel in any other thirty-year interval in American history. Table 2, therefore, represents the same reported salary information in real dollars. The data demonstrate that the early years of the century were difficult ones for the clergy. While clergy salaries were not immediately cut when general prices and wages fell in panics and depressions, congregations found it difficult to honor their commitments in such times and then were very slow to increase minister's salaries once the economy recovered. Indeed, by working in small institutions depending on voluntary support, clergy were sheltered somewhat from the short-term impact of price volatility, but their wages were probably depressed in the long term.

On close inspection, both census tables reveal substantial salary differentials correlated to race, region, and class factors. The data tables are ordered by average annual salary, but looking at the names of the denominations represented one sees that the first three churches are historically African American denominations. Ministers in those black churches earned on average less than

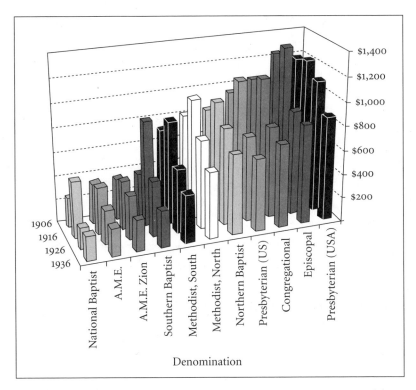

Figure 1. Ministers' salaries in 1906 constant dollars. The data are from United States, Bureau of the Census, *Census of Religious Bodies*, 1906, 1916, 1926, 1936 (Washington, D.C.: U.S. Government Printing Office).

half of what their white counterparts made, except in the case of clergy in the Southern Baptist Convention. Proceeding through the list, one sees that in every instance ministers in southern churches (the black churches, the Southern Baptist Convention, the Methodist Episcopal Church, South, and the Presbyterian Church in the United States) made considerably less than their counterparts elsewhere in the nation. Southern economic deprivation, therefore, was felt by the clergy. Southern preachers, black and white, may have been among the most respected members of their communities, but they shared in their people's economically depressed condition. Finally, this list of eleven denominations ranked by the annual salaries of their ministers also reveals the class hierarchy among the denominations, with Baptists at the bottom, Methodists in the middle, and the old-line denominations—the Congregationalist, Episcopal, and Presbyterian churches—at the very top (see figure 1).

Even in the case of the relatively affluent denominations, however, the purchasing power of ministerial salaries was deeply eroded by the middle of the

TABLE 3. Annual Wages in Selected Occupations (Nominal Dollars)

Job classification	1890	1926	Increase (%)
Public school teachers	$256	$1,277	499
Coal miners	406	1,247	307
Factory workers	439	1,309	298
Street railway workers	557	1,566	281
Clerical-mfg. and railroad workers	848	2,310	272
Farm labor	233	593	255
Postal employees	878	2,128	242
Ministers	794	1,826	230
Gas and electric workers	687	1,477	215

Source: United States, Bureau of the Census, *Historical Statistics of the United States, Colonial Times to 1957* (Washington, D.C.: Superintendent of Documents, 1960), Series D-779–793.

Great Depression from its high point only twenty years earlier, before the United States entered World War I.

The hierarchies within the ranks of the clergy along the dimensions of race, region, tradition, and class, therefore, appear to have held up even as the absolute purchasing power of the clergy declined. But this leaves aside the question of whether the clergy as a whole were losing position relative to other walks of life or whether everyone was suffering to a similar degree. Table 3 illustrates that other occupations, some as well paid as the ministry, were seeing consistent gains in income far in excess of those received by the clergy for the years 1890 to 1926, during which an increase of 190 percent was needed just to keep up with price inflation.

Thus the clergy were getting only modest increases in comparison with middle-class clerks in manufacturing and railroad jobs and working-class coal miners. What is more remarkable is that wage increases for most of the occupations listed in table 3 were occurring while work weeks were decreasing. Coal miners and factory workers each shaved more than 10 hours off their work weeks from 1890 to 1926. Postal workers, ministers, and farm laborers, on the other hand did not.[25] New consumer goods from washing machines to automobiles to ready-made clothing were introduced during this period. Participation in that new consumer economy was dependent on income increases above and beyond the level of base inflation. Workers unable to offer productivity increases tended to get left behind, and the clergy were among these.

A classic study by Paul H. Douglas showed that clergy wages did not fully recover after downturns in the business cycle or after years of high price inflation. That is, in the early years of a recession, clergy wages held up better than those of hourly workers because congregations tended to honor their commitments if at all possible. However, congregations were slow to raise their commitments when a recovery began to occur. Price spikes further eroded the real wages of the clergy. By 1926, the clergy were making, in real dollars, just 98 percent of their 1890 wages, while in the same period schoolteachers had seen their real weekly wages increase by more than half. There were three dramatic economic reversals for wage workers from 1890 to the depression of 1929–40. In each instance, the clergy experienced the effects of the downturn in a delayed manner.[26]

THE METHODISTS

The third historical case, that of the Methodists, enables us to look at clergy salary patterns over a 120-year time frame that begins in the late nineteenth century, overlaps the period covered by the census materials, and ends in the contemporary period. The Methodist *Discipline* provides a way of thinking about the kinds of ministers, ministries, and support for each that helped to guide that tradition's accounting over time to be more stable in definition than the accounting of any other large Protestant body studied in this book. The methodology used here for establishing an accurate average figure for direct ministerial support (salary and cash allowances) over 120 years, during which time the denomination merged and reorganized several times, was to track as closely as possible the ministerial support figure recorded in the Methodists' General Conference annual reports and recapitulations and to match that figure to those who would have been paid out of those funds. The Methodists have generally been careful to distinguish full conference ministers (those who are ordained and available for assignment to pastoral charges within the conference, sometimes called itinerants) from, on the one hand, bishops and district superintendents and, on the other, local pastors (individuals who serve as pastors in particular places, but who are not full members of the conference). Consequently, the Methodists have tracked the number of each of these sorts of ministers (plus retirees) separately and also segregated the amount of financial support given to each. The data series we have created follows full effective

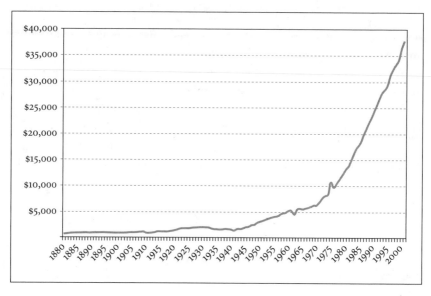

Figure 2. Average ministerial salaries in current dollars, 1880–2000. The data for the Methodist ministers' salaries are from appendix A.

members of the conference (not retirees) and the support they received from their churches. As such it represents the best available data series for clergy compensation of a large middle-class Protestant denomination over the late nineteenth century and the full twentieth century.[27]

The full data series produced for this study appears in appendix A. In this chapter, we examine graphs that trace the average ministerial pay over the period, the real value of that average pay after the effects of periodic inflation and deflation are taken into account, and then finally for the period since 1947 the relationship between average ministerial salaries in the United Methodist Church and the median household income for a family of four.

Figure 2 shows the average salaries of Methodist ministers to be constantly and consistently rising. This is the view that congregations, denominational leaders, and even most ministers would have perceived working as they did (and still do) with budgets and salaries in current dollars. In figure 3, a different picture emerges as the real salaries of ministers grow much more slowly and even decline at various points in time. Periods of price inflation and periods of recession both reduced the real incomes of these ministers. A comparison of the growth in median household income for a family of four with the growth in Methodist ministers' salaries also demonstrates a widening gap over time. As late as 1960, Methodist clergy made close to the median household income for a

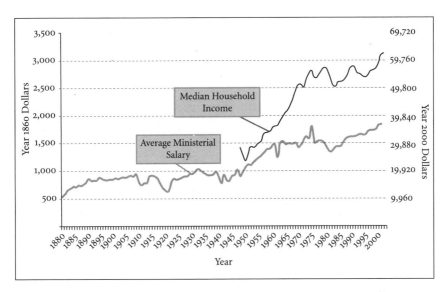

Figure 3. Average real ministerial salaries and median household income for a family of four. The data for the Methodist ministers' salaries are from appendix A; the data for median household income are from U.S. Census Bureau, <http://www.census. gov/hhes/income/histinc/fo8.html> (May 25, 2005).

family of four. By the year 2000, their average annual income of $36,464 was just 58 percent of median household income. This growing gap represents how it felt to receive the nominal salaries paid to ministers relative to the standards of living displayed by their neighbors. Moreover, from the Census Bureau data cited above, it appears that this negative differential growth between ministerial and general incomes has been going on at least since the 1890s.

Once the lines in figure 3 crossed, clergy went from being less well off than the doctors and lawyers they liked to compare themselves with to being less well off than most people in their communities. A sacrificial mind-set has been part of the Protestant ministerial ethic since at least 1800, but evidence of a sacrificial lifestyle has only grown more intense during the last forty years. The sense that the clergy lost ground in the 1960s and 1970s is confirmed by a comparison of various professions' wages from 1963 to 1973 (see table 4). Thus, in ten years of enormous economic growth, clergy incomes barely increased over the cost of living. At the same time, people in other professions achieved nearly triple the clergy's wage gains. All of this occurred before the years of runaway inflation in the 1970s. Over subsequent years, from 1974 to 2000, the cost of living (as determined by the Social Security Administration) would rise 339 percent, while Methodist minister's average salaries would rise only 255 percent.

TABLE 4. Average Salaries of Ministers and Other Professionals, 1963–1973

Profession	1963	1968	1973	Ten-Year Increase (%)
Accountant	$7,668	$9,367	$13,058	70
Attorney	12,300	15,283	21,767	77
Chemist	10,248	12,751	16,486	61
Personnel director	10,620	13,215	18,766	77
University professor	10,650	14,070	16,830	58
Clergy	6,863	8,037	10,348	51

Source: Manfred Holck Jr., *How to Pay Your Pastor More and Balance the Budget, Too* (King of Prussia, Pa.: Religious Publishing Co., 1976), 37.

Note: The cost of living index rose from 91.7 in 1963 to 104.2 in 1968 to 133.1 in 1973, a ten-year increase of 41 percent.

UNITED LUTHERANS AND PENSIONS

When American Protestant ministers addressed their congregations on Sundays, they mostly spoke of God and the gospel. When they met with one another, however, they characteristically spoke of the support for the ministry. The records of conferences, assemblies, and conventions over a period of two hundred years yield a remarkable trove for those interested in the economic history of American Protestantism. When Protestant leaders gathered, how they would pay for the enterprise in which they were engaged was rarely far from their minds. At the national denominational meetings of various traditions, church leaders often considered employment issues with respect to missionaries, superannuated clergy, and expected norms for parish clergy. These are curious meetings in part because, in every instance other than Baptist conventions, at least half of the attendies at national assemblies were clergy, and because the clergy and their concerns clearly dominated the proceedings. The reports and minutes of such meetings are full of rich detail, by way of observations and aspirations, for researchers wanting to know what ministerial incomes represented for those who paid and received them.

United Lutherans (now part of the Evangelical Lutheran Church in America) left a substantial record of discussions about how to pay the clergy fairly and who should pay. What becomes clear throughout the record is that clergy did not expect to get rich, but they hated to be gypped, and often suspected they were. In the 1940s, such feelings about the pay pastors, as distinct from church staff members, should receive and about pensions ran especially strong, as in this 1940 pension board report:

> Old age is the front line of life, moving into No Man's Land. No Man's Land is covered with mist. Beyond it is eternity.
>
> For the past biennium, your Board, according to your action at the last convention of the Church, regardless of an accumulating deficit, has continued to minister to those moving into "No Man's Land."
>
> It has not been a work of charity, it has been a work of love. When the Church ordains a man to the work of the ministry, she says: Separate yourself from the sources of worldly gain. Minister to us in spiritual things and we will minister to you in material things.
>
> The Board therefore declares concerning its work: Justice demands it; Honor enforces it; Gratitude compels it; Self-respect requires it; Expediency suggests it; Sympathy directs it; Religion urges it; obedience enjoins it; The Love of Christ constrains it; The Example of Jesus guides it.
>
> The support of the ministers of the Gospel is not a matter left to the whims of men. It is according to the Divine order.[28]

Though the Lutheran rhetoric about the just deserts of pastors is especially strong, statements like the foregoing one appear in the deliberations of many denominations between 1870 and 1960; they speak to the fears of ministers at a time when increasing numbers of them lived to retire rather than died while still in the active ministry.

THE MEANING OF LESS MONEY

In *Money* magazine's 1994 ranking of jobs for growth potential, job security, prestige, and stress, the ministry was rated as "average" in all categories except prestige, for which it was deemed "good." Clergy ranked well behind doctors, architects, and dentists in these job opportunity measures. In the Bureau of Labor Statistics survey of median annual earnings the clergy made $26,000 that year, lagging behind dental hygienists ($28,600), social workers ($26,600), and flight attendants ($26,300), and barely edged out auto salespersons. For ministers who were carried on the Internal Revenue Service's rolls as self-employed proprietors, things were even worse. In 1994, those with net income averaged less than $8,500 to report on their returns.[29] All of this suggests that clergy had moved from a conception of the ministry as an office to one of a profession and on to something else that paid even less well. Indeed, Protestant clergy through-out the last two hundred years were more comfortable with the idea of having a calling rather than being in a profession. As such, they became captive to the willing acceptance of an economic lot that a more professionally motivated group in society would not have accepted. Even when offered the chance to make more money, they sometimes rejected the terms as unchristian. A Lu-theran pastor reported: "Instead of a raise, I was offered a $1,000 bonus if I could raise worship attendance and giving levels a certain percentage over a given time. That taints with suspicion every act a pastor does. After I got them to rescind the bonus offer, it was suggested that if we didn't meet the goals, I could have the amount withheld from my salary."[30] Seeking to abandon the image of ministers as managers, they took on the mantle of servant leaders. Partly as a consequence, in the year 2000, they found themselves paid in many places accordingly—as servants.

In recent years, there have been several sophisticated attempts to use selec-tively chosen denominations' clergy salary and congregational data to try to establish the determinants of a minister's income. In all such studies, the lead-ing determinant has turned out to be the size of the congregation, far eclipsing still significant factors like denomination, amount of education obtained, and sex of the minister.[31] In general, throughout the last two hundred years, pastors of rural churches have made considerably less than their city and suburban counterparts, though in large measure this has been principally related to the size of the congregations they serve. Likewise, the ministers of African Ameri-can churches have made less than the white clergy with congregations of a similar size, though this lag has attenuated somewhat since 1965.

Size and location matter. In mainline Protestant churches, dropping depen-dency ratios since the mid-1960s have helped slow clergy wage growth. To put it another way, mainline churches have given up significant numbers of members but have not closed many congregations. The result has been congregations of fewer people still trying to support a ministry and a minister. Many ministries have been maintained with pastors or nonordained leaders earning lower wages. The two-earner household has probably buffered this drop in ministers's real wages far more effectively than any other factor in the economic life of the churches, but questions about the quality of people who will consider the ministry, given more prestigious and more remunerative options, have not been squarely faced. A recent study shows that the ministry is one of the few fields whose members can expect negative income returns to advanced educa-tion.[32] That is, clergy earn less after they attend seminary than had they never gone and chosen some other work. Attending law school and medical school—

even obtaining advanced degrees in education—can be said to "pay" positive income dividends. It is fortunate for the churches that clergy do not enter their profession on a rational consideration of the long-term growth potential of their earnings, or on examination of a decades-long trend in ministerial wages. Clerical incomes show a pattern of peaking earlier than others because the practice in which clergy are engaged rarely grows to any considerable degree based on the minister's own effort in a particular congregation. Ministers who do get ahead economically for a sustained period after their mid-forties generally do so through moving to more remunerative posts and not by receiving increased returns on their efforts in the pulpit they already hold.

At the beginning of the new millennium, a researcher by the name of Matthew Price depicted a future after the collapse of the professional model of ministry. One path was the "entrepreneurial mission," in which ministers "grew" their own churches and received compensation that closely tracked that "growth." The other path he saw becoming dominant was the "meaningful vocation," a self-sacrificing move available only to those who, after a successful prior career, chose to "step down a class level or two" for the sake of achieving meaning-filled work at midlife and beyond. For all the talk about a post-Constantinian church and a return to the New Testament model church that was in the air, Price concluded that the "reward structure of today's churches is creating a few well-endowed livings for ambitious pastors and a mass of poorly paid positions for pastors with independent means." If that trend continued, Price concluded, then the American church would soon "resemble not so much the first-century church of the apostles, but the 18th Century Church of England."[33]

I n the final analysis, the centuries-long slide of Protestant ministers' incomes and economic standing from near the top of colonial-era communities to a diminished hold on middle-class status today is the product of multiple factors, none of which has accrued to the clergy's benefit. The evangelical conception of a minister as one who pours out his life for the gospel—which began with Methodist circuit riders making less than $100 dollars a year in the early nineteenth century—has continued as a romantic ideal down to this day. This ideal and a ready supply of substitutes for clergy who ask for too much have proved to be enduring features of American Protestant church life. Increased lay leadership of congregations has had a dampening effect on setting salaries, particularly when lay leaders come from a wider range of economic backgrounds than previously and utilize the market calculus for setting salaries to which they are subjected in their places of work or retirement. The detrimental effects of periods of price or wage instability have been repeatedly passed along to the clergy as structurally reduced incomes for the same work as they performed previously. While other industries and professions boost wages by increasing productivity, the scope of a minister's service to a congregation of a few hundred people on average has not increased. Indeed, for many older denominations, the average size of congregations has actually decreased significantly since the mid-1960s. For at least three hundred years, members of the clergy have asked, "Why are ministers so poorly paid?" Given all of the factors working to lower clergy incomes, the historian marvels that Protestant trust in the ordained ministry has managed to maintain generations of men and women in full-time service. John Adams noted the decline of "the Divines" relative to lawyers, but over the ensuing two hundred years, the real story for the clergy proved to be that they had joined the ranks of the "Common People" and then moved steadily lower in those ranks.

CHAPTER FIVE

Stewardship in Crisis and Technique in

Ascendancy, 1920–1945

y 1920, stewardship as a way of both raising money and building
true Christians had so triumphed in the thinking of Protestant
leaders that it had achieved the status of a panacea. Like other
cure-alls, however, stewardship would fail to deliver on its most extrav-
agant promises. And as this failure became noted, different techniques
for raising money and different ways of thinking about giving for
church causes began to be advanced more freely. By the end of World
War II, stewardship concepts returned in a highly modified form in
American preaching. Meanwhile, fund-raising techniques in Protestant
church circles had been honed with businesslike precision.

In the 1920s, despite growing domestic prosperity, missionary agencies at
home and abroad began to notice significant declines in receipts. This troubled
mission leaders, and at their annual Foreign Missions Conference of North
America in January 1928 they voted to ask the Institute of Social and Religious
Research to make a study of foreign missionary giving by Protestant churches
since 1900. The institute itself was closely connected with mission interests, and
its board members included Kenyon Butterfield, W. H. P. Faunce, Francis J.
McConnell, and John R. Mott, who served as chairman. The research task was
assigned to Charles H. Fahs, who proved to be an excellent choice for several
reasons. In a short time he mounted the first study of church giving to employ

any real economic data, and he subjected denominationally gathered data to relevant comparison such as the relation of components of giving (e.g., benevolences and ministerial support) to one another and to trends in prices and incomes. By separating the denominations out and plotting their spending and receipts levels over time, he was able to pay attention to contextual factors specific to particular denominations while demonstrating that the main trend —diminished giving to overseas mission—was general and not related to the particular fortunes or policies of any denomination. Fahs also proved more than equal to the task of resisting the most popular interpretation repeatedly urged on him by the study's panel of advisers from the mission finance community. He managed to demonstrate that the fundamentalist controversies were not the source of the reduced funding. Instead, he showed that building programs and debt service for the great building programs of the early 1920s were displacing foreign mission giving. In the Methodist Episcopal Church alone, $4 million in interest was being paid each year out of receipts of roughly $100 million. Methodists were paying more interest to banks each year in the late 1920s than they were giving their Board of Foreign Missions. Total Southern Baptist indebtedness of $44,783,102.76 on January 1, 1927, exceeded the prior year's total receipts for all purposes by $4.6 million. The mission boards had suffered not for valiantly exploring the truth but rather because of a surge in local building priorities and attendant debt repayment.[1]

As Fahs set out to answer the foreign mission board leaders' question of whether giving was in decline generally, or only on the decline for foreign missions, he turned up other relevant insights into the state of church finance in the first three decades of the century. Special campaigns for funds, like the Presbyterians' New Era Movement and similar campaigns for the northern Methodists and the Southern Baptists, resulted in real gains, but pledges among some groups were apt not to be paid in full. Spending pledges before they had been paid had given the Southern Baptists, in particular, a crippling debt load on buildings started in anticipation of gifts. Church-related educational institutions and orphanages in this country were continuing to attract larger sums of money for buildings and endowments, while foreign mission giving was declining. Meanwhile, united budgets and unified promotional campaigns for all denominationally related causes, which had been the local churches' answer to prayer for relief from too many appeals, had resulted in many of the well-established mission boards giving up their immediate contacts with constituencies, only to find their appeals somewhat removed from the human needs that had formerly attracted giving. The absorption of separate women's boards for home and foreign missions into more general boards in many of the denominations had likewise cut foreign missions off from a considerable source of constituency support.[2]

Finally, because Fahs was examining several years' data in context, he noticed that the trend between benevolence giving and local spending had moved toward greater giving outside the local context during the war years, and then abruptly began to shift backward in the twenties to its prewar relationship. It was perhaps this last insight that was the most devastating to the leaders of the missionary advance, for their plans had been laid in the days of World War I and its aftermath, when their receipts were on the increase. In the years immediately before World War I, increases in annual giving beyond the local congregation averaged 5 percent; they then spiked from 14 percent in 1917 to 53 percent in 1920; thereafter annual giving tended to decrease by small percentages, although in 1925 giving fell by 8 percent and in 1927 by 7 percent.[3] Church giving had seemed to go up almost 260 percent from its 1913 levels, but purchasing power had only increased a modest 50 percent.

STEWARDSHIP IN DECLINE

Not only was stewardship failing to produce lasting change in the behavior of the Protestant masses; it was also beginning to attract critics. A northern Methodist writer, John M. Versteeg, thought that the meaning of stewardship had been stretched beyond recognition, and particularly so when it simply meant tithing. He sought, instead, to push stewardship away from an ironclad proclamation of the tithe and toward an understanding of stewardship as the Christian attitude toward material things. In *The Deeper Meaning of Stewardship*, he was one of the first writers to argue that perhaps the stewardship movement had gone too far: "When our leaders saw some years ago that moneydrives were necessary if the church were to meet postwar needs, they fell upon the word 'stewardship' with avidity. Here was a word that could lend itself to any enterprise! They worked it for all it was worth. In every major appeal it was given prominence. Talk was made of the stewardship of prayer, the stewardship of time, the stewardship of money, the stewardship of life."[4] One could talk about being stewards of these various blessings, Versteeg allowed, but stewardship was in danger of being expanded into meaninglessness. Rather than have it mean everything Christian, he preferred to reserve its use to the discussion of possessions. "When stewardship is mentioned people at once think of money," he wrote, adding, "We dare not forget life-service, or time-investment, or worship, and we should seek for terms to express these properly. But let us reserve the word 'stewardship' for that which it best fits. Let it be applied to possessions, to the things which we call ours."[5] He also took aim at his contemporary stewardship advocates, arguing that "stewardship is not so simple as some folks seem to think." The most simplistic thinking he found operating in the church consisted of the way advocates of the tithe had interpreted the Bible. Versteeg attacked their most cherished and basic claim that tithing was God's law and had actually been consistently practiced throughout the biblical era. Versteeg's was the first stewardship book to be written from a historical-critical hermeneutic. "With singular unanimity biblical scholars agree," he wrote, "as to the confusion touching the tithe," and he cited the great biblical exegetes of his day to the effect that the data simply did not support any consistent account of the tithe in biblical times. Versteeg accused tithing advocates of twisting the evidence, maintaining, "that in the face of this men should assert for the tithe binding authority seems incredible! A fair perusal of Scripture fails to bear out their claim."[6]

As he sought to mount a constructive claim for stewardship, Versteeg went even further to question the orthodoxy of the day: "Tithing itself is not Christian; only the viewpoint of Jesus can ever make it so." Rejecting the Bible-as-laws-and-precepts hermeneutic for what might be called the Jesus hermeneutic, which centered on the life and teachings of Jesus, Versteeg's theology of stewardship was even more comprehensive than that which it replaced. "Jesus has a disquieting habit of thinking in totality," said Versteeg. "His mind always unified concepts. He saw things steadily and he saw them whole. He knew that our hearts and our treasures keep steady company. He does not get us until he gets ours. Hence the testing exaction placed upon the fine young man who had always kept the law: 'Sell all you have; give the money to the poor and you will have treasure in heaven; then come, take up the cross, and follow me.' This command proved too much for the youth; it makes us squirm to-day! It is, alas! not true that a fool and his money are soon parted."[7] Versteeg sought to be biblically honest, but just as demanding in his theology of stewardship, and his book was the first of many to try to offer theological reasons for generosity beyond the older legal obligation view. Yet, just as the older precritical biblical hermeneutic would continue to be used in addressing issues like Sabbath-keeping, gender relations, and evolution, tithing as God's law would maintain its partisans' loyalties throughout the twentieth century.

The concept of stewardship had its first heyday from the 1890s through the early 1920s. But, as was true of other ideals of the Progressive Era, its luster dimmed as time went on. One of its key defects was that after years of hearing stewardship theology from the pulpits, most members of the business class continued to operate as before. Reinhold Niebuhr, no friend of the overheated idealism of Social Gospel liberals, took on the concept in an article for the April

30, 1930, issue of the *Christian Century* titled, "Is Stewardship Ethical?"[8] In it, he argued that most ethical theory in the Christian church was compromised by its assumption that a perfect society could be made by socializing individuals to check their lusts and expansive desires. This was natural, for after all Jesus too believed in the power of individual regeneration. But Jesus was not out to re-create universal society, and the plain fact was that no religion had ever "developed a sufficient number of individuals with so perfect a passion of love as to change the main facts of history." These "main facts" were that people almost always took advantage of what power they had to promote their own self-interest. The church, in Niebuhr's opinion, had been "singularly oblivious" to this lesson of history. While stewardship sounded good in theory, it was not insisted on in practice. Forty years of preaching the doctrine had not made Christian factory owners different from non-Christian manufacturers. Instead, the church with its unapplied ideal of stewardship served to "sanctify power and privilege as it exist[ed] in the modern world by certain concessions to the ethical principle." Thus an honest and generous businessman could regard himself with the church's blessing as a Christian and view his power in his factory "much as kings of old regarded their prerogatives." Casting his workers into the insecurity of employment was simply not a matter for stewardship as practiced in the churches to touch. "Meanwhile your man of power and privilege is generous," continued Niebuhr. "The degree of generosity varies in different cases. Sometimes his philanthropies represent a mere bagatelle in proportion to his income. It is only in rare instances that philanthropic giving changes standards of living by a hair's breadth. The church with varying degrees of sophistication and naiveté accepts these philanthropies as fulfilling a righteousness."[9]

I nterpreting the doctrine of stewardship realistically was not impossible for Niebuhr, but if done it would require the discussion of displacement of workers in mechanization, income disparity, the rights of workers, and so forth. Niebuhr did not harbor many hopes for contemporary churches in this regard, but he warned that if they failed to address such issues, then any thought of the church as a "moral guide in our civilization" was idle. If justice were the aim, there were more realistic measures of social control the church could endorse that would achieve the effect far more satisfactorily than by promoting the chimera of a world made whole by stewardship. Niebuhr, the critic, effectively spelled the end of the move to place a large concept of stewardship at the center of the church's life. The word *stewardship* would continue to be used, but for most of the rest of the century it would mean the time, talent, and treasure one brought to the church for the church.

TECHNIQUE: EVERY MEMBER CANVASSES, PLEDGE CARDS, AND THE DIVIDED ENVELOPE

Three techniques defined the state of the art of church finance in the 1920s through the 1940s in the United States. The Every Member Canvass was the first of these techniques. Its success was based on the strength of a personal appeal for support; it achieved higher levels of membership participation when compared to more passive approaches. Three calls an hour for, at most, four hours on a Sunday afternoon by a team of at least two laypeople also created a fairly large cadre of leaders who had considered their pledges beforehand. This was one of the most serious and potentially difficult things many church members would ever do in the cause of their faith commitment. The large number of persons who had to be prepared to go out and canvass the membership also created the opportunity for an esprit de corps to develop, and some churches took the opportunity to sacralize this service. The West End Congregational Church in Bridgeport, Connecticut, held a commissioning ritual in the midst of its Sunday morning service, which included these words from the minister:

> In the first place, you go not to extract a pledge from unwilling or reluctant givers. You go, rather, in the name of the Church to the friends of the Church to receive their freely given promise of cooperation.

> Again, you go out this afternoon, not as judges of what share anyone should take in the support of the Church. It is the task of every member to encourage every other member to a loyal, generous, and earnest stewardship of strength and time and money. But whether the prosperous give little or the poor give much, it is a transaction, in the last analysis, between each one of us and God. You go, rather, as those who are yourselves joyfully and wholeheartedly devoted to the work which we here are trying to do. And you go to say to others, "Come, let us join heart and hand in this great enterprise."[10]

At the end of this homily, the minister asked for a commitment, saying, "If it be now your purpose to do this work upon which so much depends, to the best of your ability, in the spirit of our common Lord, and for the building of his kingdom, will you make it known by saying, 'I will'?" The pastor then shook hands with each of the men and commissioned them using a Trinitarian formula, and then the men returned to their seats while the congregation, unprompted by the pastor, sang the hymn "O Zion, Haste." This ritual had no parallels in the worship of Congregational churches except admission to membership of the church and the ordination of clergy. For West End Church in the 1920s, the Every Member Canvass was a very serious business indeed.[11]

Pledge cards provided the basis for securing a commitment from church members to the cause of their churches. Pledge cards were indispensable for the Every Member Canvass since they gave canvassers something to attempt to collect from the homes of those visited, thus providing a concrete reason for the visit. The extent of the collection of pledges also provided a measure of the level of participation in the annual campaign for funds. Even without an Every Member Canvass, most churches were adopting pledge cards in the years after World War I. Some smaller and more conservative churches—particularly smaller churches in the South—resisted pledging. They did so either because a definite sum was inconsistent with the older principle of paying according to how the Lord had prospered them during the week or on the grounds that any giving was between the Christian and God alone. Still, pledging was found nearly everywhere, and the pledge cards themselves took a variety of forms, as the examples from the 1920s in illustration 8 show. Some looked like promissory notes (and were treated as such by courts in the South, which may account for the slower acceptance of the practice in that region). Others, by offering boxes to check, subtly suggested an acceptable range of pledges. And other cards had on them promotional information, thus reminding church members of where their support would go.

The most common feature of pledge cards and church finance more generally after World War I was the inclusion of two separate pledges—one for current congregational expenses and another for benevolences—into the giving process. Benevolence giving beyond the local congregation had long been thought of as a morally distinct category of giving. But the innovation of the 1920s was to try to unify all congregational benevolent giving into a common budget that would be subscribed to on an annual basis. In some respects, this development represented the attainment of a 100-year-old dream for pastors; the separate appeals from agencies outside the local church were under congregational control at last. At another level, however, the separation of money given to the church into World Service and Local Expenses, as the Methodists put it, reified the moral sentiment of most Protestants that it was more blessed to give to others far away than it was to support one's own local church.

Paralleling the development of two-part pledge cards was the widespread adoption of the duplex weekly envelope. Though offering envelopes had been available from some church publishing concerns since the end of the previous century, by 1920 most Protestant churches were using or considering the use of preprinted duplex envelopes as a means of securing regular contributions to

8. Pledge cards, as reproduced in William H. Leach, *Church Finance: Raising, Spending, Accounting* (Nashville: Cokesbury, 1928), 76; and Leach, *Here's Money for Churches*, (Nashville: Cokesbury, 1936), 42.

local church support and benevolences. Among the last to adopt these methods were the ethnic churches that were then in their first generation of English worship. The Reverend Samuel Stein, pastor of Zion Lutheran Church in Springfield, Ohio, wrote a book in 1920 to promote the use of the duplex envelope among Lutherans. *A Guide to Church Finance,* published by the Lutheran Book Concern in Columbus, sold out and was already in an enlarged second edition one month after its July 1920 publication. Stein worried that lack of a successful method in church finance was hampering the work of the Kingdom of God, and particularly had allowed Lutherans to fall way behind in support of their pastors, churches, and missions as their giving failed to keep up with the rapid inflation of the period immediately following the World War. He compared Lutheran finances to those of the United Presbyterians, a group with small average congregations but high rates of giving, and argued that the difference that accounted for the higher giving of the United Presbyterians was that they collected their offerings to the Lord systematically every week. Meanwhile, Stein's own Lutherans were apt to have ten special offerings a year, together with a mission festival, which all too often was "verregnet," or spoiled by rain.

Pastor Stein hastened to point out that having envelopes was not the same thing as having a duplex envelope system, but at best a way station. His claims for this better system were calculated to get Lutherans to adopt the program that was working for the Anglo-American Protestants:

> The one and best envelope system to introduce is the Weekly Duplex Envelope System. This system is recognized practically by all Protestant denominations as the most successful method at the present time for congregations to raise money for their own up-keep and for benevolences. About forty religious bodies, comprising twenty million members, advocate it. Thousands of Protestant churches have adopted it. It has been stated that if all Protestant churches (not including the colored) would adopt it, it would add eighty million dollars for local church support and twenty-five million for benevolences.[12]

Stein went on to show a sample of the duplex envelope at use in his church (see illustration 9) and then described the benefits of the system. First, the envelopes told the giver fifty-two times a year what "the Lord needs His moneys for" with varying messages on each side of the weekly envelope. Second, the average church member could give a great deal more by giving just a bit at a time, rather than trying to save up a significant sum each year. Third, weekly envelopes made for regular giving, and "regularity here means good order." Regularity was a virtue in work, at school, and in the state, so why not in the church? Stein's fourth claim for the superiority of the duplex envelope was that it encouraged personal giving, since not just household heads but women and children, too, were to have their own envelopes, and any Christian who had money ought to be giving. "And why should the husband not give his wife money for the Kingdom of God as well as he gives her money for a new hat?" It encouraged religious giving as well, for while people might be said to go to church to "get religion," Stein thought that what they got was not worth much unless they paid something for it. Finally, duplex envelopes encouraged the great end of proportionate giving, for like the home mortgage payment they encouraged church members to attain great goals in manageable increments.[13] Samuel Stein added one additional wrinkle to the duplex system to make it work and that was to suggest that an annual report might be printed following the close of every church fiscal year. In a ledger showing what it might look like, he showed a Mr. and Mrs. F. Ahfeld having paid up their generous pledges, while Mr. and Mrs. Always Arrears were predictably delinquent.[14] Doubtless, the joke was not lost on this German pastor's readers.

The adaptation to all of these methods of systematizing church finance can be seen in the experience of a Chicago congregation that was making a postwar transition from a German- to an English-speaking church. First Evangelical St. Pauls Church had until 1919 operated with loose understandings of membership and finances. Though it was a large church involving as many as two thousand parishioners, most of these people did not really consider themselves members of the church. Instead, they were most likely members of one of the organizations in the church—the Men's Club, the Junior or Senior Society (both young peoples' groups), the Frauen-Verein (the women's society). They paid their dues into their respective organization's treasury, which then paid some funds into the church treasury, but also made allocations to outside causes. The leaders of households, mostly fathers, paid pew rentals into the church treasury. And those who regularly attended church gave to special offerings on the holidays. Things began to change around Easter in 1919.

The April 1919 issue of the St. Pauls Church's newsletter announced that this year there would be no Easter Collection. For that matter, the role played by collections was to be sharply curtailed. That is, the plate would still be passed, but not with the expectation that the collection would provide the necessary funds to run the church. Instead, the newsletter indicated that every member was asked to contribute a certain amount per year, to be fixed by him or herself, to be paid as may be convenient, monthly, quarterly, semiannually, or annually. For this contribution a pledge card was enclosed and intended for use. The article went on to inform the congregation:

```
335  MAY 9 1920 | MAY 9 1920  335
```

THIS SIDE IS FOR OURSELVES

$............My Offering for the Week

For CURRENT EXPENSES of

Zion Lutheran Church
SPRINGFIELD, OHIO

For Pastor's, Organist's, Janitor's Salary; Coal, Gas, Light, Water, Insurance, Printing, Taxes, Up-keep of Property, etc., approximately $3,600 is needed.
"Upon the first day of the week let Every one of you lay by him in store, As God hath prospered him."—I Cor. 16:9
Please seal write amount of offering And bring to your church every Sunday. The number on your envelope agrees with your name on church record Careful record is kept of all offerings.

THIS SIDE IS FOR OTHERS

My Offering for the Week. $..........

BENEVOLENCES

For Our Institutions, Home, Foreign, Negro and Inner Missions, building Mission Churches; Quota; Poor Students for Ministry; Orphans; District Treasury; etc. Our Synod needs more this Year.

"But to do good and to communicate forget not: for with such sacrifices God is well pleased." Heb. 13:16.

9. A digital re-creation of a sample duplex envelope used as an illustration in Samuel A. Stein, *A Guide in Church Finance* (Columbus, Ohio: Lutheran Book Concern, 1920), 15.

The Pew Rent System at present in use shall remain undisturbed. The amount pledged shall be in addition to the Pew Rent.

Explanation: for some time it has been apparent that the financial resources of our Church, as represented by Pew Rent, Special Collections (Christmas, Easter, Anniversary, etc.) and Freewill Offerings at the services, are not sufficient to meet the demands of the present day. Operating expenses are greater in all lines of activity, including the Church, than they were formerly.

Again, it seems advisable and necessary, not only for financial reasons, to rally to the support of the Church. First: The young people, who should more fully [sic] the meaning of "membership," share the duties and privileges of the Church with their elders and, secondly, the large class of people who are not now members or regular attendants of St. Pauls, and yet call her "My Church." By contributing regularly to the support of the Church they will feel more fully that they are members and they shall be carried as such on the lists of the church.[15]

The understanding of membership was being adapted at St. Pauls to match a family structure in which fewer and fewer younger adults were attached to the patriarchies of the church. The next month's newsletter carried word that the institutionalization of the church was going even further: "The merging together of all the workers and members of our various church activities into one large body and the individual membership of every young and old person in this organization is the coveted goal of the promoters of this new order of things. Every member is to be personally responsible to his church."[16]

Every confirmed member of the church received a pledge card that spring at St. Pauls. The May 1919 newsletter also indicated that this was causing some confusion, since "many of our members do not quite understand the method of modern church financing, but in a little while they will understand." One of the things these members were most confused about was what the pledge meant: "Some good friends are even a bit disturbed in their conscience, lest they sign a pledge and then fail to keep their promises. It is always understood in any Christian church, that there, where sickness or adversity of any nature overtakes a church members, rendering him incapable of meeting his pledge to the church, such obligation will never be pressed, but will be held in trust, until a later day, when a member can realize his purposes and kind intents toward the fellowship, which he loves and honors." Through the summer those signing on grew steadily and church leaders hoped that soon all the societies within the congregation would be amalgamated into a single comprehensive unit. By November, four hundred pledges had been made, totaling $8,395.75.[17]

For the next few years, St. Pauls Church continued to push the new system while retaining pew rents, but dropping any other special offerings or collections. By 1924, the church was ready to take the next step and announced "The New System," which was the utilization of duplex envelopes:

> Many of our members have taken our monthly envelopes and make consistent use of them, thereby enlarging on monthly income. And now we have an increasing number of members who are making weekly offerings the rule of their lives. They are given the new duplex envelopes, which name indicates, that there are two envelopes in one. The first envelope is used to receive the dues for church membership, some remitting a small sum every Sunday and some larger amounts, as God has prospered them. . . . But there is also a second envelope that is attached and printed in a different color. This is provided for all such as desire to add an amount for other Christian purposes within and without the circle of the local church activities. Thus the habit of regular, joyous giving is formed and the givers are conscious that they are real members of the church and not occasional visitors, who come and go as their comfort and desire may dictate.[18]

By the spring of 1924, 250 households were giving weekly, and church leaders had ordered 100 more sets of envelopes in hopes of shifting still more of the roughly 1,000 households over to the new system. Finally, in the fall of 1927, St. Pauls adopted its first Every Member Canvass. In his pastor's report twelve years later, George Scherger indicated that the canvass had made for a great step "onward" in the church's finances. On the other hand, his closing words seem to indicate that the struggle for improved financial systems was eternal: "Miss Atzel deserves great credit in helping achieve these results. Some have rebelled. Her work has not been easy. The old cards will be good until definitely canceled. We should continue this."[19] And so they did. The Every Member Canvass constituted the chief vehicle for getting out the pledges of church members in the Protestant mainline from the 1930s through the 1960s. In two churches, the Protestant Episcopal Church and the Presbyterian Church in the United States of America, it became nearly sacramental. A pamphlet from the Episcopal Church, titled "Eight Thousand Master Churchmen," argued that the men who led their parishes' campaigns constituted nearly a second order in the church alongside its clergy:

> The time has come to recognize this order in our Church, the nearly eight thousand laymen who annually direct the Every Member Canvass in our parishes and missions. The contribution which they can make to the well-being of the Church and the effectiveness of the Church's work, is second only to that made by Her six thousand clergy. The annual canvass is usually decisive. It is a fairly safe index as to whether a parish is to be a joy and satisfaction to every one in it and a glory to God or whether its value is to be discredited in the mind of the community, the religious life of every one in it marred and God mocked.[20]

H. C. Weber, a minister in the Presbyterian Church and director of its Every Member Canvass Department, offered a hymn for the canvass:

> Let each new canvass, nobler than the last,
> Lift thee to heaven with a pull more vast,
> Till thou at length art free,
> Leaving the old devices,
> Campaigns and taxes, quotas, pew-rents, prices,
> By life's unresting sea.[21]

Weber saw asking for money for the church as a religious task of the highest order. Budget items were to be seen not as bills payable but as "release-indexes of people." Giving quotas were not money-measures; rather, they were "men-measures" that calculated people's readiness and ability to give and serve. If a church did not look forward to the annual canvass, it was doubtlessly looking at it the wrong way. Weber's prescription for such churches was to "humanize your budget and spiritualize your canvass."[22]

Mixed in with pious rhetoric about spiritualizing stewardship and canvasses, however, were stories tinged by bitterness and a minister's accommodation to the way things were in society outside the church. Weber related the story of the church treasurer who watched week after week as a lay leader in his church, "frock-coated, gold-caned, spatted and high-hatted, led his snooty family down the middle aisle of the stately city church every Sunday morning to a conspicuous pew. When the offertory plates were passed he was in the habit of depositing one envelope for the family and with great dignity. The poor church treasurer knew, however, that no anticipation on his part could change the invariable contents of the envelope. It was always one nickel, no more and no less." Weber lamented how many other treasurers shared such dismal insight into the hearts of church members. He also advised that getting to really big potential givers required approaching them on their social level. Thus he told the story of how A. F. McGarrah, another Presbyterian minister with the golden touch, had helped a church make a successful approach for an increased pledge to the richest woman in the congregation. Each year a hapless shoestore clerk was sent to solicit her pledge, only to be left waiting on the doorstep and finally informed by the butler that they lady of the manor would give the same as last year, $12 a month. McGarrah learned that the woman's lawyer and banker were each officers of the church and sent them to see her the next year. They, of course, were received in her home and were further asked by the woman how much they thought she should give. They responded from their knowledge of her affairs that they believed she should give $50 a month, to which she gladly assented.[23] The lesson for Weber was that this church had missed out on years of more adequate support by sending a social inferior to seek the pledge. Weber and other clergy might wish for a church where the members were as innocent as doves, but to get the money they were prepared to be as wise as serpents. The recurrent undertone of these stories, however, is a church leader's wish that such accommodations to culture were not necessary.

THE BUSINESS OF THE CHURCH AND
THE CHURCH'S BUSINESS

As strong as the stewardship movement was in the early twentieth century, there were also other ways in which church leaders sought to raise the funds to do the work of the church. It is a generalization, to be sure, but throughout the twenties and thirties there was a marked tendency for clergy and other religious elites (nonordained professional Christians like Mary Askew, John R. Mott, Robert E. Speer, or Thomas Kane) to use biblical and theological arguments for giving while lay leaders argued for the usefulness and importance of the religious cause in this-worldly terms. In short, each group used the reasoning it found most compelling.

The proclamations of businessman Roger Babson caught the attention of not a few ministers and laity in the 1920s and 1930s. Babson liked coining pithy pious sayings, such as

> $1 spent for lunch lasts five hours.
> $1 spent for a necktie lasts five weeks.
> $1 spent for a cap lasts five months.
> $1 spent for water power or a railroad grade lasts five generations.
> $1 spent in the service of God lasts for eternity.[24]

One of Babson's many clerical fans in this paramount era of the Christian layman, when business leaders were celebrated both for piety and worldly success, was the United Lutheran pastor Herbert Bosch. Bosch still used the word *stewardship*, but his use of the term significantly departed from the stewardship-as-duty school of thought. Indeed, *Not Slothful in Business*, Bosch's contribution to stewardship literature, was a tract for its times and a herald of stewardship emphases to come. The book contained new attitudes toward business techniques—particularly the practices of advertising and marketing—a new theology of stewardship, and advocacy for new techniques to raise money. Perhaps the most striking difference between Bosch and writers working before his time was a determination to return the basis of giving to "the cause of Christ." This was the first piece of sustained stewardship writing in a half century to use what might be called an economic choice model of stewardship —that is, to assert that what people give to a church is a function of what it is worth to them, or, in more religious language, what it means to them. This shift in orientation caused Bosch to begin his book not with the customary biblical explication, or early church or missionary hero story, but rather with a straightforward assertion of the value of the Christian enterprise. The authorities for the contemporary utility of the churches were the somewhat unusual choice of three recent American presidents and the millionaire entrepreneur Roger Babson. Each figure was invoked to prove the same point: that when Christian civilization was at stake, the church was a real bargain. For Teddy Roosevelt, the reasons for "church going" were practical; they made one a better man. For the high-minded Woodrow Wilson, the value of Christianity was that "unless our civilization is redeemed spiritually, it can not endure materially." And for Calvin Coolidge, religion was the very essence of conservatism: "We do not need more national development, we need more spiritual development. We do not need more government, we need more religion. We do not need more of the things that are seen; we need more of the things that are unseen."[25] Finally, for Roger Babson, the nation (and indeed the world) was in love with material progress, having "gone daffy" over its innovations in steam, electricity, water power, buildings, railroads, and ships while neglecting the development of the human soul. Babson, in his book *Fundamentals of Prosperity*, had argued that it was not bankers that the American people had to thank for their security and prosperity of the 1920s, but rather the preachers in the churches. He wrote: "It is the Church which has created America, which has developed our schools, which has created our homes, which has built our cities, which has developed our industries, which has made hospitals, charities, which has done everything worthwhile in America."[26] Bosch, as a religious writer and United Lutheran pastor, seemed to love this approval from men of substance in business and statecraft. He agreed that religion was the source of every good thing in American culture, but he also asked, if the church was so essential to prosperity, education, and the progress of civilization, why were church members so scanty in their support?

Church members were the first to underestimate the worth of the church, Bosch believed, precisely because the real work of the church was so often obscured from them. To church members, too much of what the church was about seemed to revolve around getting enough money to keep the church going. What then was the real work of the church? Bosch asked. It was the gospel of God in Christ, "the only reason the church has for its existence, and its sufficient vindication."[27] He compared money and the getting of money to a coal furnace. It was essential for a church to have a furnace, but it belonged in the basement, not the chancel. Likewise the money problem was best dealt with out of the garish spotlight it too often occupied. In its place belonged the cause of Christ.

From Bosch's insistence that the worth of the church derived from being a mediator of the gospel to men, women, and children stemmed a radically different kind of stewardship program from the one that had been recommended by most Protestant church leaders. Bosch was aware that through the 1920s most Protestant bodies had experienced a decrease in gifts to benevolences. Along with other stewardship advocates, he believed that the proper presentation of stewardship needed to be given. But he wondered whether putting stewardship by itself at the center of the Christian life constituted part of the problem. For Bosch, the key theological challenge was to put evangelism and stewardship together at the center of the church's understanding of its work in missions. "The world needs Christ," Bosch wrote. "He must be brought to the world and the world must serve Him." "Evangelism brings the message: 'This has Christ done for thee!' Stewardship presents the challenge: 'What hast thou done for Christ?' An appreciation of the former is necessary before the latter awakens any response." For Bosch, the new stewardship differed from the old, legalistic one in that it did not start with an insistence on the demands of the gospel before the gracious facts of the gospel were presented. The spirit of Bosch's stewardship was derived from 1 John: "We love him, because he first loved us." People spent freely, Bosch believed, only when they experienced something as having great value. People buying homes would obligate themselves for many thousands of dollars and constrain their spending in order to obtain and keep their homes. But church members, due to their partial evangelization, "were apt to practice partial stewardship and hence treat the gospel as a mere trinket," and not as something of ultimate worth. Bosch's use of scripture consequently also differed from that of other stewardship writers. He did not begin with the Old Testament or the writings of Paul, but rather with the teachings of Jesus and the interactions between Jesus and his disciples. Bosch's stewardship metaphor was not the tithe put away in the storehouse but rather the pearl of great price for which someone would sacrifice all to obtain. This difference in attitude explained, for Bosch, the often observed phenomenon of church members of modest means nevertheless being generous and happy givers to the work of the church: "Within this statement lies the explanation of the gift of humble folk. Their gifts are greater than those of the many well-to-do; they are far greater in proportion than those of the wealthy. Why? Because Christ has touched and filled their lives and they in return are able to give something of value to Him. Christ means much to them; therefore they shall mean as much as possible to Christ."[28]

From the new stewardship theology flowed ideas for revising stewardship technique. The Every Member Canvass was too often, for Bosch, crippled by the not-so-subtle message that churches were more interested in people's money than in people themselves. Bosch suggested that Every Member Canvasses continue, but that they be canvasses for people to join the cause for Christ. The Every Member Canvass had been theoretically offered as an opportunity to enlist both people and money for the church, but the larger purpose had usually failed because the dollar inevitably dominated the day, given the pressing need of the church for funds and the tendency of canvassers to present the more tangible cause.[29] A visitation for enhanced membership commitment might ask people to commit to attend meetings, or become members of groups of organizations within a church, to establish the family altar, to read the Bible daily, and to cultivate a prayer life, but it probably ought to hit only one or two of these messages each year. Bosch suggested how such a visitation might go:

> "Mr. X., we are here to see you about the church!"
>
> "Yes," said Mr. X., "I knew that and I know what you want."
>
> "What do we want?"
>
> "You want money for the church."
>
> "No," said the worker, "we do not want money. We want you. We want you to come to church, to attend its services, to be an active member always. . . . You need the church. . . . The church needs you, and only as you try to value the church, will it mean more to you. The church is interested in you. The church wants you. . . . Come next Sunday. . . . And your many friends there will be glad to see you."[30]

Changing the orientation of the Every Member Canvass gave a new twentieth-century spin to the words of the Apostle Paul "we seek you, not yours!" But it was important for such visits to be sincere, and sincerity required that they be repeated, so that evangelism be a "fixed motive" and have a "definite aim."

As for money, it was important that the church solicit for its cause with a sense of decorum and seriousness of purpose. Businesses might resort to deception and wily strategy to sell their wares, but it was beneath the church to be "a buffoon and a jester." Christians could be and had been kidded and bullied into larger donations, but none had ever been forced into a "greater liberality, which is a state of the heart."[31] Again taking a page from the business practices of the day, Bosch urged church leaders to learn from the fact that institutional advertising was far more effective than price advertising. The suggested maxim for constructing appeals was "we must plead the cause, not the cost." The church should never raise money by arguing that it was not very much that it was asking. A correct motive is established when churches emphasize the following thought: "For Christ's sake and in Christ's name your contribution is solicited that this part and that phase of Christ's work may be done."[32]

Herbert Bosch also cataloged what he saw as the prevalent and disgraceful practices of money raising in the churches of the 1920s. There was the pastor as clown, a man who could jolly people out of their money. There were endless numbers of companies offering the "gift" of money-making schemes to churches by which church members acted as unpaid salespeople for the sales of the companies products in return for a share of the proceeds. Bosch was appalled by the amount of energy the churches and their subsidiary organizations poured into such sales, often with incredible naïveté as to the economics of the sales proposition. Nearly as appalling as this false philanthropy was the list of products being pushed on churches from various sources for their sale. Saving brochures over a period of months, Bosch listed the following money-making sales opportunities that had been offered him through the mail as a pastor: chocolate pudding; candy bars; mints; tea; cookbooks; slaw cutter (a booklet on salesmanship was included to "help break down sales resistance"); milk bottle caps; furniture polish; mops; rust and stain remover; bluing paddles (Bosch pointed out that the sale of one gross of the paddles netted a church organization five dollars); handkerchiefs; washcloths; dish clothes; dust clothes; Christmas cards; Christmas wrapping supplies; stationery; shaving cream; cold cream; hand Lotion; laxatives; magazines; toys; and lingerie.[33] The lingerie brochure was particularly vexing to Bosch, for it noted that the lingerie items were made in a mill that employed church members, and thus any church that sold the lingerie was in fact helping two churches at once. In Bosch's opinion, the damage such sales did far outweighed the help they gave to churches. They introduced a mercenary psychology whereby people were urged to buy something for the church. And they undermined a legitimate spirit of giving. Worse yet, such sales often became the chief activities of some auxiliaries within the church; and when it became the only occupation in which laypeople were enlisted, it became a real impediment to the work of the church. A congregation's members were supposed to help proclaim the riches of God's grace "rather than the merits of kitchen and toilet requisites and utensils."[34]

If Bosch was dubious about sales to support the church, he was, by contrast, very positive about advertising and direct marketing in service of the church. Brochures stating the evangelistic and stewardship claims of the church together with opportunities for service and articulations of budgets helped churchgoers make informed decisions. People were becoming sophisticated consumers, and Bosch saw no reason for the church not to be sophisticated in its approach to them. He suggested innovations such as a church night program in which the consideration of the financial needs of the church might be presented amid social features, a supper, and a short program involving a forceful presentation of the opportunities for service that members could have. He also suggested that the culmination of such an event might be to pass out pledge cards matching well-designed promotional materials that could then be prayerfully and deliberately considered at home and then returned on a "subscription Sunday." Indeed, ritualizing a definite pledge for the coming year was becoming increasingly prevalent in Protestant churches that were embracing business methods such as annual budgeting, accounting for gift receipts to donors quarterly, and urging weekly gifts on the analogy of an installment plan of credit.

The system was coming back into vogue, and just as the positive allusions to people such as Calvin Coolidge and Roger Babson suggested, being businesslike in the Protestant churches was not thought to be at all a bad thing. Herbert Bosch and others valued business methods, rejecting only those that were a distraction to the main purposes of the business of a Christian congregation.

One of the church leaders most eager to embrace modern business methods was the Reverend William H. Leach. Leach was the editor of *Church Management* and the author of such books as *Church Administration, How to Make the Church Go*, and *Putting It Across*. In 1928 he published the book *Church Finance: Raising, Spending, Accounting*. Leach approached his topic of church finance with a great sense of realism. Religious leaders might agree that the Bible taught the stewardship of wealth, but church history revealed no evidence that the primitive church had any fixed idea of the tithe or an approved plan for dividing wealth for the support of the church. Leach allowed that this was probably less of a problem for the early church since there were no salaries for preachers or expenditures for church buildings.[35] Already Leach was off on a different tack than that taken by most stewardship writers up until his time. (Indeed, my copy of the book borrowed from a Methodist seminary library contains extensive marginal notes in which one reader took issue with Leach's rejection of the fixed biblical tithe.) Leach's purpose was not to do theology or biblical interpretation, however, but rather to introduce better methods in the financial realm of church work. He presented his book of "methods and techniques" without apology, writing, "methods are a necessity in church administration. And they are not a necessary evil, but a necessary virtue. Unless the technique had improved, the church would have profited little from the growing spirit of Christian stewardship."[36]

A modern program of stewardship began with sermons on stewardship and the introduction of lessons on stewardship in the Sunday school and adult Bible classes. But for Leach, stewardship needed to be made concrete if it was to achieve application in the local church. He suggested that the model of the Delaware Street Baptist Church of Syracuse, New York, be used. Budgeting had become a very popular topic in the 1920s as Americans sought to manage their growing incomes and spend money on an ever-greater variety of durable goods and luxuries. Home ownership was expanding, and owning an automobile was fast becoming a widespread goal. Most Americans were also investing in an additional wardrobe of casual clothing because of their increasing opportunities for leisure activities, including sports, movies, and interstate travel. Discussions of the family budget could be found in lots of popular magazines. Very few of these budget advice articles, Leach noticed, contained any recognition of "the Christian proportion for giving."[37] The Delaware Street Church had come up with its own recommended budget and presented it as the basis for a Sunday night fireside discussion at the church. The budget read as follows:

BASED ON INCOME OF $166.66 PER MONTH

Necessities:

Rent 25% $40.00
Food 25% 40.00
Clothing 15% 25.00
Fuel 10.00
Light, car fare, replacement 9.00

For Others:

Church, charity, etc. 16.66

For Education:

Newspapers, books, magazines,
school expenses, etc. 3.00

For Recreation:

Movies, parties, concerts, trips,
entertainment 4.00

For Savings:

Insurance, Home payments, fraternity
membership, savings bank 12.00

For Incidentals: Wife $4.50, husband $4.50 .... 9.00

People were urged to compare their own finances to the discussion budget.[38] Leach had other ideas as well. He suggested holding a school of stewardship in which materials derived from such books as Harvey Calkins's *A Man and His Money*, Julius Crawford's *The Call to Christian Stewardship*, or David Mc-Conaughy's *Money the Acid Test* might be used as a basis for study and discussion.[39] Another was the stewardship ballot, in which the whole congregation was challenged to "vote" for one of four options, as shown in illustration 10. The stewardship ballot amounted to a constrained apparent choice: all members of the gathered community were forced to make a choice and could not escape signing on to at least one of the options before God and in the presence of their fellow church members. Even though the stewardship referendum was akin to voting in a one-party state, Leach thought that the value of afflicting the conscience of the congregation was well worth the exercise. He wrote, "It is hardly possible that one will secure one hundred percent response to this ballot. But it will, at least, have the effect of making people think upon the question."[40] Budgets and ballots were one compromise with the American culture of the twenties; another was Leach's willingness to allow proportionate givers to have some latitude in allocating their contributions. In a direct counter to the storehouse tithing movement of a generation earlier, Leach advised those who would be stewards to set up a box for themselves into which to put all the money they were to give away. "It does not necessarily all go to the Church. Other obligations and charities will have consideration," for, Leach advised, "it is an unwise Church which insists on receiving the full tithe."[41]

Leach was not the only figure in the stewardship world adapting the techniques of stewardship to the trends and aspirations of the broader public. The United Stewardship Council, the ecumenical body in which most large white Protestant denominations and boards of foreign and domestic missions were represented, promoted budgeting as a discipline of Christian stewardship by selling a small leather bound budget book entitled the stewardship diary. Its system of stewardship contained some by now familiar elements. God was to be put first as the owner of all; the whole of one's income was to be treated as a sacred trust. People were urged to give generously and in a definite proportion to their incomes. But they were also encouraged to embrace the middle-class virtue of saving, and the little red book contained this admonition: "*Provide for the future*, practicing self-denial to-day, and exercising foresight and providence for to-morrow by saving. For this purpose make a budget, always remembering what is saved is to be wisely spent and generously given. Only about one-tenth of all Americans are self-supporting after 65 years of age. And yet ten percent saved by the average young worker up to fifty years of age would from that time bring in more, in a savings bank, than the worker can then earn."[42]

This practice of disciplining one's stewardship through budgeting was so compelling at the time that the northern Presbyterian Church's Department of Stewardship prepared a small version of the book especially adapted for children, which it sold for a penny. With the aim of encouraging children to form the stewardship habit early, the booklet introduced the youngest Christians to an accounting system by which they could reckon the amount received and the amounts given, saved, and spent. Indeed, this three-part division of the allowance and personal accountability for it was part of the moral education of Protestant children who later became known as the G.I. generation of World War II and the so-called "silent generation" that attended college in the 1950s.

Like Bosch, Leach urged churches to embrace budgeting in order to articulate needs before asking for money. He also argued for increased sophistication in making appeals. Direct mail experts started with the assumption that the mails would be crowded and people's attention had to be captured. Why could-

10. A stewardship ballot, as reproduced in William H. Leach,
Church Finance; Raising, Spending, Accounting (Nashville: Cokesbury Press, 1928), 47.

n't the churches learn, Leach wondered, to make their appeals more compelling
and to print them well rather than using their messy mimeographs? "It pays,"
he argued, "to invest in good physical appearance when you start mailing
letters."[43] If the promotional material was to be printed, it ought to have bite.
Leach evaluated some slogan possibilities—"Tenth Anniversary Campaign"
(lacked punch), "Over The Top" (good, but overdone), "Loyalty Campaign"
(gets results), "It Is Now Or Never" (splendid for new building campaigns).[44]

RAISING MONEY IN THE GREAT DEPRESSION

Although church leaders believed they had financial problems in the 1920s,
things were about to get much worse. As the depression deepened in the 1930s

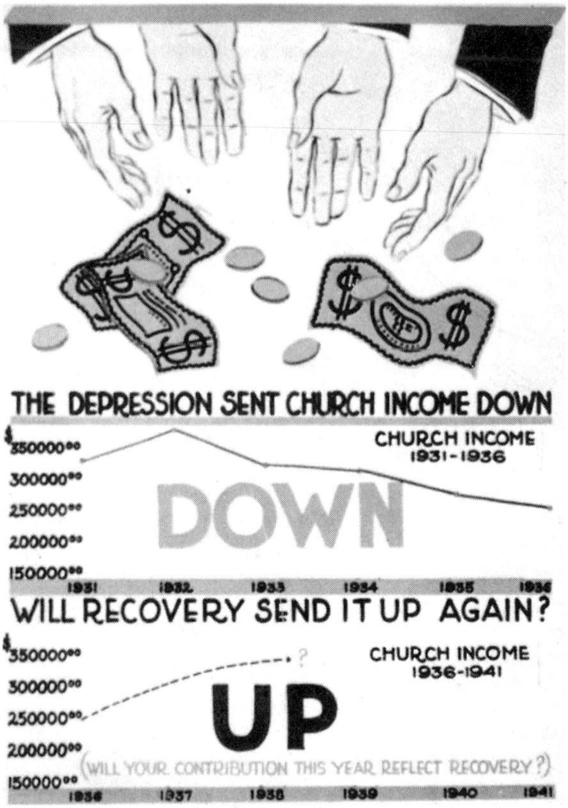
THE DEPRESSION SENT CHURCH INCOME DOWN
CHURCH INCOME 1931-1936
DOWN
WILL RECOVERY SEND IT UP AGAIN?
CHURCH INCOME 1936-1941
UP
(WILL YOUR CONTRIBUTION THIS YEAR REFLECT RECOVERY?)

11. A promotional poster from 1936. The Riverside Church Archives, used by permission.

and the churches found themselves hard hit for funds, the advice given by church financing experts became even more practical. A poster from the Riverside Church in New York from 1936 shows how blunt local church fund-raising had become, as shown in illustration 11. Julius Crawford, returning to the theme of church fund-raising in 1934 advised pastors to tithe themselves. He also provided a pointed list of common things not to do:

FINANCIAL NEGATIVES

1. Never assume the attitude of the pastor who displayed his lack of spiritual insight by saying, "The money business of my church is no concern of mine. I am a spiritual minister and have nothing to do with its temporalities."
2. Never be officious or dictatorial nor assume all the responsibility for raising the finances of your charge.

3. Never present any aspect of stewardship or of the financial program of the Church apologetically.
4. Never consider that you really know your people until you are aware of the spiritual conditions which the financial records of your charge reveal. Jesus sat over against the treasury and took special note of how the poor widow, the rich, and the multitude contributed.[45]

Two years later, William Leach believed that the depression had bottomed out, but he also thought that it would be a long time before churches again saw the kinds of budgets they had enjoyed in 1929 and 1930. In the meantime, local churches were keeping for their own use more of the funds they did get. For better or for worse, the duplex envelope helped this process. Leach wrote that "the experience of the past few years has shown that in time of economic pressure co-operative agencies, such as interdenominational federations, suffer first; next comes the denominational work; the local church suffers last. With all the propaganda of several denominations [that the church had but one true budget], churches still insist on thinking of giving in two classifications—viz., 'For Ourselves' and 'For Others.'" He suggested several fairly aggressive techniques for keeping people giving in the lean years. One technique was the so-called Belmont plan, named after the Belmont Presbyterian Church, which had popularized it. In the Belmont plan, members were asked to pledge to tithe not for a whole year, but only for two or three months. Since many more people were willing to make a limited commitment than an open-ended pledge of 10 percent, the plan usually resulted in a substantial immediate boost to church income. But its real benefit was long term insofar as it made tithing conceivable for many church members, who having managed to do without a tenth for a couple of months responded favorably when asked to just continue giving their tenth to God. Leach also endorsed Vincent Dee Beery's use of a mock trial to get the message across. Beery, a minister in Philadelphia, staged a trial titled "The Church vs. John Doe," in which Mr. Doe was accused of neglecting his obligations to the church. Church members and the benevolence treasurer all got a chance to testify, and Doe's flimsy excuses for not giving were held up to ridicule. Leach believed in dramatizing the plight of the churches in other ways as well, and he particularly liked the chart from the Golden Rule Foundation shown in illustration 12. Leach praised how the Lakewood, Ohio, Congregational Church and the Riverside Church in New York City used commercial art to articulate the needs of the church in graphic ways.[46]

In the same year that William Leach was recommending the use of contemporary marketing techniques to put the cause of the church before the people,

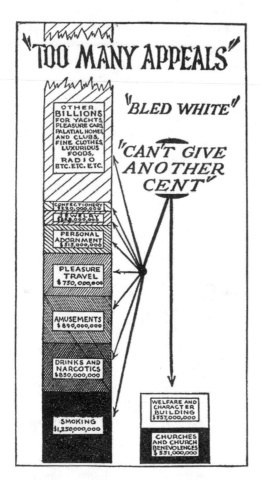

12. "Too Many Appeals," a poster from the Golden Rule Foundation, as reproduced in William H. Leach, *Here's Money for Churches* (Nashville: Cokesbury, 1936), 38.

another Methodist, George Morelock, was issuing a call to resist many of those techniques in the name of "spiritualizing church finance." The Methodist Episcopal Church, South, had decided to designate the second Sunday in June "Laymen's Day" and named the theme for 1936 "spiritualizing church finance." In a booklet designed to help prepare pastors and lay leaders for the upcoming festivities, Morelock, general secretary of the General Board of Lay Activities, provided a suggested order of worship, scripture readings, and extensive notes for featured speakers on the theme to use in preparing their remarks. Among these notes was a remarkable critique of most of the devices used in contemporary church finance:

> It would be impossible to name all of the "expedients" that have been used but we mention some: high pressure campaigns with the money object only in view ; the teaching of legalism with particular reference to the tithe with only the idea of securing money for the Church in mind; "bringing home the bacon," or the individual "cork-screw" method for the purpose of getting money out of an individual regardless of the effect upon him; the high powered collection at the public worship service where the only objective in view is to secure a particular sum of money needed at the moment; the use of pink teas, ice cream suppers, dinners, bazaars, auction sales and other kindred devices of raising little sums of money here and there for various causes; temporary tithing campaigns to raise church debts; the careless indiscriminate giving of "loose" change in various groups and at various services of the Church. None of these "expedients" will ever spiritualize Church finance because they are all primarily centered on "raising money" and leave out of account any thought, or plan, to develop the spiritual life of the individual.[47]

Having gutted Leach's most effective approaches to getting money, Morelock sought to put in their place a primary concern for the spiritual life of the individual. If the person were to give from a sense of coercion, or out of a desire for popularity, or "to pay for something," or to do his share, or grudgingly, then the giving could not, in Morelock's view, ever be spiritual. "But," Morelock wrote, "if the person gives cheerfully; if he brings his gift regularly to the Church as an act of worship; if he makes the matter a subject of prayer; if his gift really represents his ability to support the Kingdom and is consequently sacrificial; if he really feels that he is giving unto the Lord"; then the gift would inevitably result in that individual's spiritual growth.[48]

Leach and Morelock were setting the terms of the next half century's debate on church fund-raising. The debate was between those wished to talk about *motives* for giving and those who were more interested in discussing the *means* for attracting gifts to the church. Neither side's proponents saw themselves as promoting anything other than the church's welfare. Nor did either think that the churches would lack for funds if their plans were embraced. Yet the conflict between means and motives for giving would become a staple of the literature through the end of the century. Often it was the motive-centered writers who best represented clerical hopes for a church filled with people doing the right things for the right reasons.

PRINCES OF THE PULPIT AND
THE LOYALTY SUNDAY SERMON

The era from 1910 through the late 1940s saw an extraordinary number and range of popular Protestant preachers working in America's cities. These princes of the pulpit, as they were known, served large congregations, were frequently on the radio, had their sermons reported on in Monday morning newspapers, spoke to large followings beyond their own congregations, and often turned their sermons into books that sold briskly. Though their sermons often ran to forty minutes, they were much more likely to tell stories with compelling images and memorable morals than the preachers of previous eras, who were inclined toward the detailed exegesis of a biblical passage or a minutely argued excursus on a fine point of theology.

While the word *stewardship* still figured prominently in their presentations, the great preachers were apt to deliver their "money sermons" on a day called "loyalty Sunday." Loyalty as a moral category partook of a somewhat different motivation for giving, that of being true to one's church for all that it had done and could do. The reciprocal relation emphasized in stewardship was that between God and individuals, but loyalty emphasized reciprocity with the church. Thus the most famous of the pulpiteers, Harry Emerson Fosdick, could urge Riverside Church members in New York City to "stand by the church." A great deal of contemporary support for Christianity was, Fosdick thought, quite vague. But Christians who gave actual dollars to actual churches were engaged in a concrete form of witness: "On Budget Sunday, we celebrate another type of Christian, a man whose money is to him, as it were, a part of himself, so that what he does with it he is, in a real sense, doing with himself. For a man's money is an extension of his body, an enlargement of that material, physical equipment through which his spirit works. Money is another pair of legs and, lo! it can go where otherwise we could never go, walking amid the need of China today or ministering in India and the islands of the sea."[49]

George Lundy, an active layperson and a principal in the church fund-raising firm Martz and Lundy also helped speak to the emerging new cause-centered philosophy. As he looked around him he still saw preachers trying to persuade people to give more money by trying to prove that they were selfish. Lundy, meanwhile, thought that putting people on the defensive never worked as well as positive reinforcements, for people did not really give to institutions per se, but rather they gave "money *to* the church in order that the Gospel may be preached, the sick visited, the bereaved comforted, the young taught the story of Christ."[50] Lundy believed that pastors needed to work harder at presenting the great purposes accomplished by the church as opportunities for giving so that people wanted to give. Lundy would have approved of Fosdick's evocation of exotic missionary laborers in China and India to help raise the Riverside Church's annual budget. Lundy emphatically disapproved of the Every Member Canvass presentation that relied too heavily on the budgetary needs of the church. He also found some of the innovations of the last half century counterproductive. "We appeal to people to give more," Lundy said, "then do about everything we can to prevent them from doing so. We have forgotten, or we have not realized that people like to give to causes, rather than have them lumped into a sort of ecclesiastical community chest, so we have developed the one-budget system and we have said to the people, 'we will have only one appeal in our church during this year.' "[51]

Lundy also disliked a practice he found all too common, that of preachers discouraging their members from making charitable gifts to outside causes. In his experience as a fund-raiser, people who gave to charities outside the church were more, not less, generous with their churches because such people tended to fall into what he called " 'giving-habit' tracts." Preachers who understood this and understood the spiritual uplift that came from the act of giving had nothing to fear from the dreaded act of preaching about money. Such preachers— who recognized that when a man or a woman gave money they gave something of their personality—could, Lundy argued, "preach on giving from [the] pulpit every Sunday, without causing offense to anyone."[52]

The prominent preachers of the day showed great facility at articulating cause-based rationales for supporting the church. George Arthur Buttrick, pastor of the Madison Avenue Presbyterian Church in New York City, preached a sermon, "A New Day for Our Church," to kick off a capital campaign for renewing his congregation's fifty-three-year-old building. He grounded his plea in history; since 1834, the church had built and renewed property to meet the needs of the time, the last major addition being a ten-story church house building, including two gyms and a swimming pool built in 1916, when there were no recreational facilities in the Yorkville section of Manhattan. But that was in the teens, and now, Buttrick argued, there were new needs: "Our social service program is obviously being assumed more and more for weal or woe by government. But what increasing call for Christian friendliness in this raucous and lonely town! And for Pastoral Counseling, preventive as well as curative! And for the Christian nurture of children and youth, not forgetting the rest of us, who are only grown-up children! And for the stillness and praise of worship!"[53] Church officers had asked, Buttrick reported, "What does God require of our church now?" And had concluded that the building needed to be renewed. But what of those who would say, how can the church raise and spend vast sums of money in a world filled with hunger and need? Buttrick parried the objection, saying, "I could not heartily espouse this new venture in our church life if I did not believe that it will give us a new bell to win more people to give more money for every needy land. I do believe it will do just that, for we have reached a juncture in our history when we must go forward or slowly fail."[54] Buttrick went on to describe the practical needs that would be addressed, such as leaking lead pipes, but he also proceeded to sell the greater vision of the service that the congregation could be to its neighbors in spiritual terms with a new building. Finally, Buttrick clinched the sale by making the oldest of all real estate agents' claims, that the buyers can afford the house they really have come to want: "Can we do it? Yes, on a three-year basis for pledges so that the payments can be spaced. This is what has already happened: I have gone to eight or ten friends in the church, and they have promised amounts that total about $250,000, one quarter of the total outlay required. Yes, it can be done, granted that we deny ourselves luxuries, and give ourselves the joy of building a house worthy of God's works; and granted that everyone gives as little or much as he is able."[55]

Another New York City pastor, Albert A. Chambers, rector of the Church of the Resurrection, preached a Loyalty Sunday sermon titled "That Your Love May Abound," which articulated an exceedingly common theme during this era, that of giving time to the church. Clergy such as Chambers made the case that dedicating a portion of one's energy and time back to God, who had given them through the church, was both necessary and best accomplished by giving money. If one earned one, two, five, ten, or twenty-five dollars an hour and gave accordingly one, two, five, ten, or twenty-five dollars a week to the church, then one was giving one hour of his or her time per week to the church. Chambers and others thus sought to simultaneously naturalize and spiritualize the financial support of the church. Since people were not notably reluctant to give time to the church, donating the proceeds of some of their wage-earning time was made to appear natural. In Chamber's sermon the contribution of money also took on spiritual significance. He argued that "through the gift of your money you give your time in the missionary field since that money pays the salaries of missionaries—of priests, doctors, nurses, teachers who are representing you wherever your church is at work, at home in the home missionary field, or abroad in the foreign missionary field."[56]

The leading ministers of the day who were comfortable preaching about money also gave themselves substantial freedom to seek out new biblical texts to support their broadening theology of stewardship. The Reverend Charles H. Hagadorn, minister of the Community Church in Chautauqua, New York, argued that the right use of possessions was the subject Jesus talked about most. The Reverend J. Wallace Hamilton, minister of the Pasadena Community Church in St. Petersburg, Florida, preached a sermon based on the text in Matthew 26:8–9 in which Judas complains, "Why was the waste with the ointment made for it might have been sold for much, and given to the poor"; Hamilton argued that people needed to develop a sense of beauty, devotion, and generosity that the "Judas mind" would never understand.[57] The dean of Christ Church Cathedral (Episcopal) in Hartford Connecticut, Lewis M. Hirshon reinterpreted 1 Corinthians 4:2 to try to redeem stewardship from its captivity to fund-raising and instead render it as the substance of faithfulness.[58] The minister of the First Union Congregational Church in Quincy, Massachusetts, John P. Jockinsen, kicked off a stewardship campaign with an unusual text, that of the Shema. Just as ancient Hebrew parents were guided to teach the words "Hear, O Israel, the Lord thy God is one" to their children, so Jockinsen believed this central imperative for the church in his time, and particularly in Quincy, was to provide a place for an effective teaching ministry to train children and youth. Jockinsen rang on the themes of juvenile delinquency, quoting FBI director J. Edgar Hoover as saying, "The Sunday school is undoubtedly the most effective means in our country for fighting juvenile crime and delinquency."[59] Jockinsen wound up his appeal for money for a new educational wing with a tug at the emotional heartstrings: "We had a picture of 150 of our children and youth in front of this church, with a caption, 'What are they worth?' Well, what *are* they worth? Just how much would you be willing to take for that 5-year-old boy or girl? One of those little boys in the front row was stricken with poliomyelitis last summer and died. His mother would not have taken a million dollars for that boy. I doubt if there is a single parent here who would give up the life of his child for any price."[60] Jockinsen didn't have to test his proposition, for the funds poured in to the First Union Congregational Church of Quincy, and the new educational wing was soon built. Robert James McCracken, Harry Emerson Fosdick's successor in the pulpit of the Riverside Church in New York, choose 2 Corinthians 9:7 and rendered a familiar text as "God loves a hilarious giver."[61] Far from wanting to make people give until they hurt, McCracken hoped that like St. Francis, David Brainerd, William Carey, or even God, people would give generously and with joy without thought for cost. Christianity's central assertion about God, McCracken preached, "is that He so loved the world as to give His only Son for its redemption."[62] Since it was more blessed to give than to receive, in Christianity giving was a spiritual act, "as truly religious as praise or prayer or preaching." Thus, for McCracken, the mention of money belonged in the pulpit.

The Reverend Richard Pacini, minister of the Fairmont Presbyterian Church in Cleveland Heights, Ohio, took the idea of single-minded devotion even further than McCracken. Without ever mentioning money directly, Pacini went for the jugular in an attempt to get people to accept God's assignment of a trust in them through life. "The thought which looms large at our funeral services is," Pacini told his parishioners, "'what kind of a man was he?' It doesn't seem to matter then what he had, it only matters what he was. Did he understand that he was in debt to life? That the great world around us belongs to Another, whose we are, and to whom we owe both gratitude and allegiance? That, after all, is the best in life   to know that we are debtors to the Lord of life!" Pacini's steward-ship text for that year was from the twenty-first chapter of the Gospel according to John, in which the resurrected Jesus asks Peter three times if Peter loves him and receiving assent asks Peter to "follow me."[63]

The new rector of St. Luke's Episcopal Church in Jamestown, New York, in 1951 was called upon to preach in such a way as to secure pledges for a church in chronic debt with a bad habit of undersubscribing its approved budget. He chose as his text the feeding of the five thousand with five barley loaves and two small fishes. In his treatment of this text, George Francis O'Pray made it clear in a number of ways that he was a good level-headed Episcopalian. First he argued that the miracle did not supersede any laws of nature, but rather "it simply superseded the natural tendency of man to look after himself."[64] A miracle had occurred since the food that apparently had not existed was there when the hearts of the people were opened. O'Pray was, himself, preaching toward a modern-day miracle, that of getting $19,000 or more out of Jamestown Episco-palians, who, he knew, were spending more collectively on cosmetics, tobacco, entertainment, alcoholic beverages, and other luxuries. But, in an unusual twist on the sin sermon, O'Pray spoke directly to his parishioners without becoming holier than thou:

> Now I have no grievance against any amount spent on luxuries and no intention whatsoever of preaching against them, but I do think the amount spent for them as compared with the amount given to the churches is badly out of line. Episcopalian women are quite attractive—that's good—and if cosmetics help, I'm all for cosmetics. Episcopalians smoke—I do myself. Episcopalians go to the movies, plays, concerts, and enjoy other forms of recreation; nothing wrong in that—recreation is helpful, not only for the body, but for the mind and spirit as well. Episcopalians have been known to have a cocktail or a social drink and who is to condemn them if they are temperate about it? Episcopalians buy some jewelry, fur coats are wonder-

ful against the cold winter winds, and taking a chance on something when the gain or loss doesn't hurt anyone else can't be called evil.[65]

O'Pray made it clear that he would be the last one to preach against luxuries, in and of themselves, but he argued that just as the food was there all the while during the feeding of the five thousand, so there was money enough in the pockets of St. Luke's parishioners that they could give to the church if they wanted to do so. In fact, O'Pray went further: "Anyone belonging to the church who spends more on these things than he contributes to the Christian cause is selling his Lord short, and might better pledge his allegiance to Coty perfumes, or Liggett & Myers tobacco, or Metro Goldwyn Mayer, or Hiram Walker." For O'Pray it came down to this: was there going to be a cross on the altar or a carton of Lucky Strikes—was Christ or were luxury goods to be worshiped? O'Pray hoped for something better than that. Indeed, he hoped that this day when the pledges were to be made could be called "the miracle at St. Luke's."[66] Humorously shamed and bluntly guided as they were, St. Luke's members that day pledged a total of $25,000 for the 1952 budget.

Another Episcopalian with a gift for raising money was Samuel M. Shoemaker of the Calvary Episcopal Church in Pittsburgh. He based a sermon on increased and sacrificial giving on Luke 6:38, in which Jesus says, "for the measure you give will be the measure you get back." The meaning of the text, Shoemaker pointed out, was that simply put one's spiritual blessing would be equal to one's degree of stewardship. Just as in the best of Christian homes where there was free exchange about the family budget, so in the household of faith there needed to be some talk about money. Shoemaker expressed his displeasure with those who wanted it otherwise, saying, "I have no patience with the people who never want churches to talk about money. They are always the people who want to get out of doing what they should." And with a combination of direct speech and shameful comparisons, Shoemaker told church members exactly what they ought to be doing. He noted that the Church of the Brethren, which ministered largely to people of moderate means, was receiving $75 per capita each year while Episcopalians, largely people of economic privilege, gave on average $26.51. Meanwhile, mission giving was less than $2 per head a year. "Think of it," Shoemaker related to his parishioners, "you can't get two good haircuts in Pittsburgh for that—you pay more for one good necktie—it goes out the window when you sit down for a drink with a couple of your friends." Then Shoemaker ended with a soft-sell approach for tithing, noting that people who practice tithing always said, in his experience, that it blessed them. He related the experiences of two of his wardens at Calvary Church in his former parish in New York. Tithing was really best seen as part of one's spiritual discipline and only derivatively related toward raising the church budget. Still, Shoemaker reminded his hearers, "the measure you give will be the measure you get back."[67]

Anson Phelps Stokes Jr., rector of St. Bartholomew's Church in New York City, which had wealthy parishioners, was also blessed with a large church endowment. The stewardship that Stokes preached was based not on the church's need but on the human motivation of gratitude. Fundamentally, Stokes said, "God is not asking for our money. He is asking for ourselves. If we give ourselves and all that we possess to Him, then our money will be at His disposal."[68] Across town at Christ's Church, Ralph W. Sockman also asked church members to present themselves as an offering unto God. He quoted the Apostle Paul: "I beseech you, therefore, brethren by the mercies of God, that you present your body as a living sacrifice, holy, acceptable unto God which is your reasonable service" (Romans 12:1). Sockman asked whether today's Christians could pass a loyalty test. In the midst of the 1950s red scare, Sockman's choice to ring the chimes of patriotism doubtlessly had an effect. A Methodist, he followed his denomination's interpretation of the living sacrifices involving four things, namely, to pledge one's prayers, one's presence, gifts, and service to the church.[69]

The sense that Christian stewardship was somehow tied up in the great contest between the capitalist West and the communist East appeared frequently in the writings of the day. Episcopalian Bernard Iddings Bell, preaching from Washington, D.C., argued that the church stood in some sort of judgment over all economic or political systems and offered to anyone God's revealed truth about human life, saying in effect, "Here are the principles which Almighty God has laid down for mutual living."

Peter Marshall, minister of the New York Avenue Presbyterian Church in Washington, D.C., preached a money sermon on the theme of Zacchaeus the tax collector. Fifteen minutes into a very dramatic presentation of Zacchaeus's story, in which hearers were led to identify with Zacchaeus and were moved to celebrate his restoration to wholeness and right relation with God and his community in his joyful pledge of restitution, Marshall finally linked the account with the issue of money and the call to pledge generously. He argued that it was significant that it was only after Zacchaeus decided to make financial restitution and further give over half of his fortune to the poor that Jesus confirmed the fact of his conversion. Zacchaeus was restored to wholeness or health by virtue of his willingness to give up that which he had hoarded:

A man who loves money, who is a miser, who does not use his money as God wants him to use it, is a sick man.

He is not "whole"—not spiritually well. Jesus always looked with troubled eyes on rich people because He knew what money can do to them.[70]

Peter Marshall also knew what money could do to the spiritual health of rich people. And he invited them to be like Zacchaeus—to leave the crowd and overcome limitations of self. Those who gave themselves to the Lord, Marshall said, would like Zacchaeus find that giving their money would be easy. "Why not," Marshall asked, "as you leave this service—take Jesus home with you? Zacchaeus did—why don't you?"

Though stewardship and church administration writers would have had it otherwise, the great preachers of the 1930s, 1940s, and 1950s tended toward a lighter touch. For an older preacher like Fosdick, money was a way to engage in mission; for a younger preacher like Marshall, being freer with money was a way to become closer to Jesus. Where once preachers might have universally railed against smoking or the use of alcohol, the Episcopalian preachers made light of their parishioners's habits for the sake of a relatively larger pledge. Indeed, even the Methodist preachers had begun to strike a more pragmatic tone. By the end of World War II, the theology of stewardship was in eclipse, and few preachers expected all members to start tithing. But raising money to meet a church's budget with a few of the right words from the clergy and a lay-led organization to solicit pledges was proving sufficiently effective.

CHAPTER SIX

Changing the Nature of the Firm:

From Institutional to Consumer Churches

Amajor transformation of the function of church buildings
took place toward the end of the nineteenth century and at the
start of the twentieth. Viewed economically, expectations for
the building as a productive capital asset were increasing. In the eighteenth century and most of the nineteenth, the church building was
expected to provide shelter for the worshipers on Sunday and be a venue
for lesser services throughout the week. The studies or offices of the
clergy were invariably located in the minister's home, parsonage, manse,
or rectory. Some of this, of course, was simple efficiency. Heat and light,
precious commodities, were needed throughout the week in the pastor's domicile. So it made great sense to heat a small physical plant
instead of a large one, except in cases where numerous people needed to
be accommodated. Prayer meetings conducted during the week would
take place in the manse or in private homes. More than just frugality,
however, was involved; the lack of shared meeting spaces and offices in
church buildings reflected the absence of a larger conception of what a
religious congregation should do, be, and provide. Church buildings
were not widely used even as staging points for the works of charity

common to religious life in the nineteenth century. People engaged in the work of this so-called benevolent empire preferred to erect dedicated buildings for religious-based social services such as orphanages, poorhouses, academies, and mission stations for sailors or railroad workers.

The Progressive Era and the Social Gospel furnished Christians of all sorts with fresh imagination about what a congregation ought to do for its members, both socially and devotionally, and for the world at its doorsteps. Important to the renovation of this congregational imagination were changes wrought in late nineteenth-century industrial cities. Just as the the building and makeover of dozens of cities in the British Isles during the Industrial Revolution in the early nineteenth century had brought problems of previously unimagined scope and scale, so in American cities during the late nineteenth century the construction of factories, the influx of immigrants, the pressing need for housing, and public goods shortages put new problems before religious leaders. The prevailing moral conception of life was focused on persons productively engaged in the countryside or small villages in pursuits related to agriculture or trade; one's fate was then tied to the work of one's own hands and diligence. This conception increasingly failed to do justice to the experience of urban Americans. Freeholding prosperous male farmers were not the norm. Instead, the typical late nineteenth-century American was working in a wage economy and living in close proximity to large numbers of people who were anonymous to one another and could inspire in each other fear. At the turn of the century, the moral world of the United States was increasingly centered on the country's rapidly growing cities. In Cincinnati, Chicago, Columbus, Pittsburgh, and San Francisco, together with the industrial cities of the eastern seaboard like Lowell, Massachusetts, and Paterson, New Jersey, religious people faced new realities for which the model of the church on the village green was inadequate.[1]

It was in Akron, Ohio, that the future of American urban church architecture and the key to a revised conception of the nature of American Protestant congregations began to take shape. Akron was well suited to providing a structural solution to the needs of congregations in the industrial era. It was laid out in 1825 by General Simon Perkins as a town on the path of the Ohio and Erie Canal, which was completed just two years later, and the Pennsylvania and Ohio canal, which was completed in 1840. Akron grew quickly as an industrial center because of the water power and transportation supplied by these canals. After Benjamin F. Goodrich located a rubber factory there in 1871, the city became associated with the production of automobiles tires, but its growth as an urban center was already under way in 1869 when Lewis Miller, a Methodist Sunday school superintendent, devised a radical design innovation entailing multiuse spaces and a new conception of the social role of church buildings.

One of the things that favored the development of this new conception of the church was the transformation of the Sunday school over the course of the nineteenth century. In its first incarnation in industrial England, the Sunday school provided a time to teach working children how to read on their single day off during the week in the hope that they might read the Bible for self-improvement. When John Raike's invention of the Sunday school made it to American shores, it was quickly combined with the early Methodist custom of gathering classes of believers for mutual instruction and support. In the South, classes for adults and children meant that the Sunday school would meet before the worship hour. It became more characteristic of the North, however, for Sunday school for children and worship for adults to occur at the same time. In Akron, Superintendent Miller lamented that this arrangement meant the children would not worship. His plan to remedy the situation was to offer children's worship led by and for children during part of the church school period. In order to save time in moving children and to economize on space, he designed an assembly hall surrounded on three sides by two tiers of classrooms. Heavy curtains or wooden partitions would close off the cubicles surrounding the auditorium. (See illustration 13.) The Akron Plan, as it was called, was soon copied in churches throughout the United States, for not only did it provide for the putative needs of children but it also was a supremely adaptable space for other groups in the church. Weekday prayer meetings for men or women, missionary support group meetings, plays upholding Christian values staged in the auditorium, temperance meetings, ice cream socials, church fellowship suppers, and ladies circles could all be accommodated in the same flexible structure. It was not uncommon, in fact, for multiple activities to be accommodated on a single day.

Closely related to the Akron Plan for a divisible space in the Sunday school wing were changes occurring in the sanctuaries of American city churches. While Episcopalians and Roman Catholics continued to build their sanctuaries based on classical forms and designs, Protestant churches with evangelical roots turned once again to vernacular forms to reconfigure their places of worship. Now, instead of the home, it was to the theater and the lecture hall that designers turned. Pews set in straight rows gave way to curved pews, or even individual theater seating focusing on the space occupied by the preacher. Communion tables all but disappeared, as did baptismal fonts. The enclosed pulpit also disappeared as a relic of an outdated style, to be replaced by a stage with a central lectern opened to the sides so that the preacher might—like a

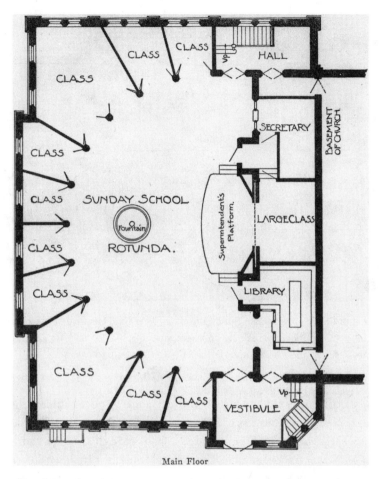

Main Floor

13. A floor-plan of the original Sunday School Building, First Methodist
Episcopal Church, Akron, Ohio, as reproduced in Marion Lawrance, *Housing the Sunday School* (Boston: Pilgrim Press, 1911), 87.

14. Plymouth Congregational Church, Brooklyn, New York, Historic American Buildings Survey, National Park Service (photographer: E. P. MacFarland, 1934). Library of Congress, Prints and Photographs Division, HABS, NY,24-BROK,31–3.

camp meeting revivalist or a highbrow Chautauqua lecturer—stride across the stage while delivering his remarks. The stage or platform, no longer a chancel, was also large enough to accommodate an organ and a choir, which had, in the spirit of theatrical showmanship, been moved from their traditional positions in a rear balcony to be up front as part of the entertainment.[2] Pictured in illustration 14 is Henry Ward Beecher's Plymouth Church in Brooklyn, New York, a typical example of the lecture hall church.

Both the Akron Plan and the remaking of sanctuaries into theatrical lecture halls were part of the still larger transformation called the institutional church movement. Institutional churches often utilized these new design forms, but they did not need to since the conception transcended new architecture. The idea of the institutional church was to meet the wide variety of needs of contemporary parishioners and their communities. In addition to worship and instruction, institutional churches offered many opportunities for fellowship, self-improvement, social service, and participation in athletics. An institutional church offered programs seven days a week and, apart from Sundays, might easily be mistaken for a YMCA or a YWCA of the era. They were a characteristic invention of an age that had learned that Christian civilization was not to be found out on the streets of the American city, but it just might be experienced in the context of a total institution that met the needs of the Christian child, woman, and man for friends, fellowship, and wholesome physical refreshment within the context of a church-sponsored program. Institutional churches could be found in every city of the nation and every ecclesiastical tradition. While smaller urban and rural congregations still were more numerous, it was the institutional churches that captured the affections of the era's laypeople and ministers. This was in part because institutional churches incarnated the dominant social theology and ideology of the day. These churches tended to be activist in orientation, often sponsoring settlement houses or off-site work with persons considered less fortunate. They were activist in another sense as well, since they represented an optimistic view of human capabilities for community and progress in the turn-of-the-century city. The large role they gave in their institutional beings to the importance of youth signaled a determination not to lose at home the gains made abroad in "the evangelization of the world in our lifetime." Institutional churches, therefore, captured the hearts and minds of Protestants, much as parochial schools had quickly captured the allegiance of Roman Catholics.

The institutional church ideal went beyond a merely bigger and better edifice. In a paper read before the African American clergy of Washington, D.C., on December 5, 1892, Alexander Crummell, a leading voice in the black church at the time, challenged the ministers of color in his city to not merely continue to build fine buildings and activities for church members but also use their churches to build institutions of charity and mercy. Some members of black churches, Crummell allowed, might be inclined to plead poverty. But, he answered, "the large and stately church edifices in every state and city, erected by our people, negatives the plea. Poor as we are as a people, we are rich in picnics, parades, excursions, church entertainments, and the upbuilding of temples. Now let some of this zeal and expenditure run in the channel of benevolence." Crummell argued that each Christian body in the District of Columbia should try to establish an orphanage, a home for widowed members of the churches, a hospital, or a home for "friendless girls." Churches might cooperate in these efforts, but they really were not optional in the institutional conception of the church. And so, Crummell argued, "the people should be called upon to aid in the effort by contributions; and the sick and dying exhorted to give legacies for the endowment of the same. And thus, and in other divers ways, we could begin, as other Christian people have done in all Christian ages, to carry on the divine command of the Lord Jesus, to give meat to the hungry and drink to the thirsty; to take in the stranger, to clothe the naked; to visit the sick; to call upon the prisoner."[3]

For the clergy, institutional churches offered the promise of achieving all aspects of church work that the Progressive Era religious leader thought necessary, in part through specialization. Because they were heavily programmatic operations, institutional churches required both larger physical plants and larger staffs to operate. It was in these churches that the use of multiple seminary-trained clergy and other professionals quickly grew. A neighborhood or rural church might, if it were lucky, have a full-time minister and a part-time caretaker. An institutional church, on the other hand, might have many full-time individuals detailed to teaching, working with youths, visiting with the elderly, directing social service work, preparing and serving meals, and keeping the building clean and open, not to mention the traditional task of preaching and the gargantuan task of administering a complex program. Not only with their retinues of many paid servants, but even in their appearance and furnishings, many of the institutional churches resembled nothing so much as the homes of wealthy Victorian era families.[4] (See illustration 15.) The God worshiped in these churches could almost have been expected to appear in white gloves and opera attire. Institutional churches, because they offered such an array of programs, often induced large numbers of members to spend substantial portions of their discretionary time in church-related activities. Consequently, they were able to appeal to these members for financial support of the programs.[5] Institutional churches not only had programmatic excitement and the appearance of vitality going for them; they also had a greater ability to aggregate members' resources in order to pay for the staff and the structure needed to produce the ministry for which they were so justly famous.

Institutional churches, because they represented such a sizable investment in one place, committed Protestants to staying in locales for the long term. The effect of all of this soliciting and spending money for buildings was not dissimilar to putting up a new, large, and efficient factory on credit. As long as the factory is in full production, the economies of scale make the facility an asset that not only pays off its debts but also bests its competition. Yet once demand falls for the products produced by the factory, scale and scope work to make the asset a very expensive albatross around the necks of its owners. Likewise, institutional churches in their heyday were large-scale vehicles for vital ministries in the great American cities. Yet their very success in the first half of the twentieth century would later blind many religious leaders to these churches' real liabilities.

The institutional churches that survived did so because of favorable demo-

15. First Baptist Peddie Memorial Church, Broad and Fulton Streets, Newark, Essex County, New Jersey, Historic American Buildings Survey, National Park Service, Library of Congress, Prints and Photographs Division, HABS NJ,7-NEARK,33-5.

graphics and judicious adaptations to their changing communities. Those that did not make it, or that remained as oversize monuments to a former glory, frequently failed not through an unwillingness to supply a vital ministry but rather because of a diminished demand for a particular ministry in a particular place.[6] As early as the 1910s, Methodist Church leaders were documenting with pins in maps the decline of Denver neighborhoods and the oversupply of congregations for the remaining residents. Like people who loved their large homes long past the time they could afford them, or factory owners sentimentally attached to wonderfully huge but obsolete factories, many American congregations found themselves attached to a place and a way of enacting their faith whose time had passed. Not surprisingly, the closing of churches, or at the very least the paring down of staff size, is often interpreted as a failure of stewardship or faithfulness.[7] More probably, such matters should be seen as a defect of the market and of American culture's long-standing preference for building on fresh farmland rather than remaining within the context of historical settlements. Thus the tragedy, if there is one, is not a religious one in the

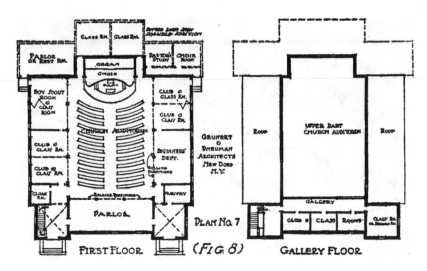

16. A recommended plan for modernizing the town church along institutional church lines, as reproduced in Edmund de S. Brunner, *The New Country Church Building* (New York: Missionary Education Movement, 1917).

narrow sense. Congregations are not so much remarkable for having some of their capital assets fail to produce with age as they are for how long they manage to keep utilizing their capital assets. Churches built in any period of the twentieth century have persisted better than the retail shopping outlets of their eras and neighborhoods.

The institutional church ideal extended powerfully to places where it was probably particularly ill suited, but its power as a model of what the church should be impressed even rural church leaders. In 1917, Edmund de Schweinitz Brunner, a pastor in the Moravian Church and a well known Christian writer of the period, wrote a book for the Missionary Education Movement's Library of Christian Progress series bearing the title *The New Country Church Building*. In it he quoted a prominent home mission secretary who, when asked what was the chief architectural need of rural American churches, remarked, "A large number of fires."[8] Brunner clearly agreed, believing that churches in the country needed to assimilate to the institutional ideal so that they might enlarge their ministries, "to include not alone the individual soul and the family, but the entire community as well. . . . We can never have a great Christian civilization in America, or in the world, if we cannot build little Christian civilizations in the smallest of our rural communities."[9] The first step in building a Christian civilization was erecting an adequate church facility, and, to that end, Brunner offered advice and plans for building smaller frame versions of the institutional churches popular in the cities. (See illustration 16.) He even provided a recommendation for using curtains to turn hopelessly old-fashioned pews into classrooms.

CONSUMER CHURCHES

The rise of the institutional church model of congregational life coincided with the revolution in the American market for manufactured goods and services. People could now obtain new suits, dresses, lamps, carriages, and machines of an array and type that were unimaginable in the antebellum period, and at prices that created the first truly mass market the world had ever known. America's first real consumer culture was also fostered by the rise of modern advertising techniques. What mass production did more significantly than anything else, culturally speaking, was to create the expectation that better, newer, preferable goods, techniques, and even ideas could be purchased from skilled manufacturers. A consuming culture did not stop at household articles; it purchased new and better engines, mills, machines, telegraphic equipment, and time recorders in business settings. The trust in manufactured culture that made Bell Telephone, Oneonta Time Recorder (later IBM), Underwood Typewriters, and the Singer Sewing Machine Company successful also spelled the beginning of the end of local, idiosyncratic solutions to human problems.

The implications of the new culture of consumption for Protestant churches might not be so readily apparent as for other areas of life, but the late nineteenth century also turned churches into consumers. A vast selection of consumables was available for sale to make a better church ranging from self-contained organs to church envelopes for systematic giving, classroom furniture for new Sunday schools, to hymn books to replace outdated Psalters, choir robes, early amplification devices, artificial lighting, factory-made stained glass shipped by rail, systematic printed charts of Bible history, and devices to record attendance and student success in memorizing parts of the Bible. All of these made the local church a consumer where heretofore congregations had been local producers of most of the items they needed. This subtle shift meant two things for the future of congregational enterprise. The first was that those churches that did not buy the paraphernalia of the church market often were felt by their pastors and members to be missing the trappings (or even requirements) of more successful churches. What could be more obviously faithful in Victorian America, after all, than a church striving to keep up with the challenges of its age? The second implication was that congregations became permanent consumers, and thus the cost of being a congregation, reflected in the cost of maintaining a customary local church lifestyle, was permanently raised to a new base.

A merican Protestant churches also came over time to express their identities in the architectural styles they favored. The greatest period of religious building in American history occurred during the twenty years following the end of World War II. *McCall's* magazine proudly proclaimed, "Not since Solomon have people lavished so much on housing for God and those who would worship Him."[10] Commissions for church building in total dollar volume in the 1950s were second only to those for hospital construction. Compared to hospitals, churches offered much richer symbolic possibilities and relative freedom from functional concerns. Architects would exercise that freedom in countless instances, finally getting their chance to make the kind of break with classical and renaissance forms that visual artists had made earlier in the century. Pietro Belluschi, whose Lutheran church commissions with their extensive use of natural and stained wood, and particularly his laminated arched trusses, would become almost a trademark of contemporary religious architecture, preached the value of experimentation in contemporary religious architecture: "It is easy to prove by any standard that imitative forms have no power to move, and that only the joyous excitement of new ideas, surging from a deeply felt experience and expressed with poetic clarity in structural honesty, can succeed in giving spiritual and emotional nourishment." By the mid-1950s it was estimated that 25 percent of all new Christian houses of worship were of completely contemporary design while for synagogues estimates ran as high as 85 percent.[11]

Though the best Gothic architecture still received the respect of professional architects due to the turn-of-the-century accomplishments of such master craftsmen as Ralph Adams Cram on church commissions and college campuses, the architects clearly turned their backs on the bulky institutional forms brought in by the Akron Plan. These churches may have efficiently served up programs from their brick and stonework urban castles, but in the eyes of postwar architects and parishioners they failed to excite. In 1957, the F. W. Dodge Corporation, publishers of *Architectural Record*, issued a volume of collected writings on religious architecture from the past decade under the title *Religious Buildings for Today*. The book was intended to instruct church and synagogue building committees on just what was possible with good contemporary design. The ax *Architectural Record* had to grind was made clear in the opening pages of John Knox Shear's introduction: "For three generations the depressing effect of bad architecture has been visited upon the worshippers of America. Because our church buildings have seldom appealed to our total interest, they failed to satisfy us. It must be acknowledged that churches share this failure with other building types, but because they are churches the failure seems more poignant." Marvin Halverson, the executive director of the Department of Worship and Arts of the National Council of Churches, was even more pointed in his condemnation of the Gothic and other received forms. He wrote, "The hiatus between architecture for the church and architecture for other institutions in groups and society exposes the shallowness of our understanding of the gospel and its relevance to all areas of our common life and all realms of society. The continuing penchant among many churches for Gothic and Renaissance denies their assertion that Christianity has significance for all aspects of man's life. It is an architectural denial of the meaning of the Incarnation and the belief that God continues to speak his Word in the language of each new age."[12] To architects and modern church leaders alike, new ways of thinking demanded a break from the past. The way in which particular churches and synagogues broke with the past, however, was by either adopting wholly contemporary designs or by assimilating to colonial church architectural forms, revised and updated according to the programmatic outline offered by Shear.

The dominant values that the structures of the postwar church building boom conveyed were comfort and size. Contemporary buildings showed these features most clearly. Sanctuaries were like open-plan living rooms, and the laminated trusses and wooden plank ceilings so prevalent in Pietro Belluschi–inspired churches created the same comfortable Friday-night-by-the-fire ambience as a wealthy family's ski lodge might. (See illustration 17.) Even colonial-style church buildings conveyed comfort. Few were built without pew cushions, carpeting, forced air furnaces, and other features of the well-appointed home. Just as in their homes filled with furnishings from the concurrent Early American craze, church members wished to attach themselves to a venerable tradition, but not to live like rustics. Here again the processes of assimilation and differentiation, described in chapter 2, were at work as congregations marked out their places in the local religious landscape.

The processes of assimilation and differentiation can clearly be seen at work in the postwar church building choices of Decatur, Georgia. (See illustration 18.) Religious building in this small city on the edge of Atlanta had been suppressed for most of the century on account of economic conditions peculiar to the South and then because of the general effects of the Great Depression and World War II. When the region was restored to prosperity and Decatur became one of the first communities outside Atlanta to benefit from a residential real estate building boom, the old religious building stock was due for an upgrade. Curiously, each of the mainstream Protestant churches in the community with the exception of some of the Presbyterians and the Episcopalians built a new church modeled on colonial/Anglican architecture. The Disciples of Christ built their church in 1950, and the Baptists built theirs in 1951. The new Colum-

17. Two 1960s churches, one Lutheran (above) and the other Southern Baptist, display the Pietro Belluschi–inspired lodge-look of laminated beams and exposed wooden ceilings. Author's photographs.

bia Presbyterian Church on the edge of town set in the middle of postwar ranch houses also assimilated to the colonial ideal in 1947. First United Methodist Church responded to tremendous growth in the 1950s and 1960s by retaining its old institutional church facility and building a massive red brick colonial church across the street in 1967, closing out the period of church building and signaling the end of new home building in the community. The older downtown Presbyterian church had likewise assimilated itself to an older ideal with its new building in 1952. But in this case it chose to build in a style identical to that employed by the nearby Agnes Scott College and the Columbia Theological Seminary, both of which were Presbyterian institutions built in red brick Collegiate Gothic with limestone accents. The remaining member of the group of churches with an antebellum heritage to assert was the Holy Trinity Episcopal church, which turned its back on a Gothic structure downtown in favor of a cruciform contemporary building (1972) that ironically distanced the Episcopalians from their colonial American heritage and allied them to the more eucharistically focused Roman Catholic and Lutheran traditions. Meanwhile, Roman Catholics, Christian Scientists, and Lutherans were also building new churches adjacent to the central business district. By contrast, however, these congregations marked off who they were in contradistinction to the old-line groups. The Christian Science Church (1963) was a completely modern structure of low-slung stained glass, aluminum, and wood. The Roman Catholic Church of St. Thomas Moore was a modern interpretation of mission architecture in sand-colored brick erected in 1947. The Lutheran Church was built in 1950 using rough-hewn granite, a nonindigenous material which, together with its massive red oak doors, made the facility instantly recognizable as Lutheran to visitors from Pennsylvania or Wisconsin.

Without identifiable forethought, each congregation used its choice of building type to articulate what it was in relation to the region's history, its own ecclesial tradition, and other congregations in the community. At precisely the same time as the leading citizens of the New South were under pressure to end Jim Crow practices once and for all, many of these Disciples, Presbyterians, Baptists, and Methodists chose to embrace an icon of the best portion of the Old South, namely, the red brick colonial church. Both defensively and constructively they forged a new future's understanding of themselves as the guardians of community tradition and virtue by finding a usable past in their houses of worship. What was, in fact, new architecture in the 1940s, 1950s, and 1960s appeared to be two centuries old and thus laid claim to a cultural supremacy and priority that did not rest on claims of racial superiority. Meanwhile, church traditions outside the mainstream of southern history differentiated themselves

18. Four post–World War II churches in Decatur, Georgia. Clockwise from top left: First United Methodist, Columbia Presbyterian, First Christian (Disciples of Christ), and First Baptist churches. Author's photographs.

by constructing their buildings in anything but the colonial style of red brick and white trim. This, too, was subject to change as when during the next thirty years after 1965, smaller, less elite traditions that were indigenous to, and prevalent in, the South adopted red brick colonial as their chief architectural form of self-expression. Today one finds throughout the South Church of God and Churches of Christ buildings along with smaller Pentecostal churches that are all indistinguishable from the antebellum evangelical denominations churches dotting the landscape.

BIGGER BARNS

Part of the significance of capital spending in American religious history can be read in the ever increasing scope and scale of church buildings. In the 1700s, the churches were clearly ordered to the purpose of hearing preaching, gathering the faithful to prayer, or celebrating the Eucharist, to degrees which varied according to the church's religious tradition. In the nineteenth century, the preacher, choir, and organ became the central focus of structure within the sanctuary itself as Protestants produced and housed their "princes of the pulpit" and developed increasingly theatrical worship styles. But churches grew even more dramatically outside the strict precincts of the sanctuary. In nearly every Protestant tradition, an increasing list of auxiliary functions can be discerned from the growing size of the typical parish plant as dedicated spaces for education, youth recreation, staff offices, and fellowship were added.

In the twentieth century, the varieties of sanctuary space became more diverse, but if anything the functions going on outside that space proliferated further. In the contemporary era, religious buildings carry all sorts of burdens. Scouting programs and twelve-step groups vie for space with mothers' support groups, shelters for the homeless, counseling centers, and office space for not-for-profits and advocacy groups. The physical plant is larger than ever, as is the number of purposes served. Yet some diffuseness has settled in with the greater number of tenants. It took the twentieth century and a culture of consumption and wild assimilation to produce the ultimate form of the institutional church, but produce it they have, and every church that does not define itself according to the programs it hosts or sponsors is either a rural, dying, courageous institution or a church of immigrant worshipers who have not yet assimilated the ideal of the twenty-four-hour, full-service church.

Four centuries of development in the investing in (and expressing identity through) the religious built environment has taken us from vernacular churches to churches that make a statement vis-à-vis modernity and received tradition. It is a move from an almost thoughtless innocence to a situation of choice that can be anything except thought-free. Once architects came into play and replaced pattern books, the process of intentionalizing religious building was well under way. Later they began to spend church money indulging their own views of a religious sensibility, but the earlier adoption of successive popular forms—Federal, Gothic, Akron Plan, Victorian—prepared the way for a distinctly American style of religious building, which we can call "consumption building." Just as Americans signify who they are by choosing the way they dress—blue jeans today, a suit tomorrow—without having to pay attention to dressing as a class- and tradition-restricted activity, so Americans in their institutional life have learned to choose whom they wish to be compared with by the building choices they make. As we have seen, in the United States it is possible for any group, however new or lowly, to consume a style of religion by building a structure like the rich Episcopalians of two centuries earlier.[13] Consumption building is a phenomenon of the second half of American history and is promoted by the rise of market capitalism and the emphasis on consumption, obsolescence, and disposability. Perhaps one symbol of the twenty-first-century church that makes a statement is Fellowship Church in Brentwood, Tennessee. (See illustration 19.) The church's name is ambiguous and nondenominational, but the form of the structure resembles a barn, a perfect family-values-friendly icon for this upscale family-oriented suburb of Nashville, whose houses dot the landscape where farms once stood.

The sheer cost of continually building and improving religious buildings has not escaped the notice of religious leaders. When they are not leading building projects, they have typically been found lamenting the waste that goes into building instead of mission and programmatic spending. The fact that it has continued nearly unabated for four centuries in the American context should cause us to wonder what deep needs are addressed when the religious attempt to materially structure their environment. What underlies this urge to build that is decried by contemporary clerical critics as the "edifice complex"? First is the deep need to make a mark in the environment—to fashion with one's hands still more perfect structures. These structures become like children in the sense that they are both part of us and transcend us—providing a kind of immortality. Second is a felt need to do something for God. Places of worship are symbolically close to where the action of the holy occurs. Even in traditions that officially discount the idea that God is to be quintessentially met in the *Domus Dei*, when the loved one of a member dies, memorial gifts used to purchase something for the sanctuary are much easier to come by than comparable gifts for, say, feeding the poor. Indeed, clerical resistance may come from the clergy's

19. Fellowship Church, Brentwood, Tennessee. Author's photograph.

own interests in redirecting funding away from capital improvements and toward programs. Or it may arise from understanding all too well the true religious significance of their parishioners' role in "improving" the place where God is worshiped as a modern-day form of ritual sacrifice.

CHAPTER SEVEN

Churches Expanding in

All Directions, 1945–1980

The thirty-five years following the close of World War II saw an enormous expansion in American life and prospects that would be measured in a variety of ways—by population, housing, educational opportunity, the end of legal segregation, and above all Americans' sense of responsibility in the world. The Protestant churches of the nation partook of the expansion by establishing many congregations in new suburban areas and by adopting the psychology of responsibility into their own thought and practice. By the end of the period, American Protestantism displayed the signs of stress resulting from the expansion as urban churches struggled to survive, and liberal, moderate, and conservative Protestants diverged in their convictions about the fundamental purposes of the church and even the role of money in the Christian life.

STEWARDSHIP AS RESPONSIBILITY

The watchword of the postwar era was responsibility. Responsibility is the peculiar province of those who can do something—or at least think they can. A victorious American culture asked itself in countless *Time, Life,* and *Look* articles how the United States was responsible for the world in new ways after World War II. The Marshall Plan represented a concrete act of taking on world responsibility, and the "loss" of China to Communist control was seen as a failure of responsibility. An elevated sense of American responsibility drove foreign policy to mount the Berlin airlift and to intervene in Korea. This idea of responsibility also powerfully reshaped postwar definitions of Christian stewardship. Stewardship became less about ritual submission to God, the giver of all good things, than it was about human beings discharging the responsibilities laid before them. A minister and author like Roy L. Smith might literally see hundreds of biblical texts as stewardship texts. Even though Smith was a great believer in "the tenth" and always made it a point to preach tithing at least five times each year, he argued that stewardship meant responsibility. Consequently, a text like Deuteronomy 4:32–40—"he loved your fathers and chose their descendants after them, and brought you out of Egypt with his own presence, by his great power"—became a stewardship scripture lesson, the point of which was that all were born with obligations: "Much effort has been expended on the subject of human rights, and much still remains to be done in that field before all men's rights have been made safe. But we dare not lose sight of the fact that every right is matched by a responsibility and that our privileges all come to us on a cash-and-carry basis. They must be paid for in service to the generation of which we are a part."[1]

In like manner, the story of Hannah was a stewardship text, for she demonstrated she was a "responsible mother" by giving up Samuel to the Lord.[2] Though Roy Smith went further than most in his expansive view of the meaning of stewardship, the idea that stewardship was about human responsibility was becoming prevalent. George L. Hunt read responsibility as the central Christian message. Jesus preached the message in parables such as that found in Luke 19. For Hunt, the parable of the pounds was not a lesson in smart business practices, nor did it teach shrewdness with money. Rather, it was "a lesson in using the abilities which God has given us. The man who uses wisely and faithfully the 'pound' which God has given him will be rewarded with increased responsibility according to his proved ability. However, the man who fails to use his God-given abilities will meet God's inexorable judgment. The 'pound' will be taken from him and he will be spiritually ruined." Moreover, after Jesus had introduced the idea of stewardship into the vocabulary of the Kingdom of God, it remained for the Apostle Paul to make it a fundamental dimension of faithfulness.[3] In this sentiment, Hunt was joined by a prominent biblical scholar of the era, Ernest F. Scott, who wrote of the apostle:

Paul's favorite image for Christian fidelity is that of stewardship, and this term as he uses it is meant to carry its full implication. The steward was a servant, working in the interest of another, but he was a trusted servant, who held a place of authority. He was free to choose his own tasks and to perform them in his own way, and part of his duty was to exercise his judgment boldly and intelligently in his master's service. "This only is required of a steward that he should be found faithful" (I Cor 4:2). So long as he discharged his trust he could think out all the details for himself.[4]

Christians as stewards were as free as they pleased, another idea in keeping with postwar notions of liberty and democracy, as long as they were responsible. The critique of the stewardship writers toward contemporary Christians in the immediate postwar years was that too many exercised their responsibility thoughtlessly. Thus Hunt would complain that too often churches wasted the precious resource of time. As a case in point, he noted his experience during the recent war when "a certain Women's Association which met only four times a year wanted to devote an entire program to the subject, 'The Differences Between Limoges and Haviland China.' The world was burning up and literally dying because men did not know the Christian message. Yet here was a group of woman willing to spend valuable time on a secular subject!"[5]

Secularity, "being conformed to this world" in an older, more biblical language, grew as a concern for mainline Protestant clergy and writers as prosperity increased. Wesner Fallaw observed that the home was failing its modern mission to be an arm of the teaching of church and life behavior, since in most homes the occupants were, like their society, basically secular. How would children and youth grow to be good, Fallaw wondered, when most of society was "preoccupied with superficial conduct characterized by the decadence of swing-bank exhibitionism and jitterbugs."[6] Though Americans were experiencing ever greater levels of income and wealth, they continued to give at the rate of about 2 percent of aggregate income to philanthropic causes, with the poorest people and the extremely rich being the most generous. The most grudging givers were those with incomes of between $10,000 and $25,000 per year.[7] Since this group was also the upper stratum of mainline Protestant churches, the comparison hurt. George Hunt noticed that the $3 billion given to all charities in a year just after the war neatly equaled the nation's tobacco bill for the same year and was dwarfed by the liquor bill. Hunt also tracked the Ladies' Home Journal series called "How America Lives" and noticed that of the fifteen families with church connections profiled in the series over three years, two were tithers, four gave 4 percent of their incomes, and the balance gave 2 percent or less, including two who gave nothing. He noted with obvious dismay that both of the tithing families were Baptists.[8] As a barometer of mainline American religious life, both the giving statistics and the anecdotal evidence revealed the same thing, how selfish Christians really were.

While mainstream Protestants continued to sit on their wallets, pastors like Roy Smith continued to preach the tithe. In 1958, two Episcopal priests and seminary professors, Richard Byfield and James P. Shaw, noticed that the message was still not getting through. They called installment buying the way of life in the suburbia, noting, "Rare indeed is the family that is not involved with a lending agency for the purchase of a washing machine, a refrigerator, a deep-freeze, or an electric range! Average installments on one such item come to about $10 per month; but the average suburbanite buys more than one thing at a time, and his payments are closer to $20 per month, or $5 per week. In 1957 the average Presbyterian gave $1.44 per week to his church."[9] Did these figures mean that the average Christian cared no more about the church than about his cigarettes or kitchen appliances? Perhaps not, but Byfield and Shaw probed:

> Let the reader ask himself the probable reaction of this same Mr. and Mrs. Homemaker if it were suggested that, by dropping the cigarette item, the church item could be doubled! Let him hear Mr. Homemaker on the subject of why it is impossible for him to carry his lunch to work in his brief case! And listen to the young Homemaker children when the family decides that the money they've been spending on the television set might be put to better use! "Let him . . . take up his cross, and follow me!" said Our Lord. "We will give the church what we can spare when the 'essential' items are all covered," is the response of our imaginary family!

Meanwhile, Byfield and Shaw thought there was blame enough to be laid at the feet of the clergy as well, for as hard as it might be to preach stewardship without talking about money, legions of pastors attempted to do that each year. Many, they noted, came from higher-class backgrounds than their parishioners and found asking for money—or revealing their own financial commitment to the church—unseemly. Others in avoiding the real topic allowed the laity to come "away from such a sermon confused and definitely in the dark as to what would constitute a good pledge! It is impossible to be specific in a sermon that is composed of harmless generalities." Still, pastors continued to fail in forming the economic mores of the laity in their care. One minister said, "I have taught tithing throughout my ministry, but no one in any of my congregations has ever become a tither!" For Byfield and Shaw, this was an all too common clergy experience. "One of the most frightening things about the pulpit ministry," they observed, was "the amount of preaching which means so much to the preacher and means nothing at all to his congregation." Preachers tended to be too easy, never really discussing the difficulties of real life—marriage, business ethics, economics, and politics—in theological terms from pulpit; or they tended to be too tough, verbally beating their congregations with "prophetic" sermons. The result was that congregations were unprepared for a concrete talk about money from the first kind of minister and reacted like the child who is always beaten—by emotional withdrawal—when the second kind began to preach.[10]

Clergy anxiety about position and status emerged in unusual ways and in unusual places. One of the most striking came at the end of George Laird Hunt's 1949 book, *There's No Place Like Home for Stewardship.* Hunt at the time was working for the Board of Christian Education of the Presbyterian Church (USA) in its Philadelphia headquarters. After spending time on the standard issues of the stewardship literature—whether the tithe should be based on pre- or posttax income and the biblical passages supporting various views of stewardship—and after criticizing women's associations and other church groups for spending time and effort on things that were not the marrow of the gospel, he offered readers a play that might be given at canvass time as an evening church entertainment. The play, "That Crazy Kid of Mine," was situated in the home of a prosperous Philadelphia Main Line family. The husband, Tom Atterbury, a forty-year-old insurance broker and his wife, Mary, have a son, Paul, who has gone to a church-sponsored camp and tells his parents that he is thinking about going into the ministry. Tom yells and Mary cries. Though they belong to a church and attend regularly, both are unhappy that their son is choosing a path that rejects their values and lifestyle. A key moment in the drama goes as follows:

> PAUL: Why, Dad? What's wrong with the ministry? (The misunderstood anger arouses Tom Atterbury to fever pitch and he replies in ranting tones.)
>
> TOM: It's just not our kind of life, that's what's wrong. We've made a nice home for you here that beats anything any down-at-the-heels preacher will ever live in. We have ideas that the Church calls wrong. We like cocktails and liquor; how would you feel preaching against something your own parents do? Our circle of friends don't take the Church so seriously; what would they think if a son of ours became a minister? They'd think you were crazy. We want you to marry a girl that's your equal, and none of the girls I know around here would feel very comfortable in a leaky, shabby manse. Someday we want to enjoy grandchildren. How will

we feel if they are a bunch of pious, mousy, hymn-singing kids that ask me to read them Bible stories? But that's not the main reason, Paul. The main reason is that I've worked hard to build up a good insurance business. Why? For myself? Partly. But chiefly so that you will have a good berth to fall into ten years from now. It's the second-best insurance business in the city today. Ten years from now it will be the best. And that's when it will be all yours. You're downright crazy to give that chance up for the uncertain, drab life of a poor preacher. If I can help it, you won't make that mistake. (He sits down heavily. Mary is, as usual, sobbing loudly. But Paul has regained his composure. He looks at his father calmly. The arguments are so flimsy that even his youthful mind knows they hardly deserve an answer. He is relaxed as he speaks.)[11]

Paul promises his parents that he would not do anything to hurt his father and mother if he could help it. But he also defends his choice: "It just seems to me that the world is in a mess today because too many people have thought only of themselves—right people, soft jobs, and all that—and not enough about others." Hunt's attitude toward the middle-class Christianity he knew as a pastor was transparently critical. It just was not real biblical religion. He spoke for the ranks of pastors who, like himself, made the kind of sacrifices and life commitments the gospel seemed to require of all Christians, and then watched as church members regarded the clergy as a different, useful, but socially inferior species.

FUND-RAISING TECHNIQUE AS THE SUBSTANCE OF POSTWAR STEWARDSHIP

After World War II, the majority of the books about church finances concerned technique rather than theology. This could be expected in the great age of how-to books. After all, the great lesson of World War II for victorious Americans was the triumph of American ingenuity. One such how-to offering was Weldon Crossland's 1947 *How to Increase Church Income.*[12] Theology faded to the background in these guides to success, and Crossland's book was no exception as it turned its primary attention to issues like developing the habit of giving in the young by securing a pledge from every child over the age of seven. This change in emphasis from theology to know-how was consistent with Crossland's view that "the raising of the budget ranks high among the important religious services any church renders to God and humanity."[13]

Crossland also believed that the key to recruiting adult givers was stressing the

PLEDGING RECORD OF

HENDERSON, MR. AND MRS. JOHN B.

This Pledge was made through
☐ The Church ☐ The Church School.
This Pledge can best be secured by
Henry Sheffield

YEAR	AMOUNT PLEDGED		SOLICITED BY	REPORT
1939-40	Cur.$ .50	Mis.$	Wk. Mo. Qu. Yr.	H. Sheffield	
1940-41	Cur.$ .75	Mis.$	Wk. Mo. Qu. Yr.	Loyalty Sunday	
1941-42	Cur.$ 75	Mis.$ 10	Wk. Mo. Qu. Yr.	Loyalty Sunday	
1942-43	Cur.$ 75	Mis.$ 25	Wk. Mo. Qu. Yr.	Loyalty Sun	
1943-44	Cur.$ 50	Mis.$ 10	Wk. Mo. Qu. Yr.	H Sheffield	Illness, death of father. In debt Sorry to cut.
1944-45	Cur.$ 75	Mis.$ 25	Wk. Mo. Qu. Yr.	Loyalty Sunday	

PLEDGING RECORD OF

HENDERSON, MR. AND MRS. JOHN B.

This Pledge was made through
☐ The Church ☐ The Church School.
This Pledge can best be secured by
Henry Sheffield.

YEAR	AMOUNT PLEDGED		SOLICITED BY	REPORT
1945-46	Cur.$ .75	Mis.$ .35	Wk. Mo. Qu. Yr.	H Sheffield	
1946-47	Cur.$	Mis.$	Wk. Mo. Qu. Yr.		
1947-48	Cur.$	Mis.$	Wk. Mo. Qu. Yr.		
1948-49	Cur.$	Mis.$	Wk. Mo. Qu. Yr.		
1949-50	Cur.$	Mis.$	Wk. Mo. Qu. Yr.		
1950-51	Cur.$	Mis.$	Wk. Mo. Qu. Yr.		

20. A pledge canvasser's record card, as reproduced in Weldon Frank Crossland, *How to Increase Church Income* (Nashville: Abingdon-Cokesbury Press, 1947), 52–53. Used by permission.

concept of loyalty. Together with ideals of stewardship and service, it was loyalty that would "Christianize the entire campaign."[14] Not surprisingly, Crossland and a good many others sought to press the loyalty concept as far as possible and used "Loyalty Sunday" as a sacralized occasion for receiving pledges from members and friends of the church. The Loyalty Sunday, if worked well in advance, assured that members of a congregation would be present and ready to place their pledges in a basket or on an altar (and, yes, advocates often used the term *altar* even when their theological traditions insisted there was no altar, but only a table on which to share the Lord's Supper) in front of God and one another.

Working the principle of loyalty to its greatest effect required that increasingly sophisticated records of past giving be kept in order to stimulate pledgers to "move up" when possible. (See illustration 20.) Crossland advocated that each prospect be rated according to interest and ability to give, and that the fellow member most likely to secure a good-sized pledge be sent to get it. This practice he called the "askings" phase, and he encouraged the minister to be one of the four individuals involved in preparing the "asks." Finally, borrowing a page from the Red Cross and Community Chest playbooks, Crossland suggested that it was crucial that the largest givers (and givers with the largest incomes) be approached for their gifts by other generous givers of like means before the stewardship campaign ever entered its public phase.[15] Once the public campaign had begun, the message was to be reiterated weekly from the front of the church with "Minute Men" talks, which took the basic form of commercials for the church as a product, delivered by lay spokesmen.

The techniques of the postwar Protestant mainline worked so well that they have been retained, at least in vestigial forms, for more than half a century. On the other hand, part of the reason for the subsequent decline in financing must have been that few church leaders in mainline Protestantism in the latter part of that half century had the confidence (or perhaps audacity) necessary to "work them" as ably or as shamelessly as religious leaders did in the 1940s and 1950s. Tapping actual motives for giving played a tremendous role in the successful campaign. Weldon Crossland noted the motives that worked:

- Because I love my church and want to help her.
- Because First Church does so much for my children.
- Because my church stands for the best things in the community.
- Because I believe that money given through my church is my best investment in happiness and human welfare.
- Because I like to support all good causes and the church is one of the best.
- Because I find help and friendship in my church.
- Because I wouldn't want to live in a community where there were no churches. If people didn't support them there would be none.
- Because God needs even my small help in his work.[16]

Crossland steered the churches away from appeals based on need, pity, and keeping up with other churches. Loyalty worked best as a theme for increasing giving to churches that were expanding their programs and growing in membership. And loyal members needed to increase their individual pledges, too, as suggested by the "stepping up" leaflet shown in illustration 21. As a church grew, its members were encouraged to make their giving grow by "stepping up" to a pledge higher than the one of the previous year.

With Crossland and others like him, the historian sees many of the most

---

OUR GLORIOUS GOAL: 560 PLEDGES FOR $14,755!

	AMOUNT PLEDGED WEEKLY
Let's All "Step Up"	$10.00—$11.00
Our Pledges	$8.00—$10.00
One or More Steps	$6.00—$8.00
Loyalty Sunday!	$5.00—$6.00
	$4.00—$5.00
God will increase	$3.00—$4.00
your prosperity	$2.50—$3.00
as you prosper	$2.00—$2.50
his work!	$1.75—$2.00
	$1.50—$1.75
	$1.25—$1.50
	$1.00—$1.25
	75c—$1.00
	50c—75c
	35c—50c
	25c—35c
	15c—25c
	10c—15c—Church School pledges
	5c—10c—Church School boys and girls
	1c—4c—Pledges by Church School children

LET EACH MEMBER DO EVERYTHING TO "STEP UP"!

21. A stewardship leaflet, as reproduced in Weldon Frank Crossland, *How to Increase Church Income* (Nashville: Abingdon-Cokesbury Press, 1947), 80. Used by permission.

common features of church fund-raising over the next half century already firmly in place: the Sunday for pledging, advance literature, stepping up, a campaign mentality, lay appeals from the pulpit, and rituals designed to increase participation. One also sees other forms of sophistication—such as securing large advance pledges during a quiet phase and segmenting the appeal for annual support among types of givers—that are common in nonchurch charitable fund-raising, but are virtually unknown inside congregations except in the course of professionally assisted building campaigns.

In 1948, the General Board of Lay Activities of the Methodist Church published a book written for a popular audience by William F. McDermott. The book, *Everlasting Treasures*, was by turns theological ("Who would take a can of gasoline, bow down before it and adore it?") and modern ("We must keep pace with our ways and means of serving God. We must use the efficiency of the airplane age, not the methods of oxcart days"). Most of all, *Everlasting Treasures*'s tone was can-do and practical. McDermott was full of suggestions ranging from how to set up a stewardship committee to how not to negatively think one's way to defeat by viewing the church's budget in survival terms. "Avoid defeatism as we would a pestilence," he advised. "Christ's promise is for victory."[17]

William McDermott also believed that his time was ideal for breaking the patterns of past church life:

> One of the encouraging marks of this generation is that if people know, they will generally act. For the first time in history, the masses are not afraid of anything just because it is new. A new invention, a new treatment, a new way of living is accepted if it has the stamp of authority. A church that would guide its people into larger areas of service must keep them informed as they go along. That is why we stress at this stage of the work what we might call the "period of information." The impressive truth about Kingdom advance unfetters the mind and pocketbook of many a Christian who is earnest, yet who is not awakened to the enormous spiritual changes going on in the world today.[18]

The line drawings used to illustrate *Everlasting Treasures* were the book's most striking aspect. (See illustration 22.) The cross of Christ was juxtaposed with the mushroom cloud of the atomic bomb; the American dream home was weighed in the balance with the church; the church was placed at the center of the community crossroads (as the author so clearly wished it was); and a stack of pledge cards was shown adjacent to the important accoutrements of the modern life, the clock and the appointments calendar. That stewardship was serious business could be seen in a picture of men in suits gathered around a table. The result, however, was a happy one, with both the church and the parsonage radiating a well-cared-for aura.

The way to get this kind of commitment from church members was through their stomachs. "Feed 'em and win 'em" was a motto that seemed psychologically sound to McDermott, and he defended the view biblically, writing, "Plenty of scripture is also available to back up the custom. Jesus fed the five thousand before He preached to them. Why can't His Church do the same? We make no argument, simply chronicle a fact." Later, McDermott reminded his readers that where food and stewardship were concerned, actions must follow in proper sequence: "That means the dinner *first*, and the pledging *afterward*. Good food produces an amiable mood even among the most reserved."[19]

Churches in the postwar years increasingly used printed bulletins to convey not only the order of worship but also announcements of church activities. Taking a cue from the then wildly popular *Reader's Digest*, they began to include brief aphorisms and quotations, often humorous in character, designed to make parishioners think. Not a few of these sayings concerned giving, the use of

22. Illustrations from William F. McDermott, *Everlasting Treasures* (Chicago: General Board of Lay Activities, Methodist Church, 1948). Used by permission of the United Methodist General Board of Discipleship.

possessions, and one's financial relationship with God and the church. The following "Bulletin Fillers" were suggested by Lawrence E. Brooks in a Church of God (Anderson) book titled *Better Church Finance*:

- It is never safe to trust God's business to the man who neglects his own.
- When a man is asked to become a tither, he is asked to establish as a life principle the habit of putting God first.
- There are no records of failure among tithing churches. The examples are legion.
- If a church has a lot of "flinty givers," it may take a lot of knocks to get the "fire."
- Wonder what the Lord thinks when a woman with a twenty dollar hat gives five cents to his glory.
- Some people try to get something for nothing and then kick about the quality.
- Our credit in heaven is not determined by what we give but by what we have left.
- There is enough of the Lord's money in the purses of Christians on Sunday morning to do all the work God expects them to do—if He could get his own money back!
- Our money will testify concerning us in the Judgment. Whether our checkbook is to be summoned by the defense or the prosecution depends upon us. We are the ones who make His testimony for Him. He will only say what our stewardship tells Him to say.[20]

Many stewardship books continued to take the high road of theological approach to raising funds for the church, but increasingly others began to appear that reflected how the churches actually raised their funds. A 1952 book by Ralph Seaman exemplified the how-to genre. *101 Ways to Raise Money for Your Church* included a royalty-free Christmas pageant called "The Living Light." Seaman prided himself that his layman's approach to raising money in the church had never been "inhibited by any theological handicap." Indeed, he observed that there was a real difference between clergy, whose "preoccupation is theology," and laypeople, who felt quite differently about ways of raising money.[21] Seaman's book provides insight into how mid-twentieth-century Protestants employed fund-raising devices in their churches. Seaman cataloged the many possibilities for raising money, including exhibits (quilt sales, embroidery sales, hobby shows, collections of rare objects, sewing parties, and the sale of donated art), banquets, and dinners (such as the "$5.00 Dinner"—the food was grossly overpriced, but entertainment was provided, and Seaman advised,

"Try to find a first class, charming accordionist, male or female, but don't have two accordionists"). One could obtain separate funds to support the music program of the church, sell cemetery lots on commission, engage in unit selling of the budget (where people are challenged to buy one or two units of a 500-unit budget, for example), and make toys for sale. Not to be forgotten, of course, were bazaars, cookbooks, and rummage sales.[22]

Significantly, Seaman recognized the appeal of honoring donor preferences to a high degree and advised readers that the greatest success for a "white Christmas special offering" was to be obtained when each class in the Sunday school retained "the right to dictate just where their total fund shall go." On the surface, this might seem as though a lot of money might be getting away from church coffers, Seaman allowed. But, he argued, this was not true, for it was "inescapable that the church board must administer to certain such charitable needs anyhow." The old bait-and-switch routine was alive and well in the American congregation.[23] Seaman also had no difficulty with making direct appeals to the pocketbook interests of wealthy potential givers; he reminded them that a gift to the church could be an income tax deduction and thus could cost them little indeed. "Here," he wrote, "the appeal is made directly to the selfish side of an individual rather than to the philanthropic."[24] Using birthday and anniversary boxes was recommended along with encouraging tithing, and money could be saved by having Boy Scouts and volunteers perform various services whenever possible. Seaman even advised congregations who paid taxes on their parsonages to physically connect the pastor's residence to the church building so the whole structure would count as unratable property. After all, a penny saved was a penny earned. To his credit, Seaman advised consulting with a local attorney before acting on his riskier suggestions. Finally, Seaman advocated raising money for hymnals and flowers by tying their purchase to memorials of the dead.[25]

Taken as a whole, Seaman's list of fund-raising techniques constituted a kind of antistewardship treatise, a guide to how money was actually brought in and how people *liked* to raise funds. Moreover, it disclosed the ways in which congregations perpetuated their ties with their members, adherents, and well-wishers. If these were not exceptionally theologically refined ways to raise funds, then at least they were religious ways of obtaining support. The ritual of dropping coins in a bank to mark a birthday, or a wedding anniversary, placed the recognition of personal life events in a communal context. Likewise, memorial flowers placed behind the altar extended the caring of family and community beyond the realm of the living to the dearly departed. What could be more religious?

Books by ministers about stewardship continued to be written in the 1950s, but even these tended to be less doctrinaire in their approach to the subject. In 1954, W. E. Grindstaff published *Developing a Giving Church*, which he hoped would be a new kind of stewardship guide; for while there were many books to inspire Christians to become better stewards, he had been unable to find any that satisfactorily addressed the "mechanics of financing a church."[26] Grindstaff approached his task from the assumption that every clergyman knew that tithing was good for their churches, but the trick was how to entice more members to tithe. Grindstaff made his case for the tithe by drawing on Henry Van Dyke's story "The Mansion" and argued that the most effective way to teach the truth about tithing was to show that it amounted to investing in one's eternal home. If people failed to send a tithe ahead to God, then they might expect, like the wealthy Mr. Weightman of Van Dyke's story, to be shown to a shack and told, "Here is your home." If Christians wanted to occupy heavenly mansions, it was up to them to send enough material ahead.[27] Grindstaff was an utter pragmatist when it came to testing the tithe; he observed that "there are a great many superficially pious people today who say we are living under grace and have given all that we have to God. But you will notice that they still keep practically all of it for themselves." Given this level of cant, it seemed reasonable to Grindstaff that "God would still prefer the tithe in cold cash."[28]

Not only did God prefer cash tithes, but Grindstaff believed his plan called for one-point collection. This was, of course, a revival of "storehouse tithing." Grindstaff labeled any other type of giving "promiscuous tithing." The church, he argued "is the rightful custodian of God's money. The church and the church alone has the right to say how such money shall be used."[29] To obtain the commitment of a tenth of a modern American's resources, Grindstaff knew, required a skilled solicitor. After first recommending going out after dinner on Monday nights when people were likely to be home (Sunday afternoons having already ceased to be good times to catch Christians at home), Grindstaff suggested ways to be as efficient as Jesus in one's witness: "Always try to visit under the most favorable circumstances. Usually this is in the family circle. One can create a friendly environment, if necessary. If the radio or the television set interferes, the visitor should lower his voice until the prospect cannot hear clearly and turns off the set. Adapt yourself to the situation. If there is company, it may be best to excuse yourself and return later. Lead your prospect to talk. Never do all the talking. Direct the conversation."[30] Many of Grindstaff's suggestions involved using the family as a source of social pressure to do the right thing. For instance, he maintained, "It is generally easy to win a child to tithing in the presence of his parents. The parents will be impressed by the child's response to Bible truths." The parents were also likely to be converted to tithing by their children's example. Another key to a successful stewardship call was avoiding the topic of money for at least fifteen minutes. "Talk Christ, the Christian home, and missions before you talk about tithing," Grindstaff advised. "When Christ is welcomed into the heart and home there is no real problem in stewardship."[31] Nor was Grindstaff above using invidious comparisons to urge the tithe on those who were slow to adopt it. He suggested at least twice that when people tried to excuse themselves from tithing, they should be asked to compare themselves to Jews. He urged people soliciting the tithe to answer excuses with the question, "If God expected a Jew to tithe under law, would He expect any less of a Christian under grace?"[32]

In treating other issues related to the mechanics of church finance, Grindstaff proved himself thoroughly modern. Missions ought to be financed through a cooperative program, a system whereby "everyone gives to everything" and where the Kingdom was advanced by means of large-scale budgeted finance. "Abraham was rich because he banked with God," Grindstaff wrote, "he channeled all his investments through the trust company of heaven." Unified denominational mission giving was the modern way to make similar investments.[33] Likewise, building campaigns fit into the theological scheme of storehouse tithing, for the command "Bring all the tithes into the storehouse" inevitably posed the question "Do you have a suitable storehouse?"[34] Grindstaff also advised pastors and other leaders to introduce programs of "Stewardship beyond Death." Such stewardship of "deathless dollars" was practical, sensible, and democratic, he argued. Moreover, he wrote, "If we deposit deathless dollars to carry on the work of the church we shall bless mankind forever."[35] And to those who had complained that memorials and bequests partook more of a family piety than Christian discipleship, Grindstaff had a ready reply: "Perhaps those of us who make bequests will not long be remembered as individuals. We may rest assured, however, that the cause to which we have given and the Christ who heads that cause will be magnified forever."[36] Either in Seaman's world of sales and benefits, or in Grindstaff's more traditional approach toward stewardship, new avenues for church finance were opening.

If W. E. Grindstaff rang fresh changes on the tithe, a Methodist bishop, Costen J. Harrell, represented a change in key. In his 1953 book, *Stewardship and the Tithe*, Harrell tried to eliminate the minor tones of biblical law, duty, and obligation altogether. In their place he wrote about how the tithe was best viewed as an "acknowledgment" of God's sovereign ownership of all things and a response to grace already given.[37] Harrell also thought giving could be best categorized theologically as "a means of grace," that is, a way of making oneself more available to awareness of God's presence just as when one prayed, accepted the Lord's Supper, or read the scriptures.[38] The way in which Harrell was perhaps the most modern was in his determination to return the conversation about stewardship to the question of possessions. A generation of leaders after Harvey Calkins had talked of "spiritualizing stewardship." By contrast, Harrell wanted to despiritualize stewardship if by their use of "stewardship of life" his contemporaries meant to avoid the point at which stewardship was most severely tested: "All that may be said about the stewardship of prayer or influence or talent may result in a doctrinaire or sentimental attitude. Our insistence on the stewardship of life, though ever so true, may be so general that we lose ourselves in the gloriously indefinite." By contrast, Harrell thought, the stewardship of possessions was definite and constituted "the door by which we may enter into a true appreciation of the whole concept of stewardship." Property was one of the leading questions of the day, as was witnessed by the conflict between the Eastern communist bloc and the Western capitalist states, but it was also a question for each servant of Christ: "His account books will reveal whether or not he is a faithful steward in the use of money. If one will not diligently apply his stewardship in the things that are seen, can he be expected to do it in the gifts of the spirit that transcend the art of bookkeeping? For this reason the stewardship of possessions is the crux of the whole matter."[39]

In the mid-1950s, an English theology student traveled to Evanston, Illinois, to complete a fourth year of theological study and to investigate the giving practices of the American Anglicans that might have application in the United Kingdom. Brian Rice, like many foreign observers before him, was stunned to see how much money the American churches collected. As was the case with other travelers to United States, the things he found remarkable serve as valuable evidence of what was distinctive about the American religious scene of the era. The first of his insights was about the ubiquity of the Every Member Canvass for raising operating funds and the prevalence of professional fund-raising firms when buildings needed to be erected or augmented. Money appeared to be everywhere, and Rice remarked that an English observer "may feel that some American churches think of evangelism almost primarily in terms of efficient fund-raising, of Christian witness as confined to making regular donations." To support this contention, he cited a saying he found in a prominent church publication: "The Church that quits asking for money is dead."[40] Rice found the church in America neither dead nor shy about asking for funds.

There were at least twelve major national fund-raising counsel firms at work in the United States in the 1950s. Rice quoted some of their prevailing fees. Campaign Associates charged $1,800 for a very small church and $10,000 for a very large one. The Wells Organization, meanwhile, estimated that approaching a church with 200 to 275 families would take four weeks of service and cost $3,000 to $4,000. The leading firms disagreed about how best to raise funds. Wells Organization preferred to raise money before the building plans were begun, while the Ketchum Company believed that afterward was the right time inasmuch as people "give much more understandingly and willingly because they can visualize how their pledges will contribute to the work of the Kingdom."[41] All the consultants agreed that it was the role of the clergy to make pace-setting pledges. This led to Rice's other key discoveries. In the Episcopal Diocese of Chicago, he found a culture of giving that surrounded the Bishop's Pence, a practice begun in the depth of the depression. Bishop George C. Stewart in the 1930s had challenged each Episcopalian to give a thank-offering of one penny at each meal in conjunction with saying grace before eating. Bishop Stewart set forth an ideal when he said to his diocese, "The Bishop's Pence has gone into the home and says 'don't eat as if *you* had made the food: eat and be thankful that God gave it to you.' " Rice was as much impressed with the way this small practice became part of the daily piety of Chicago's Episcopalians as he was with the funds it generated.[42]

In the Diocese of Michigan, Rice experienced something even more dramatic. There, Bishop Richard Emrich had challenged clergy and laity to become tithers in an open and modern way. He recognized that to tithe was to give a tenth to the church, but he suggested the modern adaptation most in keeping with the social organization of contemporary America was for each Episcopalian to "adopt in gratitude to God the idea of devoting 1//10 of his net income (after income taxes) to selfless purposes—5 percent for his church and 5 percent for general charities."[43] This regimen was practical and did not depend either on a view of biblical law or restricted social obligations that Episcopalians would have found difficult to abide. Nevertheless, the ideal set by the popular and respected Emrich was widely adopted, and the Michigan diocese ranked first in per capita giving to the church of all Episcopal dioceses in the United States.[44] Some of the reasons for "Modern Tithing" given in diocesan promotional literature provide a sense of how the tithe could be theologically updated:

6. By making us responsible with a fixed percent of our income, it teaches us responsibility in the handling of all our possessions.
7. Like all truly Christian living, it brings to us the joy of an honest and important participation in God's work in this world.
8. It places us in a mighty tradition because it has Scriptural authority.

9. It helps us to see that all of living, even the making of a personal budget and the spending of money, can be done to God's glory.[45]

Rice believed most of his fellow Church of England members were mere "tippers" in comparison with American tithers.

Throughout the postwar responsibility years, a culture of accountability grew in Protestant churches. The congregation's annual meeting grew in importance from a short meeting at midweek to a major afternoon or evening event on Sundays, at which a "loyalty dinner" was served and a printed report detailing the past year's accomplishments was handed out. These "annual reports" came to resemble corporate annual reports with their combination of audited statements and boasts about the organization's feats. The reports of ministers, however, were often an exception to the "big picture" rule. The genre of the pastor's annual report took on the character of a justification for the employment and payment of a full-time person to labor on the congregation's behalf. Just below the surface of the statistics usually lay a minister's hope that his activities would be judged worthy of a salary increase to be voted on later in the annual meeting. One instance of this kind of accounting comes from a 1959 annual report of a Church of God (Anderson) congregation:

PASTOR'S ANNUAL REPORT

This is my first report in an annual business meeting. God has given me ample strength to serve as a happy pastor with this church.

This is not meant to be a "brag" sheet but a page on which you, the member, may see some of the work for which you remunerate your pastor. Since I do not punch a clock or have a timekeeper, this page will be of service to all.

I traveled approximately 31,017 miles this year for the ministry; 6,800 by planes, 217 by bus, and 24,000 by automobile.

I delivered about 181 sermons: 128 in this church and 53 in other engagements, over radio stations, in youth conventions and camps.

There went out from our offices 31,585 pieces of mail. Besides these, we printed 22,075 bulletins and programs. Study courses, Sunday school classes, youth and visitation evangelism had us print 9,830 in addition. Thus, a total of 63,490 pieces came off our machines in 1958!

Your two ministers made approximately 3,380 pastoral calls in their visitation work, calling on the sick, the bereaved, and new families, and making calls pertaining to church business.

I officiated for seven weddings, twelve funerals, and one pastoral installation. I conducted approximately 35 midweek prayer meetings.

Sixty people were converted this year, and of these, I baptized forty-seven. Your pastor taught six study and leadership courses this year. Also, he conducted six workers' conferences. Your minister met with the two major church boards at least eighteen times.

In behalf of this congregation, your two ministers attended three camp meetings, two youth camps, three youth conventions, two missionary conventions, one leadership retreat, and six ministers' meetings.

Your pastor completed his Master's Degree (one trip per week) in June. Work is now being done on his doctoral studies in religion and biblical literature.

We have completed a wonderful first year, and look forward to 1960 as a "banner year for Christ."[46]

This annual report was offered as a model to pastors to demonstrate their accountability and to eliminate any question that the minister was not worthy of his pay. Perhaps no other postwar practice so clearly demonstrated how entwined with one another money, accountability, and clerical identity could become in the responsibility years.

DEVELOPING A MODERN ATTITUDE TOWARD OLD-TIME GIVING

By the late 1950s and well into the 1970s, giving and Christian stewardship became topics of earnest intent. Christians were to demonstrate their care for the Kingdom of God's purposes by their dedicated stewardship. Charlie W. Shedd, a minister and author of numerous practical guides for the faithful on daily problems, approached church finance in much the way he had weight loss in his 1957 classic, *Pray Your Weight Away*. That is, he saw the issue as one of attitude. The right attitude toward giving or any other problem was to commit oneself in one's church to the right program. Echoing Jesus's words "Where your treasure is, there will be your heart also," Shedd worked with his congregation to put their treasures in the right place. He called his solution the "Program toward a tithing church." Through this program, Shedd reported, "dollar-a-week members had become highly blessed percentage givers and eventually tithers."[47] As in all of Shedd's books, there were testimonials by laity and statistics to back them up. In nine years of the program, the congregation's operating budget increased 400 percent against a membership increase of just 26 percent. Benevolences rose from 13 to 50 percent of the annual budget.

Shedd went to another church and made his program work there too. The program had four basic rules:

(1) Develop a program of church finance which will be focused on the soul and not on the purse.

(2) Develop a program of church finance which will be focused on what the Lord wants and not on what the church needs.

(3) Develop a program which will be projected over a long-range and not limited to the requirements of a yearly budget.

(4) The church member may become a follower of Christ in that moment when he begins his first commitment, but to become a full follower may take a full lifetime. That is why our program moves away from demands for set amounts to call for "growth in grace."[48]

People who canvassed for the pledge were guided in classic salesman fashion to deflect objections: "Common questions associated with percentage giving in tithing talk are, 'Do you mean I should figure my income before taxes or after taxes?' 'Should I count what I give to Red Cross and other charities?' 'Are you talking about gross or net?' The list grows large." Shedd said, "Our official answer is, 'Your percent of giving is between you and your Lord. You decide with him what is right for your right relationship to him who gave his all for you.'" The number one rule was not to get drawn into an argument. The program was also supported by saturation marketing. Weekly, monthly, and biennial messages reinforced the point that giving generously was an essential part of the Christian life. Some of these messages to the congregation used negative comparisons to foster even greater commitment to give sacrificially rather than merely tithing 10 percent. One example of this rhetorical device reads this way:

Have you ever thought how your giving would change if Jesus stood before you waiting to receive your gifts? Would you give him exactly the same amount as you now give for God's work? Before you close your eyes tonight, ask yourself, "What would my Lord have me do about tithing?" Jesus, in reproving the proud Pharisees, gives them no credit for tithing. He says "These ought you to have done." Does he mean that I must give one-tenth of my income to his Church? There may be some question at this point but there is no argument here. Matthew 23:23 is a call for me to respond fully to divine grace. Am I doing all I *ought*?[49]

Even in using negative comparison and guilt as motivating techniques, Charlie Shedd could strike a positive note. Treating the same topic more philosophically, John A. McMullen made a similar claim. God was "interested in all our money."[50] Calling money "congealed sweat," McMullen argued that all money was a product of God-given abilities and efforts; thus Christians as stewards were accountable to God not for a tenth but for all their money. "There is nothing for which we spend money," he wrote, "that is not a part of our life as a steward, or that is beyond the interest of God."[51] McMullen wanted to get away from the tithe, not because it was too much, but because it was not strenuous enough as a standard. Indeed, the tithe was more an artificial rule than the standard of giving, imposed as it was from outside the believer's own conscience before the Lord.[52] But McMullen also entered into the question of whether Christians should calculate their tenth before or after income taxes, an increasing fact of life in the postwar era. Here he argued that since the average American household had five times as much discretionary income as in 1940, the ancient tithe was not enough.[53] McMullen's book, *Stewardship Unlimited* (1961), also demonstrated a tendency that would grow in subsequent years. In arguing that stewardship was the basic form of the Christian relationship to God in the world, he extended the category of stewardship to previously uncharted territory, including the institution of marriage. Christians were responsible for the "stewardship of sex," McMullen argued, but then he also quickly went on to discuss the stewardship of children that naturally followed: "The Christian steward does not need to escape the 'burden' of children, but gladly accepts the gift of them and plans the stewardship of sex for the best interest of the child and of the parents."[54] Somewhere in this veiled reference to birth control and planned parenthood, the definition of stewardship was being stretched.

Stewardship's rapidly expansive definitions could also be seen in Helen Kingsbury Wallace's *Stewardship for Today's Woman* (1960). Wallace, an American Baptist, conceived of a woman's stewardship in terms of women's roles and life stages. She did not organize her book by the familiar biblical warrant/contemporary application style common to most clerical writers; instead, she had successive chapters on "the career woman," "the wife," "the mother," "the widow," "the retired woman," and "the church woman." Like much older guides to the care of souls, Wallace's book was premised on the idea that each role-identified person has a typical besetting situation or problem. In her case, a proper understanding of stewardship was always the answer. Career women were most often self-absorbed, independent, and lonely. They needed to stop reading the paper on Sunday, join a church, and give of their time and money to something larger than themselves so that they might find themselves.[55] The Christian career woman might also "exercise her stewardship" in her job by exemplifying Christ to her work associates.[56] Wives, meanwhile, were economic contributors to their households, wherever they worked. The wife's need was to appreciate her economic power as an earner and consumer, to shape the household in keeping with Christian principles and values. Women who wanted their families to tithe could use their power within the household to do so. Wallace drew on the usual source for this protofeminist message, the Women's Missionary Union at the Southern Baptist Convention. She quoted approvingly from one of the Union's leaflets, "If the wife really wants to tithe, she can prove to her husband that she is willing to make any sacrifice in order to tithe."[57] Mothers most needed to make sure the habits of stewardship and prayer were taken up by their offspring. The widow had to renegotiate financial matters. The retired woman needed to volunteer more and set her affairs in order with a will so that the church might be perpetuated. Women at all stages of life were finally challenged to be committed to church work so that they might enlarge the ministry of Christ.

A book published two years later took the stewardship of the self even farther away from money. Almost any other term could have appeared as the main title of Virginia Ely's *Stewardship: Witnessing for Christ* and not affected how one read the book, so intense was Ely's focus on the need to witness. Yet her use of the word *stewardship* gave it a particular meaning: that the believer needed to use the self to greatest possible advantage in witnessing for Christ. She advised readers to use their wealth, influence, good looks, pleasant dispositions, and personalities to win others for Christ. Among her key points were the following:

- Good health and personal hygiene are important factors in personal attractiveness.
- Appropriate attire is an important feature in one's social appeal.
- Attitudes are a determining factor in personal attractiveness.
- Christians should be cheerful.[58]

Ely's book illustrated a growing trend in the 1960s. *Stewardship* as a term began to be used so broadly as to lose its connection with giving and money. Meanwhile, writers who discussed giving and financing the religious enterprise were becoming more concrete in speaking of money and less dependent on either the theory or theology of stewardship.

In 1962, Luther P. Powell published a history of fund-raising in the Christian church titled *Money and the Church*, in which the term *stewardship* had a greatly diminished importance. Instead, training his attention on how the church in former and contemporary times went about getting money, Powell was led to focus on motives and techniques. As one would expect of a book by a Methodist preacher, it ended with a note of hope that people would give generously for right and faithful reasons. Powell provided a comprehensive catalog of mid-twentieth-century religious fund-raising techniques. Looking around him, Powell saw a pervasive spirit of merchandising that raised rather limited amounts of money. Variations of the lottery and bingo were present in many churches; group buying and sales schemes for products from candy, to soap, to cars kept church people busy from coast to coast (these were the years before discount pricing, when up to 50 percent of the final price of most goods went by fair-trade distribution standards to the final retailer). Pancakes, antiques, crafts, and labor were sold to raise church budgets and particularly the budgets of men's, women's and youth groups within churches. Not a small amount of a total benevolences budget of the typical church was raised through these forms of enterprise.[59]

Powell heaped a fair amount of scorn on the Lord's Acre scheme that had caught on in the rural South during the Great Depression. Farmers' families who had difficulty making cash contributions to their church were urged to plant an additional acre for the Lord and to bring in the full proceeds from that land. The clergy championed the Lord's Acre as their economic salvation during the lean years, and enthusiasts defended the acres as biblical. Powell was disturbed by the folk magic that seemed to cling to the practice. As far back as 1924, Georgia farmers participating in the earliest Lord's Acre program were claiming that "the acres devoted to the Lord produced better crops than were produced in surrounding acres." A "Biblical wheat" experiment of the 1940s yielded well, except in 1942, when pheasants were threatening to eat all of the wheat. Fortunately, the planters recalled Malachi 3:11, "And I will rebuke the devourer for your sakes, and he shall not destroy the fruits of your ground," and waited five days for open hunting season to begin, when, they knew, the Lord would solve their pheasant problem.[60] Wherever Powell saw these rural and other, more urban, schemes to go into business with God as one's partner, he detected superstition and veiled self-interest. But Powell's own experience with the Lord's Acre as a pastor may have played a role in his jaded view of the plan. The year he and his church planted the Lord's Acre, the crop died in a drought.

Luther Powell also documented the wide use of the Every Member Canvass at midcentury and the growing trend of using professional fund-raising counsel for the purposes of raising large sums in capital drives to build new and enlarged church facilities. Of these techniques Powell was far less critical. Finally, he produced an honest catalog of the reasons why people gave to religion. Some gave out of fear; some because tithing was the law of their churches; some for personal glorification; others with hope of personal profit or out of marked self-interest. Powell preferred those who gave out of missionary zeal or love, but he recognized the range of motivations present in the church and its members.[61]

The publishers Fleming H. Revell and Association Press (the latter being the YMCA's press) produced much literature in the postwar era on how to raise money for churches and the reasons for doing so. This is not surprising, since fund-raising was a job that laity shared with clergy, and in the period between 1945 and 1965, there were countless building campaigns that provided tens of thousands of new church starts and many more building additions. The title in Revell's Better Church Series by C. Harry Atkinson sought to help churches do the capital campaign right. In *How to Finance Your Church Building Program*, Atkinson laid out the perils and promise of a building campaign.

> A RIGHT BEGINNING is a major factor in the success of any enterprise. It is of crucial importance when launching a Campaign for church building funds and a half hearted, bungled beginning is almost certain to blight any hope for complete success. On the other hand, the church may rightly expect the people to respond with surprising generosity if it begins with adequate preparation, deep religious conviction concerning the merits of the campaign, selection of competent leadership, and a program designed to present the needs and to enlist the support of every member.[62]

Atkinson advised leaders to employ professional fund-raising counsel, while predicting that in most churches some leaders would object to spending money on counsel or to facing pressure. While not wanting to "blackjack people into contributing," Atkinson thought there was real value in some kinds of pressure that came with professional guidance. "There will be the pressure of self-study," he wrote, "self-appraisal, incentives to do better things in better ways."[63] Above all, the context Atkinson wished to create was one where people gave most generously because they were challenged not to build bricks and mortar, but to attain some great prize through a building. For these great things, members of the church would "rise to new heights of self-giving and break their alabaster boxes of precious ointment."[64] Critical to such successful campaigns, however, were generous lay leaders and an enthusiastic pastor. "If the pastor drags his feet," Atkinson wrote, "because he fears a vigorous campaign might offend some of his parishioners, or that the appeal may appear too mercenary if mentioned in the pulpit, you can be quite certain that the campaign will not reach its goal."[65] Atkinson had seen many promising campaigns fall short because of faint support from the clergy. In the years ahead, with greater pressure to apply congregational resources to relevant causes, mainline clergy would become even less able representatives of the big capital campaign. For now, Atkinson was firm about the indispensable role of the clergy as cheerleaders for big money.

Another of Revell's how-to books was David W. Thompson's *How to Increase Memorial Giving*. In it Thompson developed the view that memorial gifts were both an important way to remember the deceased in their church homes and a means of meeting the needs of the church. Thompson suggested a menu of items, arranged by price, that might be offered to those who wished to remember a loved one. He also suggested that the best memorials paralleled an individual's interests and activities in life. From altars to tapestries, and from hand bells to bulletin boards, twentieth-century American churches were filled with amazing amounts of material goods, and Thompson hoped to make it possible for congregations to acquire their church goods while keeping alive the memory of a departed member. His suggested techniques began with a committee to cultivate such gifts, to work with children and youth to develop an appreciation and reverence for the gifts gracing their building, and to enlist the pastor as a sales agent, always ready to suggest an appropriate memorial to a grieving party. Thompson recognized that some might think some of these techniques are unnecessary. "They may think," he wrote of the idea of conducting children through an annual tour of memorial sites in the church, "[they] are too young to realize the significance of memorials given in memory of the living or the dead. The discerning, however, will come to the thought that a special meaning of the church and its continuous, generation-after-generation service will be sensed instinctively by the children."[66] More than Thompson realized, the growth of the use of memorials also pointed to the differences and similarities between the American way of death and official Protestantism. The latter had no cult of the saints and struggled at midcentury with how much to mention the dead and dearly departed in the actual funeral liturgy. Yet at precisely the moment when a mobile generation was living and dying apart from the extended family, a great need to remember loved ones on some sacred ground was reshaping religious practices so much that we can speak of a new Protestant cult of the dead, in which former members were richly present forever in what had been their places of worship. What began as recognition of very wealthy benefactors, and of men and women who had given their lives in World War I and World War II (Civil War dead had largely been memorialized in public structures outside the church), was now democratized, so that the names of any who died in the faith might soon be stamped on a pew or a table or in a hymnal. Though not exactly big contributors to church revenue relative to all other sources, memorials had become a significant fact of life in the ways churches were furnished and families transacted their religious business between the living and the dead before God and church witnesses.

One sign that church fund-raising was of general interest and not highly denominational in character in the postwar years was that there were non-church-owned presses producing so much of the church fund-raising literature of the period. By the 1960s Prentice-Hall was offering twelve titles in its Church Business Management Series. The writers in the series came from a wide variety of Protestant denominations. One of these titles was *Church Fund Raising* (1964) by George W. Harrison. Harrison (a pastor who never directly reveals his own affiliation) went right to the heart of the question as he saw it—money. People, in his view, were quick to identify money as the root of all evil and to suggest that filthy lucre must have little or nothing to do with God and by extension God's church. "The reason we have accomplished so little for God and His church is that we have conditioned ourselves to think small and to expect small," Harrison wrote, adding that "we have been extremely successful in attaining our small goals!"[67] Children in church were taught that the church was a nickel or dime institution and seemed never to get over that perspective when they grew up to deal with millions in industry, banking, and government. Harrison's essential proposal was that Christians needed to learn to think in big money terms: "[Bankers, investment brokers, and trust officers] talk in terms of hundreds of thousands of millions of dollars for their purposes. It seems to me, therefore, that we who are representatives of the greatest government in time or eternity, the Kingdom of God, and are charged with the greatest business in the world, that of saving the souls of mortal man, must think as big as do those who represent earthly government and who are interested in undertakings far less important than that with which we are charged."[68] Here then in a few short lines were the great themes of the preachers who were seeking money. Given that their work is clearly more important than most worldly activity, why then is that work not better financed? Charlie Shedd as a younger minister could still optimistically argue that getting a tithing church was at base a matter of asking and reminding the congregation to do the right thing. Harrison, as an older clergyman, wrote from a more disillusioned perspective, wondering why people continued to think in "small change terms" when it came to the Kingdom of God. Though his book is a guide to fund-raising, one cannot escape Harrison's pervading sense that the people who have the funds are living with a mixed-up set of priorities. Where Shedd sought to address the congregation with wall-to-wall religious rhetoric, Harrison preferred to move toward businesslike methods. The alternative, as he saw it, was accepting mere tips for the work of God.[69]

In the years before cable television, video recorders, prerecorded tapes, and

Power Point presentations, people of all ages in all sorts of settings were often pleased to learn that a gathering would include a movie or a filmstrip. Churches frequently offered this entertaining form of enlightenment—a story or lesson under the guise of a picture show. Stewardship films were widely produced and viewed in American churches, perhaps because like health films in the army or junior high they dealt with topics that authorities found necessary to discuss but could introduce with less discomfort in a prerecorded format. The father of many of the stewardship films was Dr. Harry Myers, executive secretary of the United Stewardship Counsel for its entire duration (1920–50) and later in charge of such work with the National Council of Churches until his death in 1963. Myers produced his first stewardship picture show with large format slides in 1903. Later he moved into filmstrips with narration provided on an accompanying record. His most popular actual film, indeed the most popular of all National Council of Churches' films, circulated for years, with over 1,200 prints of the film going from church to church through the mails. This film, *The Will of Augusta Nash*, was built on the premise that Donald Nash, a young professor, discovers that his great aunt, Augusta, has left him $100,000 on the condition that he become a tither.[70] Professor Nash struggles with what tithing means, but he arrives at a happy ending when he not only learns that tithing is just a responsible Christian response to God's grace but also gets to keep the $100,000. This thirty-four-minute black-and-white film about tithing had dozens of counterparts. In one sixty-five-minute movie, the theme of large gifts toward the end of life was addressed in the manner of a Perry Mason courtroom drama. In *All That I Have*, a retired surgeon, Dr. Grayson, finds himself in court facing a charge of mental incompetency brought by his nephews. In a series of flashbacks, it is revealed that Grayson had given away a part of his considerable wealth to help others. The most vexing gift from his nephews' point of view is the surgeon's $50,000 thank-offering given to his church. Grayson has to demonstrate his competency to the court, and in the process he shows the audience his integrity as a Christian responding to God's purposes and a good sermon by his pastor.[71] Other films stressed other stages of life. *Split-Level Family* addressed middle-class striving in a story about a family trying to finance its suburban dream house. A teenage daughter's realization of how little she is giving to the church becomes the catalyst for a reassessment of the entire family's values.[72]

The use of films by the stewardship community did not mean that other vehicles were being neglected. A 1960 competition for new stewardship hymns brought in 436 entries, from which the Hymn Society of America chose the contents of its *Ten New Stewardship Hymns*. One of these, "Give to the Lord as

He Has Blessed Thee," was written by James Boeringer, a Lutheran musician. It began this way:

> Give to the Lord, as he has blessed thee.
> Even when he seems far away,
> Know that His love has e'er possessed thee
> Shelters and feeds thee everyday.
> Heaven and earth are God's alone;
> Wilt thou hold back from Him his own?[73]

Alongside hymns that pushed guilt and movies that challenged postwar prosperity and greed, there were books of stewardship plays. "Take Five," from Robert Casemore's *There Were Twelve*, typified the genre and illustrated its limitations. "Take Five" is a play within a play, whose backstage story is about how a group of church performers in a musical called *Mutiny on the Stewardship* learn what stewardship is all about. With a script derived from *Kiss Me Kate* and *Guys and Dolls* and numbers like "When Stewardship Rules Our Hearts Again" sung to the tune of "When Johnny Comes Marching Home Again," it was virtually guaranteed to embarrass the youth groups who were its intended cast. But the mere use of young people to deliver the stewardship message was, in a new youth-oriented culture, designed to attract fresh attention to what has perhaps become a tiresome chore, the annual appeal for giving of time and talents.[74]

STRENUOUS STEWARDSHIP

While mainstream Protestants were working out culturally acceptable ways to restate the old stewardship message, there were signs that more conservative traditions were pursuing a more strenuous path. In 1965, a Missouri Synod Lutheran pastor, Waldo J. Werning, released a book titled *The Stewardship Call*, which was based on a concept of Christian vocation. Werning bet his whole hand on the "Gospel Call and Covenant." Most so-called stewardship programs, he argued, were wrong because they appealed to something other than gospel motives. Loyalty, for example, the common theme of the layperson's appeal to support the church out of loyalty was nothing less than a false idol. Even stressing the giver's need to give was "sub-gospel," an appeal to the "Old Adam." Following Luther, following the Apostle Paul, Werning favored only appealing to the Word of God. People were called to be priests of their gifts from God.[75] Entirely avoiding the topical use of the Bible to command giving, Werning hoped to show that the universal priesthood of all believers was more than sufficient to return to God what was needed for the work of the people under God's covenant of grace: "For a steward is a priest—and a priest is a steward."[76] Werning, beginning from a characteristically Lutheran theology centered on the triumph of the gospel over law, was arriving at a strenuous ethic of stewardship that anticipated some other strenuous ethics in the 1960s through the 1980s. Meanwhile, a Reformed scholar of the New Testament, Lukas Vischer, examined tithing in the early church and concluded not only that the practice had less of a biblical basis than its advocates supposed, but also that the tithe, "when adopted as divinely appointed measure of Christian giving, leads almost inevitably to the belief that it represents a fulfillment of what God expects from us."[77] Thus again, serious advocates for generous giving were calling into question the methods by which American church members liked to raise large amounts of money.

Other conservative voices in Protestantism were making a break in another direction. They began to preach what was to become known as the "prosperity gospel." Typical of this genre was A. A. Allen's *Send Now Prosperity*, which promised to offer "God's divine plan to put an end to poverty and the poor people's campaign march." Allen was a revivalist based in Miracle Valley, Arizona. Allen composed his teaching on bits and pieces of the Old Testament, as for example, "The Lord maketh poor, and maketh rich; He bringeth low and lifteth up" (1 Samuel 2:7) and "But thou shalt remember the Lord thy God for *it is* He that giveth thee power to get wealth" (1 Deuteronomy 8:18). For Allen the implication of all these scriptures was clear: "God promises you a prosperous soul if you obey Him and do what He wants. God wants you to have equal portions of health, wealth and salvation."[78] The devil had a gift to offer, too, Allen believed, and it was poverty and sickness. The Fatherhood of God, however, meant that prosperity was simple to claim. "God promised it because He has it and HE WANTS YOU TO HAVE IT!" Allen wrote, "YOU ARE ONE OF HIS CHILDREN, and He is your Father. YOU are heirs of God and joint heirs with Christ. You are the rightful owners of all HIS WEALTH! Any Father that loves his child wants that child to be comfortable, well-fed, and clothed. Surely, He loves you more than He loves the birds and the lilies of the field. Birds do not fall to the ground without his knowledge."[79] Allen never went too far without reminding his readers that it took money to get the word out about prosperity: "This gospel must be preached! It must be preached before Christ can return for the church. To preach this gospel, it takes money. In the great commission, we were commanded to preach the gospel, and thus commanded that we support the preaching of it. If Christ does not want us to have money, then HE DOES NOT WANT THE GOSPEL PREACHED."[80]

This radically different place to start an account of the relationship of money and the believer had become an increasingly common theme in the era of flamboyant evangelistic ministers who suggested that one gave to get, had faith to make things happen, and received God's blessing in direct relation to the amount of trust one placed in God and God's preacher. A typical account of faith and reward ran this way:

> Bro Jimmy Reece of Dallas, Texas, says, "When Brother Allen came to Dallas the Lord spoke to me to sponsor the meeting. At that time I owed $50,000 on a church property.
>
> "I promised God that I would fully cooperate with the Allen Meeting. Then when Brother Allen was taking an offering and pledges to buy the mission's helicopter, the Lord challenged me to prove Him by pledging $1,000.00 on the helicopter.
>
> "I took an envelope and pledged $1,000.00. Within a very short time the Lord helped me sell a lot not much larger than the tent platform for $58,000!"

Pastor Reece, Allen reported, paid his first pledge, made another pledge for a second thousand dollars, paid off his church property, and "still had $60,000 left!"[81]

Anyone's money problems, then, were simply a matter of faith. In a religious environment that was increasingly being divided into liberal and conservative forms of Protestantism, conservative voices offered a more direct approach to the themes of faith and money. Beginning with Oral Roberts, A. A. Allen, and Catherine Kuhlman, and continuing on with Jim Bakker with the PTL Club in the 1980s, these conservative voices were no longer heard only in revivals or on late night radio on the far right end of the AM dial. Indeed, part of the new faith evangelists' appeal was their direct answer to the question, "What's in it for me?" For those in doubt, Allen made it clear. God's promises were free, and the choice of health and wealth was in your hands. He urged readers to cut out and sign a "Prosperity Policy" from his own book as a constant reminder of God's promise.[82]

Even the mainline was moving its discussion of faith and money in a more strenuous direction. In New York, an Abingdon Press writer named Raymond Balcomb urged those perplexed by the winds of existentialism, the death of God controversy, calls for a renewal, and embraces of secularity, to "stir what you've got." Balcomb thought that a religious recession was under way. The faith would survive among a smaller group that took it seriously. What better way to be one to take the faith seriously than by renewing the discipline of tithing, or at least giving generously of the things one had as a middle-class individual. This was stewardship for a "mod" and confused age, and its motto amounted to "to be faithful, be sure to do what you can."[83]

Stewardship and fund-raising literature of the early 1970s reflected the orientation of the communities from which the authors came. So Missouri Synod Lutheran Charles W. Berner's *The Power of Pure Stewardship* was chiefly concerned with the theologically acceptable kinds of fund-raising. Episcopal David W. Crockett's book *Sound Financial Stewardship* spent little time on theological matters and placed a major emphasis on organization, fostering participation, and campaign technique.[84] That said, it is almost certainly the case that evangelicals of all denominations were overrepresented among the writers of stewardship treatises of the 1970s and later. The people who regarded raising money as an unfortunate necessity at odds with their understanding of their ministry simply did not write stewardship books. Those who wrote them, however, customarily displayed unusual zeal for having a "giving church," raising money for mission, or creating stewards as a way of developing better disciples for Christ. Sometimes all three enthusiasms were present, as in the case of Presbyterians Bartlett and Margaret Hess, whose 1974 book, *How to Have a Giving Church*, left no stone unturned. "None of us likes to have money extracted from us forcibly; we don't like pressure tactics," Margaret Hess noted. "But a pastor can bring his people into touch with spiritual principles of giving. The Holy Spirit can make us *want* to give. Then the church has the money it needs. Our lives have a new dimension in joy of giving."[85] The Hesses had led small, medium, and large congregations from the pulpit and the pew. Along the way they had discovered principles of giving they believed worked, for, as Margaret Hess warranted, "results have been beyond our dreams." Their critique of the way other ministers approached raising money was to assert that most failed to ever state the church's needs much less their own:

> Most ministers are happy to accept raises but can't figure out where they come from. Other ministers feel they alone can balance a wobbling budget by cutting their personal needs to the bone. Simon Self-Sacrifice, of course, renounced dreams of riches when he entered the ministry. He believes his responsibility is to preach the gospel, tend the sick, care for the poor. He feels it's up to his congregation to provide him with worldly goods. . . . And, of course, church members will provide for the needs of the minister, *after* other bills have been paid.[86]

Both Margaret and Bartlett Hess had grown up as children of the manse. Both displayed a sense of realism about what worked and what failed. Their account parodied the ministers who, like Simon Self-Sacrifice, ended up defeating themselves by the way they pursued their ministries. Simon was loved, but no one brought their friends to church because he looked so shabby. Norman Nagger wore his congregation down with special appeals. Byron Beggar raised money playing on pity, letting everyone know his church was "practically in a wheelchair." Peter Pleader told "tear-jerking stories of churches never finished . . . beams piercing the sky—monuments to a lack of faith." All of these pastoral types were wrong, as were ministerial fantasies about serving a church where an endowment or a rich uncle made up all deficits at once. Stewardship was squarely the minister's job, and the direct approach was the best.[87] Moreover, sizing people up and trying to figure out how much they could give meant very little in the Hesses' experience. They preferred to reduce the amount given to a simple algebraic equation. "Amount equals commitment in relationship to resources, A = C divided by R (Amount = Commitment/Resources)."[88] Ministers could do nothing about a person's resources, or wealth, so clergy should stop worrying about who had what. Rather, clergy needed to concentrate on church members' commitment. All other drives, pledge campaigns, and the like were beside the point. The Hesses' trick, besides sharing the church's or the mission's need, was to celebrate enthusiastically when the need was met. Congregational generosity was publicly praised and positively reinforced.

By the time Margaret and Bartlett Hess wrote their best-selling guide to having a giving church, part of the climate of American Protestantism was again shifting. The urban churches that had continued to hold wealth and pay the highest salaries began to falter and fold. Suburban congregations were becoming the normative church experience for most active Protestants two decades before a similar shift was complete in the population demographics for the nation as a whole. Meanwhile, the baby boom children and youth confirmed in the 1960s and early 1970s went to college in ever-increasing numbers, but they did not return to the congregations of their parents or any congregations like them. On campus, the Jesus People, Campus Crusade, and InterVarsity Christian Fellowship defined the options for students who were serious about their religion, though most students of the Vietnam era stayed away from even these groups, so strong was the aversion to institutions of "the Establishment."

While the student generation struggled with moral questions about the world, sex, and drugs, sometimes with the help of college chaplains, their parents experienced an economic challenge at home and in the church unlike any most had experienced in their adult lives. The presidencies of Richard Nixon, Gerald Ford, and Jimmy Carter saw unemployment rise from 3.4 percent to 9 percent and inflation rise from less than 3 percent to more than 14 percent. The stock market experienced its longest bear market since the Great Depression. And a new factor in the world economy, a cartel of oil-producing countries—OPEC—arose to push the price of energy up and supplies down.

All of these economic developments were hard on the middle class, the bedrock foundation of American Protestantism. The middle class entered a two-decade long period of stagnant or declining real wages. Not surprisingly, the economic challenges of the 1970s and 1980s hit Protestant congregations hard. Since most congregations were utterly dependent on voluntary giving from discretionary income, real-wage declines resulted in many churches struggling to keep up. Since inflation hit people living on fixed incomes especially hard, the churches struggling to manage with upward-spiraling budgets could not count on the unlimited generosity of their older membership at a time when the average age of members was increasingly approaching fifty-five. Worse yet, the energy crisis left congregations with large plants, which were built on the basis of cheap utilities, with costly bills just to heat the church. The churches worked hard to turn thermostats down in the winter and up in the summer. Ministerial compensation and giving to causes beyond the local congregation began to suffer.

Stewardship literature reflects the concerns of the time in which it is written. Writing in 1976, Wallace E. Fisher addressed what he saw as "a new climate for stewardship." Though the book eventually came to terms with issues of money and who should pay for the activities of the church and why, Fisher's leading concerns were for the "responsible stewardship of biblical truth" and for the "care of the earth."[89] As Fisher saw it, while the church's primary authority in all matters of faith and practice is scripture, "the authority of the scriptures has in fact become blurred for all Protestants and undermined for most." What one believed constituted biblical stewardship was dependent on who Christians accepted as reliable interpreters of the gospel. At the present moment, Fisher wrote, "there are wide differences on these issues in the grass roots church. Certain conservative Christians name Billy Graham, Harold Lindsay, and Earl Roberts as faithful custodians of biblical truth. Mainline Protestants look to Roger Shinn, Paul Lehman, and Joseph Fletcher as responsible stewards of the mysteries of God without feeling any constraint to agree with them fully." In Fisher's view, the single most important form of stewardship was a responsible stewardship of the gospel, in which congregations taught their members "how to discern the word of God in the human language of the Bible."[90]

Once the church had exercised its stewardship of the word of God, it could go on to care for persons by teaching them to "discern, study, and incarnate the living word of God." For Fisher this was a radical, biblical word from God to typical mainline Protestant congregations, which he believed violated biblical stewardship regularly by "their ingrained disposition and culturally conditioned practice of valuing property above persons." Still trying to come to terms with the 1960s, Fisher wrote, "Most middle-class church members in the 60s, reflecting John Locke's views on property, were more concerned about the destruction of property in Watts, Newark, Detroit, Washington, Chicago, and Kent State and Jackson State than they were about the loss of human life in those places or about the moral failures of the body politic which spawned those riots." Caring for people was more than a feeling; it would be better understood as a compassionate and competent commitment to attending to the full needs of the person, physical and spiritual. And if one cared for God's word and exercised stewardship for persons, then Fisher believed ecological concern naturally followed, for "ecological concern is an elemental strand in biblical stewardship." Here again the white middle-class church was guilty, no less than other powerful forces in the West, for the earth's deteriorating environment and an impending "premature death" of the planet. Church members, Fisher wrote, "have shared directly and indirectly in plundering the earth."[91]

The environment and, indeed, the physical climate constituted for Fisher a new climate for stewardship. And Fisher's work neatly captures the environmental turn of Christian thought about stewardship. Still, the man had been asked to write a stewardship book by a church press, and so he turned to the task nearly seventy pages into his book. When he approached the question of possessions and personhood, he noted that "the stewardship of money in the American church became the dominant strand in stewardship teaching after the Civil War." Here again, Fisher was prepared to think in big terms. Following the ethicist Joseph Fletcher, he sought to turn the church's attention to the stewardship of possessions through large-scale institutions. "Living now in this radically changed and changing society," he wrote, "American Christians must work to administer public programs more responsibly and to be more innovative in providing human services to technological man."[92]

Finally, late in a *New Climate for Stewardship*, Fisher took on what he called "some stubborn questions in stewardship." He asked, "Are apportionments or quotas valid in 1976?" and argued that denominational quotas had undermined true benevolence more than they had fostered real Christian stewardship and giving in freedom. He asked, "How shall gifts be divided between the church and social agencies?" and he argued that responsible Christians ought to contribute generously to their congregations and to educational institutions, social agencies, and political associations. While arguing that perhaps churches ought to begin paying more taxes, Fisher was unequivocal about the need to end the exemption allowed on housing for the ordained clergy in the federal income tax system. He contended, moreover, that clergy salaries ought to be standardized, by which he meant modeled on the practices of the civil service and the military.[93] He also maintained that all church members should pledge, but not everybody should be expected to tithe (some should do more, some should do less), and that pledges and annual gifts should never be publicized in the church. When it came to technique, Fisher was suspicious of the Every Member Canvass, even though he noted that it was the most widely used fund-raising method in mainline Protestantism in 1976. He was likewise dubious about pledging in the context of a worship service where it was more likely that a stewardship sermon had set up a sales pitch to underwrite the budget rather than made a proclamation of the gospel. Fisher was even ambivalent about the practice of pledging at congregational dinners. In the end, Fisher focused his book on what so many pastors of his era devoted their attention—on the environment, on the domestic problems of the 1970s, on the moral questions surrounding the Vietnam War, and on the religion of the American dream that had competed for the attentions and affections of church members. Although he had many exciting ideas to offer about the stewardship of the gospel, persons, and creation, when it came to financing the church, Fisher ended with a lament: "It is difficult to finance any voluntary institution these days—especially the church—in a truly Christian fashion. All congregations fail at it somewhere; too many congregations fail at it everywhere. What is tragic, however, is that some congregations do not care how they get dollars so long as they get enough to maintain the parochial existence and support their family chaplain."[94]

"Creative" was a buzz word in the 1970s and nowhere more so than in the church. Worship, for instance, needed to become more "creative"—and not allowed to grow stale. This usually meant experimenting with more contemporary songs that were not found in the hymnal, playing guitars rather than organs, and wearing clerical garb in colors other than black. While all of this experimentation in pursuit of a new and fresh experience of a Protestantism in keeping with a colorfully changing culture might have been dismissed if it had been known as "experimental worship," the modifier *creative* possessed a strikingly positive valence. People engaged in doing something creative were doing a new thing, not subject to judgment by the church, and perhaps even offering something fresh to God. Soon the term was showing up in other contexts and promising the same magic qualities. Preaching, pastoral care, and managing church volunteers could all be rechristened as "creative." Lyle E. Schaller, a popular church how-to series author and an editor for Abingdon Press, collectively designated his 1970s how-to books the "Creative Leadership Series." In

1979, the series published a work by Richard B. Cunningham titled *Creative Stewardship*. Inside the covers of *Creative Stewardship* was very little that was genuinely new or creative, although one did find a growing discomfort with the vast reach of global wealth in a world where poverty still was so prevalent. For the most part, Cunningham's account was a standard neoorthodox biblical theology reading of material possessions. In the cataloging of those material possessions and how they might be disposed of at the end of the individual believer's life, however, *Creative Stewardship* offered a new level of sophistication. Alongside wills and insurance policies, Cunningham noted that outright gifts to reduce inheritance taxes, revocable charitable remainder trusts, and irrevocable charitable remainder trusts were all available to people wishing to support their churches during their later years or after they had died. Indeed, as Cunningham noted, most major denominations had by then established foundations to "assist Christians in making decisions about the final disposition of their wealth and estates." In the context of his book, Cunningham meant this observation to support his final point, that it mattered "how we acquire, use, and dispose of the wealth that God makes available to us."[95] Historically, however, the fact that each of the major traditions had at least one foundation working to convert members' wealth to support for church causes indicates three striking developments in later twentieth-century American Protestant church life. First of all, it tells us that there was enough wealth in the hands of older Protestants to support the continuous cultivation of end-of-life giving. Putting the point more sharply, some members had enough wealth, there were enough of these wealthy members, and the churches stood to receive enough support to dedicate substantial resources to seeking and even managing these resources from and for their members. The development of the foundations also demonstrates that the activity of developing these gifts had been professionalized, so that people were now afforded a greater opportunity to control the distribution of their wealth after death through payment restrictions and third-party trusts than had ever before been offered to so many individuals.

The proliferation of foundations and even local church endowment committees alerts us to a significant development in late twentieth-century mainline Protestantism. Not only was a large proportion of the support for particular congregations coming from older members; an increasing amount of that support was being provided from beyond the grave. This represents something of an American recapitulation of European Christianity in which intergenerational wealth comes, over time, to maintain congregations beyond the capacity of their living membership. Of course, this pattern is not available to congregations in their first generation, and so it is not surprising that the traditions and congregations with the most "support from non-living sources" (a category actually employed by the Presbyterian Church in its annual accounting) were by the late 1970s associated mostly with former colonial powerhouses (the Presbyterian Church, the Episcopalian Church, and the United Church of Christ) or churches that had been in a particular place for a long time, including an increasing number of urban Methodist, Baptist, and Lutheran churches. Wealth, both physical and financial, kept some churches in place, while newer churches lived by their wits and the gifts of their members, but also had the advantages of flexibility when it came to location and choices concerning the scale of their activities.

CHAPTER EIGHT

Ministers' Wives: A View

from the Side of Labor

Viewed from the perspective of labor, there have been at least three constants over the last 250 years of American Protestant church life. The first is that a remarkably stable proportion of the funds raised by congregations (approximately two-thirds) has gone directly to the support of the clergy. The second constant is that Protestant clergy, of whatever denomination, have been expected to preach as their principal function in ministry, so much so that *preacher* is an American synonym for the words that antecedent European ecclesial traditions would use—*minister, pastor,* or *priest.* The third constant is that these clergy have overwhelmingly been married males. The one exception to this rule was rather short lived. In the early republic, Francis Asbury, father of American Methodism, preferred that his itinerants be unmarried so they could expend all of their energy in spreading the gospel; this preference was quickly abandoned by his successors. In a state where voluntary support of religion made consumers of church members, clergy came attached to spouses, and a spouse was one of the characteristics churches believed they were buying when they hired a man to preach.

Since the subject of this book is to see how Protestants have raised and spent their money in churches over the last two and a half centuries, it makes sense to inquire into how the large amount of resources allocated to clerical labor was received in the domestic culture of ministers' households. We have already seen the degree to which money raising seemed premised on clerical anxiety about the importance of religion and their own roles. Is there any way to get inside the life-worlds of these laborers in the church and to move beyond the begging sermon to understand their situations? Clearly, income statistics tell part of the story, as was discussed earlier in chapter 4. Here, however, we take a more indirect, yet intimate approach by looking at materials left behind by some of the affected parties on the labor side of the enduring exchange between preachers and churches. We turn to the minister's wife and ask, what can be learned about life in a Protestant minister's household and the relationship of that household's members to the employing institution, the church? Much can in fact be learned, as we shall see, for even a brief examination of these materials demonstrates the sense of economic anxiety that pervades the preacher's household.

Because of the way ministers found their mates, there was a strong chance that the role of minister's wife came with a fair degree of economic disappointment. The profession of minister was a respected calling, and a woman marrying a clergyman in the years of this study could expect to be treated with due regard. In a country with no landed aristocracy, there was, nevertheless, widespread gentility, a socially conferred right to be called "Mister" or "Missus," the former being a shortened form of "my sir." Clergy, though not possessors of great land, were called Mr. in the eighteenth century, when even successful merchants could not make an uncontested claim to the title. In the nineteenth century, clergy were still called Mr. and were often the graduates of four-year colleges and theological seminaries. Indeed, colleges often honored successful ministers in their regions and in their circle of knowledge with the further title of Doctor of Divinity (D.D.), denoting the clergy's unusually high level of education, learning, and public visibility. A young minister was marriageable in the sense that he was likely to have some degree of refinement, was well spoken, possessed a favorable reputation in the community, and eschewed many of the bad habits of other men of the age. The minister himself was also well positioned to find a suitable spouse, colleges and churches being great places to meet women of good backgrounds and breeding.

Once married, not a few wives found that they had fewer of the material comforts of life than they had possessed in their families of origin. Always in the public eye, the minister's wife was generally working to maintain appearances on a limited budget. The pressures of the manse included responsibility to raise children to be models of piety and good behavior, to dress decently without ostentation, to comport oneself with graciousness, and to never prefer any church member's company over any other in a visible manner. In short, the minister's wife, like the minister himself, was expected to be perfect, though with even fewer tools at her disposal, since the woman who exercised too many leadership qualities was seen as less than a perfect helpmate. The role was difficult enough that it generated a large amount of sister-to-sister literature. The guides written by ministers' wives to others similarly situated provide insights into how clergy families lived and the sense they made of their position within life, the church, and the community.

Unlike books produced by clergy themselves, the minister's wife's book is only partly written to offer a sermon. Whereas a minister's book typically has a fair amount of the "world as it ought to be," the emphasis in the minister's wife's book is on "the world as it really is." Four themes repeatedly emerge. The first is the burden, unfair but real, of exemplifying perfection in dress, manners, and interests. The second is the reality that while one cannot survive on respectability alone, it is the one thing a couple in the ministry most has and therefore must work at all costs to maintain. The third prevalent theme concerns the rewards of a life spent persevering in a ministerial marriage. Older and more experienced women married to ministers advise young brides that the riches that are gained in service to the church are greater than the fine young things one dreamed of acquiring as a girl. The fourth theme is perhaps the saddest, for in this literature women write of the slights one must bear in silence on behalf of one's spouse, setting forth a virtual catalog of church members' bad behavior.

In sum, this body of writing provides a subjective and mostly unvarnished insight into the lives of the principal employees of American Protestantism. On the one hand, these insiders' views confirm that it has never been easy to serve in the American Protestant church. The work and the personal toll exacted by that work have always been burdensome. On the other hand, one detects a turning point about twenty-five to thirty years ago, when the respectability that formerly compensated clergy families coping with less began to be reduced, such that the work was perhaps less well paid and with less prestige than had ever before been the case.

One of the earliest published testimonies to the life of the minister's wife appeared in the form of an anonymous novella, *The Minister's Wife; or, What Becomes of the Salary* (1861).[1] In the book, the minister's success in a small factory town leads to an appointment in Boston with nearly three times his prior salary, but also with far more than three times the expected expenses. The absolute nadir for the poor minister's wife comes when she walks in on several of the wealthy women whispering about her at a pre-Christmas party. She hears them agree that it is a scandal that their minister's wife possesses only one silk dress. Her heart turns cold toward them throughout the Christmas season, only to discover that members of means have been plotting to shower their new minister and his family with all the things their new city lifestyle requires, including a fine and fashionable silk dress. Meanwhile, butchers, coal men, and grocers are all demanding for their services cash—which the family has run out of. The novella ends with the melting of a struggling clergy family's hearts, but also with a sense of their utter dependency on members in the congregation to bridge the gap between solvency and devastating debt. A long and moralizing introduction precedes the novella that only intensifies the sense that clerical families are pressed between expected appearances and grudging, careless support. The introduction contains a catalog of calamities that befall clergy, who are expected to keep their families well dressed, shod, and fed on cast-off produce, the value of which is summarily deducted from the giver's expected church contribution for the year.

A biographical account of the life of Carrie Morrison, published by A. H. Redford in 1877, tells the familiar tale of sacrifice with an even greater sense of tragedy.[2] A Methodist minister's wife in her twenties, Carrie Morrison, moves every two years to new appointments and cheerfully suffers decreased health with each move; at only twenty-eight years of age she dies in the Lord, surrounded by a grieving husband and young son. To die young, beautiful, and faithful was potentially the lot of those called into the role of minister's wife. Next to being a beautiful flower cast early into the flames for the sake of the gospel was the plight of the minister's wife who suffered many moves over many lonely years. Loneliness and feeling different from other, more settled women was the fate of the veteran minister's wife. This was especially, but not exclusively, true for women married to Methodist preachers. Mary Orme Tucker's autobiography, published after her death in 1865, detailed the more than twenty moves her husband made to new churches, circuits, and towns. In 1840, she wrote of their "gypsy sort of life": "This is said to be a 'world of change.' To a Methodist minister's family it is indeed so. No sooner are they comfortably settled and pleasant acquaintances formed, than the inevitable fiat is received from Conference, the result of which is to 'stand not on the order of your going, but go at once.' Many years of experience had hardly reconciled me to the trials of an itinerate life. It is a gypsy sort of life, yet it has its compensations."[3]

Americans in the early nation already enjoyed the highest standard of living in the world (as measured both by commodities produced and consumed and by a diet that made the Continental army soldier a full three inches taller on average than his English and European counterparts).[4] In times of plenty in a basically agrarian economy, clergy families did fairly well, but the nineteenth century did not prove to be as kind to clerical households as had the 1700s. The economy went through a protracted transformation throughout the first two-thirds of the nineteenth century. While cash began to be the standard for all transactions, the clergy continued to receive commodities for their pay, which proved decreasingly liquid with time. In this commodity-to-cash transformation, Leonard Sweet argues, "the clergymen of America's voluntary society were caught—perhaps more than any other occupational group—in the crunch of the household society giving birth to a wage economy."[5] To make ends meet, clergy wives often taught school, farmed themselves, took in boarders, and founded female seminaries. Apart from farming, all these activities produced modest amounts of desperately needed cash for their families. Even Roxana Foote Beecher, the wife of as prominent minister as Lyman Beecher in as prominent a congregation as Connecticut's Litchfield Church, took in boarders and taught school. Beecher attributed his wife's early death in 1816 to her "undue exertions" in working off their household debts.[6]

All the while cash was in short supply, congregations continued to settle their accounts with food, new and used clothing, and, if the clergy were lucky, wood or coal. Helm Edmonds described what it was like to be on the receiving end of a donation party, where parishioners descended on a household laden with "gifts" toward their obligatory support. "We had a *donation party*, one of the episodes in a minister's life, fraught with fear, and expectations, and hope, and anxiety, and sometimes followed by regrets as well as gratified feelings."[7]

In 1887, Margaret Woods Lawrence asked whether donation parties were a good idea. She wrote, "In such cases if a fair contract is made in the beginning, inclusive of these visits, and it is understood that the pastor is not hampered by them, there may be no very serious objection to the arrangement."[8] Her use of so many conditional clauses betrayed what she really thought of forcing clergy families into discharging an honest cash obligation with surplus fresh meats and onions. She quotes a daughter as writing, "Why is it when father's salary is the merest pittance, that our people must bestow our donations in such a way as to make us feel that we are *objects of charity* giving a little tea or sugar or piece of cheese with an air as if conferring some great favor, and collecting a few dollars and cents by passing around a hat in our presence? It makes my cheeks burn for shame that they have no more feeling than to treat us as if we were beggars." For Lawrence, the time for this dynamic to end was "now, for justice is better than donation, and . . . the principle of work and wages is holier than that of pious mendicancy."[9]

Ennen Reaves Hall remembered what it was like to be the new Baptist minister's daughter in 1900 in a fledgling town in Indian Territory. She painfully recalled that a church member's first reaction to meeting the ten-year old Ennen was to deride her unusual name. From there it got worse: "Unaware of my reaction to her words, the woman rattled on. 'Are those your best clothes? I must say, I expected to see our pastor's family more dressed up—well, it's true, John, so why shouldn't I say it? You know the whole town will be judging our church by them.'"[10] Nearly sixty years later, Hall recollected with pride the integrity of her father and mother, who suffered these and many other slights with a measure of dignity and good humor. This and other memoirs have mostly the character of tales of triumph through adversity, marked by the humor of survival.

Sometimes the latent expectations in their roles could create a seething anger in clergy wives. Comparing their lot with that of other professionals' spouses made matters worse. Minister's wives in the Progressive Era like Margaret Woods Lawrence clearly wished to be their own selves, and not just an extension of a husband's job. "A doctor's wife has no responsibility in respect to her husband's patients," she wrote. "A lawyer's wife has none in respect to her husband's clients. But a minister's wife is regarded as owing special and important duties to all and to each of her husband's parishioners. There are multitudes who consider themselves entitled to find in this piece of humanity a combination of all the virtues in the calendar."[11] Women in the Progressive Era might well be more critical than their predecessors of the social role into which they were cast, but the pressures to maintain that role continued and were sometimes fostered by ministers themselves. A McCormick Seminary professor, Cleland McAfee, in a 1928 guide to ministerial manners and practices, helped keep the pressure up, writing, "The wife who is indifferent to the work of her minister-husband can do more to cripple him than she could do with any other kind of husband."[12] A few years later, Frances Sandys Elson published *Quiet Hints to Minister's Wives*. Among her hints were these: be a "pal" to one's husband, lead the Sunday school or choir, learn to speak and pray well in public (but avoid "masculinity"), and above all learn to take care of one's self. "Put a number of ministers' wives together in a group and what do you find?" she asked. "Generally, a teary and tired set of thin creatures. Admire the zeal of their souls and the acumen of their minds, if you will; but tell me why are these souls and minds housed so frequently in battered and broken temples?"[13] This theme was put more positively, if even more forcefully, by Carolyn P. Blackwood in 1950, when she reported the results of a survey she had circulated among laywomen in a wide range of churches. "Our 'first lady' should never seem overdressed. Neither should she ever look dowdy. According to lay women who responded to my questionnaires, 'she should dress as well as the salary allows.'"[14] Beyond dressing well, Blackwood recommended that sisters set an example of gracious living, provide constructive criticism to their husbands (though never on Sunday), take the *Reader's Digest* to stay current on ideas, keep track of the family budget, and take the lead in making ends meet around the manse. Alongside the advice she dispensed, Blackwood spoke of the rewards of the role: "As the 'first lady' of the church the minister's wife mingles around the *best* people in the community—not always the wealthiest, or the highest in the social scale, but those who feel most concerned about the kingdom of God. She learns to love them for their own dear sakes, and in turn receives from them loyal devotion as their queen. Her invisible diadem consists, not of gold and glittering gems, but of love from the hearts of God's people."[15]

Writing in the same year, Welthy Fischer also tried to turn the burden of marrying a man and his job into a kind of gift. Here the gift was participation and a kind of partnership, for "few, indeed, are the occupations which impose such requirements of team work on husband and wife. The diplomatic service and certain very high political positions would call for such a supporting role by the wife. But how few women are involved in these 'occupations' compared with the great and valiant army of minister's wives! It's high time the job was recognized as a special vocational achievement."[16] Such comparisons to the "first lady" and to diplomats wives suggest a search for status to compensate for the economic sacrifices ministers' wives encountered. The fact that the comparisons were offered so frequently argues for seeing that women in the postwar era had a genuinely positive appraisal of the role of the influential wife of a public figure (e.g., Eleanor Roosevelt), and aspired to such a role for themselves. But, in contrast to first ladies in the White House, experienced minister's wives often held their roles for decades. Mable Case looked back in the 1950s on her long years with gratitude: "The life of a minister's wife has held only joy for me and I can heartily recommend it to any young woman in love with the ministry. But the greatest happiness does not depend on things you can buy but rather upon the service that you can render to troubled hearts and saddened homes and the smiles you can bring to the faces of little children."[17]

Irrespective of the status and rewards offered by their role, clergy wives of the postwar era still faced the daunting task of making ends meet around the household. Lora Lee Parrott, the author of at least six cookbooks, some devotional guides, and *Christian Etiquette*, published *How To Be a Preacher's Wife and Like It* in 1956. As one might expect from the title, Parrott's book was full of advice. She celebrated the fact that ministers were better paid than in former years and no longer in need of the courtesy discounts in stores that formerly were their due. Yet when it came to money, Parrott believed the pastor's wife was more than 50 percent responsible for financial matters in the home and made eight suggestions of how to get by on a salary less than other professional men were willing to live on:

1. Do not buy everything you think you need.
2. Buy quality merchandise.
3. Watch for sales.
4. Pay cash.
5. Consider the possibility of used goods. ("It is better to swallow pride and keep solvent than to hold onto the pride and suffer financial embarrassment.")
6. Keep things in good repair.
7. Go easy on luxuries.
8. Don't worry about the Joneses.

Of all the suggestions, number six about home repairs was probably the most telling in an age when masculinity required men to be handy. "If your husband knows more about philosophy and theology than he does about hammers and nails, do not be discouraged. Get yourself a few tools at the local hardware store and learn how to make minor improvements and repairs of your own."[18] The pastor's wife's obligation was clear, to make up for a lack of income and even manly ability on the part of her spouse—with ingenuity, hard work, and common sense.

In 1974, Ruth Truman wrote an *Underground Manual for Ministers' Wives*. As the title implied, Truman sought to provide some countercultural sisterly advice to other minister's wives. Somewhat less than fully liberated, she had as her goal to help women survive in a culture that still thought it was honoring the minister's wife by letting her have first pick at the rummage sale. The problem as she saw it was that while Timothy had counseled a way to be rich in the parish—"grow with noble actions" (1 Timothy 6:18)—one could not eat noble actions.[19] That left the clergy wife in a vulnerable position: "And there you are, sweet, innocent, trusting your husband to provide (first mistake) and confident that the paycheck will come at the end of every pay period (second mistake) and it will take care of all your needs (strike three: you're out!)." Truman's tone, though humorous and patterned more on Erma Bombeck than any other writer, left no doubt she meant for her sisters to get the justice they deserved. "Your husband doesn't provide," she wrote; "the church does."[20] If the church did not or could not do enough and true budgeting and sacrifice could not close the gap, then it was time to face the "Super Frown" the church members and a husband's ecclesiastical superiors gave upon the news that one was going to work. Emancipation was made all the more necessary because of the attitude the church projected: "Everyone *knew* that a minister and his wife were hired as a team to serve the church, and somehow, by bringing income from a source other than the church, you no longer belonged to the team."[21] Beneath it all, for Truman, the problem was that it was hard to maintain a true spiritual life in the parsonage: "It is very easy to be super-religious (translate—'extra active in church work') and hate yourself—or your husband, who got you into this mess."[22]

Alongside concerns about the burdens of work for ministers and their spouses, the issue of church-owned housing continued to fester throughout the 1970s and 1980s. John and Linda Morgan produced a report titled "Wives of Priests," an inquiry into the status of clergy wives in the Episcopal Church issued in 1980. Their major finding of dissatisfaction was in the area of housing: approximately half of all clergy households lived in church-owned rectories, and of these fully half believed the arrangement unsatisfactory.[23] Charlotte Ross, writing in the same year, found that family life for clergy households continued to be a major issue. One correspondent reported running into the expectation that her children be better than others as early as when her children were two and four years old, respectively. Many objected to "life in a fish bowl." But perhaps the most poignant comments reflected the loneliness ministers' wives experienced as they tried to raise children in what were tantamount to single-parent households:

> I especially wish for more help in parenting from my husband, but he is just not physically available.
>
> I resent his endless hours. I resent that he never had time to see his children grow up.
>
> We have no weekends to enjoy as a family when our children are free from school. He is too busy Saturday getting ready for church and too busy Sunday with services to enjoy outings as a family.[24]

At the same time, absent or not, minister fathers themselves expected higher degrees of loyalty and exemplary conduct from their children, just as they did from their wives.

As was true of Ruth Truman, Charlotte Ross was not prepared to write off all matters of inequity within clergy marriages as being due to irresistible forces within the church. Ross still believed, however, that there was plenty of blame to be shared by congregations for wives' feelings of insecurity. A long-time sufferer of other people's decorating, she allowed that one of her fantasies, meant only half in jest, was that upon her death she would be at last rewarded with the words "Well done, good and faithful servant, enter into the joy of thy $5,000 kitchen."[25] The thing that hurt most was having no voice in decisions about what happened in and to the house where she lived. On limited salaries and fixed housing arrangements, many clergy wives in the last quarter of the twentieth century found themselves in the same position as women in the first quarter of the nineteenth. They were placed within a system that valued domesticity while living in a domestic cage furnished without their participation. The problem was perhaps most acutely felt among Methodists in such groups as the North Carolina United Methodist Conference; well into the 1980s, clergy families in the conference did not possess even their own furnishings, including large or small appliances. Indeed, a proposal for a reform of the parsonage system offered in 1979 suggested how deeply entrenched the system was. Based on a New Jersey Conference experiment, the proposal was that ministers have the option to buy the furnishings in the current parsonage in which they dwelt as a means of achieving a measure of "equity"! No wonder Mary Owens Fitzgerald blamed the parsonage system for fostering a culture of dependency, and a contemporary survey of clergy wives pointed to the system as a leading cause of marital discord.[26]

A Southern Baptist couple, Robert and Mary Frances Bailey, wrote of the domestic insecurity engendered by other people's knowledge of all of the clergy family's finances. "The entire church not only knows all the minister makes," they noted, "but they also subject the parsonage family to the humiliating pressure of having his compensation up for open discussion." Fear of humiliation from not proving to be worth his compensation, the Baileys thought, was at the root of the "workaholic tendencies of the contemporary minister."[27]

The issues identified by the 1950s writers for their generation of ministers' wives still persist in the literature in websites dedicated to clergy wives in the new millennium, though no one compares their role so explicitly to that of a first lady or a queen. The ongoing struggles with social-role expectations have shifted somewhat, however. The authors of the most recent guides are much more likely to identify themselves as evangelical and to work within structures related to more conservative portions of the Protestant spectrum. The issues their writings cover (Should a minister's spouse work? What kind of model should she set in child rearing?) and the difficulties of sharing her clergy spouse's best hours with others are the perennial ones of being part of the ministry by extension, yet they are simultaneously as contemporary as the latest *Focus on the Family* radio show. Indeed, work and family issues are at the center of contemporary discourse about the clergy and their spouses across the entire spectrum of American Protestantism. In liberal and moderate circles, the question of whether a woman may work was, by the year 2000, not a subject of debate. But issues of disproportionate expectations from congregations continued to rankle. Even among the conservative Protestant writers like Diane Lanberg, who believe that ministers should go before their lay leaders lovingly and ask them to pray over the problem of the minister's family's lack of adequate material support, there was a new willingness to name foes in a congregation. Lanberg herself addressed the stunted emotional development of many church members. "Some," she wrote, "like the nine lepers in Luke 19, will go on their way with no thought for you, no word of gratitude." Another conservative take on the problems faced by clergy families living in "glass houses" argued that the four great stressors on ministers' households were the absence of time boundaries, higher expectations for family members, the lack of family privacy, and continued difficulty with finances, making it impossible for clergy families to live as others did in their communities.[28]

The glass house theme continues to be sounded as new generations of women experience afresh what it means to live in the shadow of the church and their husbands' ministries. A Seventh Day Adventist's minister's wife, Claire Eva, wrote in 2000 to commend budgeting as a spiritual (and financially necessary) habit.[29] The next year, Kay A. Fuller, the wife of a Baptist General Conference minister in Cedar Falls, Iowa, wrote of her guilt in meeting a deacon of her church in a parking lot after stocking up on a month's load of diapers, paper towels and toilet paper: "I attempted to converse, but his eyes were fixed on my sacks." I just knew he was thinking: 'Our pastor's wife must be a frivolous spender. We must be paying her husband too much!' "[30]

What are we to make of the continuity and concerns of women occupying a specific role documented over at least 180 years? The fact that most of the recent writings about the difficulty of being a minister's spouse come from more conservative sources might suggest that, with the advent of women's ordination and liberal clergy spouses' working outside the church for money, perhaps the phenomenon of feeling trapped by the ministry is on the decline. Could it be that the emancipation of spouses from church service by marriage is only a matter of time since its last vestiges are only visible in the least culturally "advanced" portions of religious America? That is an interesting thesis, to be sure, but several contemporary signs point in another direction. First is the new battle over itinerancy being fought out in Methodist conferences, where the spouses of clergy, male and female, are now contributing more income to their households than are the ministers to whom they are married. How, these new clergy two-earner families want to know, can the conference move them with-out regard for the spouse's practice as a therapist or his or her tenure as a teacher? The number of small, underserved churches and churches with vacant pulpits has skyrocketed in the Presbyterian Church (USA) and the Episcopal Church, mostly in areas that offer few prospects for a second earner to cross-subsidize a spouse's ministry. What appeared, at first glance, to be a labor problem solved is a problem transmuted. Indeed, a 1993 study by Edward C. Lehman on gender and work in the clergy reached the intriguing conclusion that the best predictor of whether male *and* female clergy in the Methodist, Presbyterian, United Church of Christ, and American Baptist denominations led their churches in ways that fostered lay ownership and control was high household income. Ministers of either sex in any denomination with lower than average household income were apt to "run their churches" with a high degree of clergy control,[31] apparently because they were determined to keep what little they had. The lesson was clear: fear of falling out of the middle class characterized large portions of America's Protestant clergy labor pool into the contemporary era.

What is the enduring testimony of the ministers' wives? It is a familiar story, repeatedly experienced and retold by new generations of women. This story, at its heart, is the intimate experience of being part of a spouse's workplace. Sometimes the story is that of being given a chance to serve and earn respect far beyond the opportunities given to others in the Christian life. At other times, the larger element of the narrative is that of being judged and ruled by the job one's husband holds or by one's husband's employers and by supposed peers in the parish. The essential point to be drawn is what a peculiar workplace and economic entity the typical Protestant congregation is, as viewed by the people attached to the laborers who serve the congregation. If the early Christian church was built on the blood of the martyrs, then the economy of American Protestantism is in no small measure built on the hearts of women who gave their lives and accepted opportunity costs in order that the spiritual enterprise might succeed.

CHAPTER NINE

In America You Can Have as

Much Religion as You Can Pay For,

1980 to the Present

This chapter weaves together the strands of the story of Protestants, their money, and their churches—the strands of raising money, spending it on ministry, and investing in structures and ways of doing ministry—into a final account of the pursuit of the Almighty's dollar since 1980. Throughout the history of American Protestant church life, we have seen that the health of local congregations has been highly dependent on how the communities in which they are located are doing and how the congregations themselves respond to local competition through leadership, programming decisions, and even building choices. In the United States, it seems, you can have as much religion as you want to pay to have. The voluntary nature of church support initiated this pattern two centuries ago, and recent social and economic trends have greatly intensified the demand-driven aspects of American Protestant church life. Principal among these trends are: regional migration, the development of more nondenominationally identified congregations than ever before, and the pursuit of religious goods outside congregational settings. Through it all, Protestant churches, old and new, have sought to secure the funds to do ministry as before and with new twists on old practices to meet the challenges of the contemporary era.

MIGRATION CREATES SOME KINDS OF PROTESTANTS MORE THAN OTHERS

If the 1970s were hard years for many mainline congregations, the 1980s and 1990s were good years for newer congregations, at least financially. Many new congregations opened in the Sunbelt, part of the largest and quietest internal migration in American history. The migrants moved from the North and East toward the South and Southwest. Not all portions of the South and Southwest benefited equally. Rural areas and small town churches, for example, continued to be small and lose membership unless they were in the shadow of medium-sized and larger cities, in which case they often became absorbed into those cities' metropolitan areas as suburbs. Throughout the nation, suburbanization profited Protestant churches. All of these population movements impacted church life in a fairly straightforward five-step process.

First, more people attending churches in their new Sunbelt homes in the South and Southwest meant the balance within denominational families was shifting toward the South.

Second, people attending churches in newer residential areas, North and South, were free to pioneer new models of worship, partly out of necessity and partly out of a post-1960s and 70s dissatisfaction with the received formality of their elders' church-going mores. Rock instruments supplanted organs and Sunday casual replaced coats, ties, and dresses in the moves outward and southward.

Third, those who moved south in the 1980s were a curious mixture of retired people, who began their working lives in the 1940s, and younger people, who chased jobs to warmer climates. The retirees were already comfortable with a Protestantism of personal faith and hard work for group causes. They were less inclined to see the church as a force for radical social change than was a later cohort. Joining them in the southern migration was a group of young adults who had by and large come to faith outside the instrumentalities of the churches. Even if they had been sent to Sunday schools as small children, they entered adolescence in the 1970s, a decade in which American church leaders were unsure of their theological claims and paid most attention to things other than faith formation for teenagers. This did not mean that the so-called Me Generation did not get its faith formed. The gap left behind by mainline and even conservative congregations was often filled by college campus evangelistic fellowships and other groups patterned on them. The college students of the 1980s (and later high school students) were offered regular opportunities to claim Jesus Christ as their personal Lord and Savior, to ask Jesus into their lives, and to turn their lives over to Christ. The sum total of this trend was a gain for more conservative congregations that understood the Christian faith and how one got to be a Christian on a more personal and individual basis. The churches that grew most in the Sunbelt were, therefore, churches that catered to the older generation of personal faith retirees or to the generation that sought congregations that most resembled their campus Christian fellowships (such as Campus Crusade, Young Life, Youth for Christ, and InterVarsity).

Fourth, though the retirees and the young adults of the 1980s chose similarly conservative faith outlets, they tended to worship in different congregations in the same Sunbelt areas. The retirees in Orlando and Phoenix worshiped in churches with a formal worship structure, organ music, large robed choirs, regular Sunday school classes for adults, and a robed minister invariably referred to with a title as "Dr. So-and-So." Meanwhile, across town, the younger adults sang the praise music they had learned in youth groups or college and heard a message (not a sermon) from a minister who went by his first name (as in "Bob is our minister," "Bob's message really spoke to me this week"). Organs came to these congregations rather late, if at all; enthusiastic musicians with drums, basses, and guitars were far easier to locate in these congregations of the young.

Fifth, these two great migrations, together with a somewhat later third movement of affluent blacks to the suburbs and the establishment of so-called megachurches, furthered a movement toward a significant adjustment in the shape of American Protestantism. This adjustment was nothing less than the eclipse of the self-consciously multigenerational congregation in favor of narrowly cast congregations filling de facto demographic niches. Just as older people ate at Country Buffet restaurants and young adults frequented t.g.i. Friday's, so churches took on narrow bands of religious taste and preference. Like so many prior settlements of Protestants on American soil, the new churches meant new capital investments for property and buildings.

THANK GOD FOR LOW INTEREST RATES

The church building boom of the 1990s and early 2000s is both directly and indirectly attributable to the availability of inexpensive money. After accounting for inflation, the loans that churches could obtain to pay for their new and renewed buildings over time were nearly interest-free. This constituted a stunning improvement in the borrowing capacity of churches, which in the 1970s and 1980s had faced the same double-digit interest rates as homeowners did when they sought to build. During that earlier period, the real rate of interest reached historic highs while the high inflation of the era eroded parishioners' real incomes. It is not surprising, therefore, that booms in the construction of housing and of religious buildings go together. As of this writing, two-dozen highly dedicated church-member families can reasonably take on the project of building a new church and plan on paying it off over terms of fifteen to twenty years. Indeed, while median real wages in contemporary America are somewhat stagnant, in the neighborhoods where community churches are going up just after the residential landscapers have finished their work, incomes are on a steady rise.

Racial segregation in American congregations has long been noticed as a fact of life. Less obvious but no less real are the class and income stratifications of American congregational life. This becomes vibrantly clear in the case of new suburban congregations. The poor do not start new congregations; they join existing ones (when they attend at all). The wealthy are also likely to be members of established congregations. It is younger, upwardly mobile, and geographically mobile members on the affluent side of the middle class that are starting new churches, just as their grandparents' generation did soon after World War II. Once again, as throughout American history, development of the American religious infrastructure takes place on the margins of existing (now metropolitan) areas and among a differentially privileged population.

What difference does it make to American religion as a whole that wealthier middle-class people are establishing new churches in suburbia? At first blush, this looks like a simple extension of an old pattern, most recently featured in the move to the suburbs of the 1950s. Even a quick comparison of the postwar and millennial-era church building booms, however, reveals major differences. The greatest one is that the new churches of the present era are likely not to carry a denominational brand name, even when they are affiliated with a larger body. Countless new churches of the 1990s include the word *community* in their names. Some of these are affiliated with the Southern Baptist Convention or the Presbyterian Church of America. Many others are loosely affiliated with the Vineyard, Calvary Chapel, or Willow Creek. Still others are completely independent of any larger expression of church. To be sure, some well-organized Methodist conferences, Episcopal dioceses, and mainline Presbyterian presbyteries are establishing new churches through new church development plans, but for every one they put into operation, several more locally and entrepreneurially organized churches are being established. These latter churches are typically going up much more quickly since their clergy leaders have nowhere to move to if they fail and local lay leaders have no one to oversee (read "block") their plans to develop a congregation to their liking. In the realm of video and coffee shops, a well-organized brand like Blockbuster or Starbucks beats out idiosyncratic single-store outlets nearly every time, but a congregation is a participatory organization that is unique in appearance and in organizational features even when it carries a denominational affiliation. In sum, American Protestantism has entered an era where—at least at the margin of residential growth—a denominational family affiliation is perceived as a drag on, rather than a strength for, a local church.

The histories of two self-designated nondenominational community churches near the author's home illustrate how new-style congregations start in the contemporary era. One of the churches, the New Hope Community Church, declares on its website and in its brochures, "It is not our intention for New Hope to be an exclusive place for Christians. We understand there are Christians in different churches all across the globe. New Hope helps individuals who come out of any kind of background to appreciate those things that have brought them closer to Christ. It is a place where we focus on the primary essentials of the Christian faith, and give liberty to secondary issues of the faith. Within this context we believe we can all grow and experience different aspects from our various backgrounds."[1] In this church the senior pastor is from a Free Methodist background; the associate pastor is a graduate of a Presbyterian seminary; and the youth minister is currently a master's degree student in a nearby Nazarene college's religion program. None, however, label themselves denominationally. Like their congregation, these ministers are independent Christians. Begun in the late 1970s, New Hope has matured to the point where it has mission statements and international mission projects of its own. Worship, fellowship, and Bible study bind members and ministers together. A denominational label is seen as a problem that the rest of the church has, but not one that inhibits New Hope.

Two miles away is the Living Word Community Church. Established just a decade ago, the church tells its founding story in terms of leaders, moves, and mergers. The church was formed under the direction of Bishop Ralph H. Houston, president of the Original United Holy Church; Dan Scott, assistant pastor of Christ Church (Pentecostal); and the Reverend Hilly Hicks, a local AME Pastor; but it was Rodney E. Beard Sr., the church's current senior pastor, who is credited with the founding of the church. After moving from a small facility it had taken over from another congregation to a high school, it purchased a large Baptist church property from a congregation that had outgrown its buildings. Then the church combined its "Kingdom efforts" with those of the Cool Springs Church of Franklin, Tennessee, and Pastors Kimble and Melinda Knight. Here in the mid-South, an interracial congregation of fifteen hundred has been formed from preexisting streams on the main street of an affluent suburb. The church itself does not use the word *interracial* or mark the denominational families that gave rise to its particular understandings of ministry; instead, it celebrates becoming a community of faith by saying, "Together the two church families have taken a quantum leap as cultures have melded into a homogeneous mix of faith, hope, love, excellence and purpose."[2]

Four other Brentwood, Tennessee, churches illustrate how suburbanization and new church growth is reshaping the religious landscape. Illustration 23 shows the Owen Chapel Church of Christ, established in 1859, still meeting where it began in the same-sized building. By contrast, the Brentwood Baptist Church grew steadily with its suburban setting since its beginning in 1968 as a mission church meeting in a Baptist home for children. In the subsequent thirty-seven years, it has worshiped in four buildings, each larger than the one it replaced. The last of these buildings is the 175,000-square-foot building shown in illustration 24, located a mere three hundred yards from the Owen Chapel Church of Christ. The same distance away is the Remnant Fellowship (see illustration 25), a church that grew out of the Weigh Down Diet, created by Christian diet-guru Gwen Shamblin in 1986. The building itself resembles nothing so much as a church that has been there for three centuries, as befits a fellowship determined to reject the false church and build the "new Jerusalem." Somewhat more typical is the Community Church located three miles away. A careful eye is required to see that this new church has an affiliation with the Church of God. (See illustration 26.)

Established American Protestant denominations grew by opening new congregational outlets in the twenty years after 1945. The religious boom of the 1950s for these denominations was not so much a return to religion, in the sense of people returning to existing churches, as it was the establishment of newly organized congregations in new neighborhoods. In the years surrounding the year 2000, the new religious outlets are decidedly not denominational brands. The long-term impact of this change is probably far-reaching in two ways. The first is that the mainline's loss of market share will permanently rebalance the character of American congregational life. Just as great a percentage of the population might, in the future, be associated with a Protestant church as is now the case, but fewer people will be associated with a church whose institutional conception of itself goes beyond the local congregation to a regional, national, or even international expression. Organizing Protestants to do some-

23. Owen Chapel Church of Christ, Brentwood, Tennessee. Author's photograph.

24. Brentwood Baptist Church, Brentwood, Tennessee. Author's photograph.

25. Remnant Fellowship, Brentwood, Tennessee. Author's photograph.

26. The sign for the Community Church, Brentwood, Tennessee. Note the size of the denominational affiliation. Author's photograph.

thing beyond the local church will resemble political organizing for the 2004 presidential election more than it will the unified mission appeals of the mid-twentieth century. Every effort at collective action will require its own "follower base." Churches will not tax themselves for generalized common mission efforts so much as they will choose which individual missionary workers—known to them personally—they will support. In this respect contemporary American Protestant life seems a return to the early nineteenth century, when individuals representing good causes went begging from congregation to congregation. Leadership in this paradigm is likewise more charismatic and less representational in character. Since bishops and other denominational leaders can deliver less of a follower base in this situation, bishops (and their equivalents) will be less likely to get invited to the White House, or the statehouse, than in the past. Charismatic leaders like Tony Campolo or James Dobson will be much more likely to get such invitations.

The second related, but discrete, impact of this new configuration of American Protestantism is the way the new style of congregational life establishing itself on the growing edges of American culture is reshaping and will reshape existing congregations affiliated with denominational bodies. The realignment that is taking place more resembles the era of the early republic than it does the years following World War II. Whereas the postwar return to religion saw increases in denominationally affiliated congregations, the early republic found the colonial powerhouse traditions—Congregational, Episcopal, Presbyterian, and Reformed churches—being eclipsed by evangelical upstarts, the Baptists and the Methodists. In the process, the old-line traditions soon became more evangelical themselves. The result was that American churches became less European and established in character and instead became more voluntary and engaged in what might charitably be called competitive coexistence. Once again, innovation in religious life has rendered old patterns of organization dated while fostering even greater local autonomy than could be conceived of in the past.

THE RISE OF ENTREPRENEURIAL PROTESTANTISM

Twice before in the history of American Protestantism, the religious sector has undergone a sea change leaving congregations—the dominant form of religious organization—to deal with substantially new realities. The first was the introduction of competitive privatization in the early national period. By 1830, all American congregations competed against one another for members and sought their funding from within their own ranks. The second was the rise of the institutional church as a de facto standard for American congregations. With rare exceptions, congregations after the Progressive Era no longer considered themselves going concerns if they offered their members and the community around them only Sunday worship services. The twentieth-century congregation was in no small measure defined by its service to people in a building occupied by multiple groups each day of the week. In each of these instances, we may say that the nature of the firm—what it meant to be a Protestant congregation—was transformed.

Once again a transformation in how American Protestantism goes about its business is under way. Like earlier renovations of the American style of religion, this new form is a response to challenges from without and within. As a result of the so-called third disestablishment of the church, people have found diverse ways to be religious in a time when social rewards and sanctions for religious involvement in a standard brand of American piety have all but disappeared. I call this "Do-It-Yourself Religion" with full awareness that categorizing trends in the midst of their own unfolding is fraught with difficulty. Nevertheless, I offer this analysis because I believe that those situated inside the existing institutions of American religion misunderstand their position if they think of themselves as working in the institutional-congregational paradigm dominant in the past century.

The very phrase "Do-It-Yourself Religion" may be misleading when used to encompass both the religiosity of those who embrace New-Age spirituality and the rise of the megachurches. Yet what the many developments of the contemporary period have in common is a religious quest that is unfettered by the moorings of tradition. What "works" is, for most people, a religion that is most authentic to their own experience. The authority for determining what it is that "works" is the self. All other authorities, ancient or modern, written or personal, are tested in the crucible of personal experience and are lightly discarded when their truth does not meet the test. When traditions no longer control the use and meaning of their distinctive forms of life and practice, ironies develop. So, for example, Thomas Merton and Dorothy Day are cited as life-models for some. These two figures who were radical in their willingness to grant parts of the received tradition autonomous control of their lives, prove fascinating to many contemporary people who read their writings and about their lives for "inspiration" without the least desire to live bounded by a religious tradition themselves. Likewise, things Amish and Shaker and other forms of the simple life are consumed by people driving $75,000 BMWs.

Operating within this new state of affairs in which religious consumers—and not suppliers—decide the terms of trade has set the stage for further innovation. In addition to good old-fashioned, Sunday-morning-choirs-in-robes Protestantism, new options have arisen to compete for the time and religious energy of Americans. Sunday morning might as likely be spent reading the paper as going to church, as many ministers have been quick to note. But it would be a mistake to write the Sunday brunch crowd off as nonreligious. Indeed, Sunday brunch may take place in a Borders Books and include a visit to the spirituality section of the store. The bruncher who never leaves the table may spend time reading one of the new sections on "faith and values" that many metropolitan newspapers added during the 1990s as part of their lifestyle coverage expansion.

So what is the religion that binds the family values crowd, mainstream pew sitters, the Sunday brunchers, and the spirituality seekers? It is arguable that Americans have realized a new version of Protestantism that is nevertheless still recognizable as Protestantism nearly five hundred years after the movement began. It is a religion that insists on the right of private judgment. The acceptance of any authority or tradition is provisional. If one attends a church, pledges a respectable gift, sends one's children to Sunday school, and insists that they go through a confirmation process, it is still with the firm idea that it is because one has chosen to do this with one's life. One might have made another choice; Americans often do. Even the baby-boomer mothers and fathers who insist their child go through confirmation class may also justify their insistence in contemporary terms by saying, "It's so that she can make her own choice." The American Protestant who claims in an older mode that God has called him or her to do something, or who instructs his or her children in the Christian faith "because it is the truth" has become much rarer over the last one hundred years. This is true not withstanding the public visibility of conservative and fundamentalist Christians.

A rigid demarcation between the brunchers, active church members, and experimenters is impossible. Often, they are the same people at different stages of their lives, or even the same people on different days of the month. The message that premarital sexual relations are in some sense wrong or fraught with difficulties sounds like one thing to a nineteen-year-old in college and like something else, something wiser, to the parent of the nineteen-year-old. The idea that salvation is to be found in but one way, which is the quintessential message of the religious professional, is privately watered down in the minds of even the most regular lay Protestants in contemporary America by the qualification "for me." Thus, "there is but one way to salvation (for me)" is the oil of the American workplace and the public square. People in these settings are proud of their values, but tolerant of others even when such toleration stretches those personally held values. Perhaps nowhere do we see this as clearly as in the widespread social acceptance of gays and lesbians in the workplace and in the irony that some people who hear homosexuality condemned in Sunday's sermons and on religious television programs nurture friendships in the work setting with homosexuals. Others embrace gay and lesbian members as worthy family members no matter what their churches may publicly proclaim. Not only that, but people of homosexual orientation are to be found in all churches, irrespective of those churches' public stands on sexuality. These facts raise the question of what the real religion of American Protestants is. It appears that the dominant religious outlook is a cultural Protestantism that is not taught in seminaries but is practiced by pastors and laypeople alike. The symbol of this new cultural Protestantism is the minister-father figure from the wb network's surprise hit *Seventh Heaven*. Pete is a minister for our times, good looking, with a good but imperfect family, who tries to do the right thing, even when he is wrong, and manages with a sense of grace to muddle through the many times when the choices before him are contradictory. His liturgical activities are rarely as exciting or significant as the ministry he exercises outside the church building. In the contemporary situation, real life and television mirror one another, and religious authority is accepted only so long as it makes sense for us to accept it. There are other teachers in the spiritual marketplace, and American Protestants are prepared to go elsewhere if what they hear does not make sense. As a result, the Protestant clergy has probably never been so decentered in all of American history, but it is hard to miss the ways in which they have contributed to, indeed structured, some of the religious alternatives that Americans now enjoy.

What do the emerging trends in Protestant life mean for most churches and their members? It is hard, of course, to predict the future with confidence. Human beings show remarkably little imagination in seeing how new ways might soon become their ways. Technological adaptation is like that. The first horseless carriage was an obvious nuisance in most towns; so too was the last horse and buggy. More recently, few individuals in 1980 thought they would ever have need of a computer in their homes. Changes in the way religious life is practiced also come quickly. At different times, battles have been fought within congregations over whether to add an organ, a choir, hymnals, an educational wing, a gym, a public address system, a wheelchair ramp, and a hunger pantry. Still, all of these have become standard parts of our mental furniture in picturing how churches should be equipped and what they should do. Despite pockets of continued social resistance, the widespread adaptations to the new modes of church life came rather quickly. Not every innovation in technique succeeds. Drive-in churches failed long before drive-in theaters vanished. The fate of current innovations—Saturday night come-as-you-are services, cyber-prayer lists and newsletters delivered by e-mail, bands replacing organs, light rock replacing Bach, and seeker services—is by no means so clear. What is certain is that once a group has embraced a form of religious observance it will soon reify that form into "the way things are." Meanwhile, older forms will persist alongside the new. After all, formal religious adherence and attendance, though reduced compared to the high-water mark of the early 1960s, are not so bad when judged in historical terms. But that is just what goes on inside congregations. The supply of religion outside congregational settings has become pervasive, and its entrepreneurial suppliers are legion. Will chat groups replace small groups? Will spirituality stores and vision quests replace congregations? One doubts that they will provide entire replacements, but these religious alternatives represent strong competitors to congregations cast in the traditional mold.

In contemporary America, books outsell every other form of media, and many best-selling books feature religious themes or subjects one is unlikely to encounter in the typical Protestant congregation. So, for instance, out of the top ten best-selling books for 2003, two were thrillers written by Dan Brown, *The Da Vinci Code* and *Angels and Demons*. Both books derived their plots from unflattering speculation about intrigue within the Roman Catholic Church. The top-selling book for the year was the fifth Harry Potter book, *Harry Potter and the Order of the Phoenix*, which like its predecessors imagined a world enchanted with spirits and magic, but free from organized religion. The fifth best-selling book on Barnes and Noble's list was Mitch Albom's *The Five People You Meet in Heaven*, a book in which a comforting new myth about the afterlife, again without conventional religion, is introduced. The seventh book on the list, *The Purpose Driven Life: What on Earth Am I Here For?* by Rick Warren, the pastor of the 50,000-member Saddleback Church in Lake Forest, California, took a theme drawn from a previous book, *The Purpose Driven Church*, and turned it into a self-help book for individuals seeking a way forward in life. Even this book by a minister illustrates the new, more entrepreneurial commodification of contemporary spirituality, for inside the first chapter and final sections of *The Purpose Driven Life* one finds Purpose Driven Life–branded items one can buy along with the book. There are Purpose Driven calendars with inspirational quotes, Purpose Driven datebooks, Purpose Driven mouse pads, Purpose Driven coffee mugs, and so forth. Gone from the best-seller list are the ministers from mainline churches and prominent pulpits reaching a national audience with the same material as they preach Sunday by Sunday. Indeed, out of the top one hundred books on this particular list, only one by Mister (Fred) Rogers, weighing in at number fifty-three, was written by a clergyman from a mainline tradition, and even his book is an exercise in providing a set of value lessons from an undisclosed religious position.

What happened in organized religion was not unlike what was happening in television broadcasting as bandwidth was increasing. The television story is well known. In the 1950s and 1960s, there were but a few local channels, and only slowly did the networks even move their programming to color from black and white. The 1970s saw a proliferation of UHF stations in major local media markets, followed by an explosion of cable channels in the 1980s and 1990s. The singer Bruce Springsteen could lament that there were "57 channels and nothin' on," but the fact remained that television's vast audience was fragmenting itself across dozens of channels, and "mainline" television in the form of ABC, CBS, and NBC was no longer being watched in so many homes simultaneously so as to provide a common culture for Americans as they once did in the 1950s and 1960s. For religion, a similar transformation was under way. Whereas religion in the early postwar years meant "let's go to church," by the mid-1980s there was a proliferation of outlets for religious interest and even involvement that undermined the mainline franchise.

I have used the term "entrepreneurial Protestantism" to describe the emerging religious ethos in contemporary America, but some might wonder in what sense this religion can be termed "Protestant." I believe the term applies insofar as Protestantism is historically distinguished as a form of Christianity by its insistence on justification by faith, scripture as the essential source of revelation, and the priesthood of all believers. For all the claims of new and emerging groups that they are nondenominational or "not into tradition," American culture is so steeped in the fruits of Protestantism that these groups have, in effect, reinvented Protestantism while rejecting the label. Some new Bible churches, coffeehouse fellowships, and even the people who cannot quite find a church in which they are comfortable have managed to retrace paths that earlier Protestants trod. From Anabaptists and Restorationists to the isolated piety of Roger Williams, it has all been done before. But what makes it so American and so Protestant is that it is being tried here and now by new people on a quest for religiously authentic experience of their own, who reject any priest between themselves and the divine, but who will easily turn to religious entrepreneurs for help.

In the contemporary period, no prior method or argument for raising money in the Protestant churches has disappeared. The persistence of past methods and rationales through the close of the second millennium was all the more striking when it is remembered how many other major aspects of American church life and Protestant thought had changed. The Bible, for instance, was no longer used to argue for slavery, but rather for liberation. Gone was the curse of Ham. Protestants, by and large, still drank grape juice and not wine at the Lord's Supper, yet no one seriously entertained the idea that Christ drank the unfermented fruit juice at his last meal with his disciples. Instead of looking for Biblical warrants for their practice, churches seized on pragmatic justifications. Grape juice was just better for children and those in recovery from alcoholism. Finally, in many traditions the Bible was no longer used to prohibit women from speaking in church, and women in many of the Protestant churches were eligible for ordained offices of ministry. But the tithe, giving proportionately, and even sermons about robbing God and Gideon's fleece were as common as ever before. As one popular sermon line ran, "God's law of the tithe has never been repealed." Neither, apparently, had sermons favoring 10 percent giving gone out of style.

To the contemporary historian, the Internet is an amazing medium of popular democracy and opinion. On issues related to church finance, the World Wide Web features opinions about the right ways to raise and give money in the churches that simply have no parallel in published literature, including pamphlets and church bulletins. The Internet has eliminated both external editorial controls and private inhibitions. In regard to this study, there is no hotter topic on the Web than tithing. Whether on official denominational websites, leadership resource sites, or Christian chat rooms, contemporary Christians have an urge to push opinions about tithing. Given the historical finding of this book that tithing in American Protestantism represents a nineteenth-century recovery (or even the invention) of a questionable biblical era precedent and practice, it perhaps comes as a surprise to the reader how much giving 10 percent of one's income and assets to the church is defended as Christian law and by whom. A belief in tithing makes for odd bedfellows in American Protestantism. On the other hand, those who oppose tithing are also an interesting lot.

Positions on tithing and the people who take them reveal much about the beliefs, hopes, and focus of contemporary American Protestants. The official Assemblies of God website has, at this writing, a major page on the position of the denomination on tithing. "The Assemblies of God has always," the site reads, "been a proponent of tithing (or giving one-tenth of one's personal income to support the work of God). We believe tithing is a recognition that everything we have comes from God. The practice checks our greed, promotes personal discipline and thrift, testifies to our faith, promotes God's work in the world, and alleviates human need." Later, the Assemblies addresses concerns about people who withheld tithes when they did not like decisions espoused by their spiritual leaders: "While we may designate some of our offerings (beyond the tithes) to ministries outside the local church, the tithes rightfully belong in the church with which the Christian identifies. And if one is not identifying with a local body of believers, he or she disregards God's instruction that we not forsake assembling together with believers (Hebrews 10:25)."[3]

What the Assemblies of God tries to argue by scripture and reason, the Church of God's Department of Stewardship seeks to illuminate with nine proffered sermon illustrations. The first of these attempts to shame hearers into tithing: "If every church member in the United States were suddenly to lose his/her job and went on Welfare, and yet were willing to tithe from the minimal amount received from public assistance, giving in the nation's churches would immediately increase over thirty percent." If pastors do not wish to use the welfare example, they might choose to use a positive example drawn from the innocence of a young African Christian: "There was a knock on the door of a hut occupied by a missionary in Africa. Answering, the missionary found one of the native boys holding a large fish in his hands. The boy said, 'Reverend, you taught us what tithing is, so here—I've brought you my tithe.' As the missionary gratefully took the fish, he questioned the young boy, 'If this is your tithe, where are the other nine fish?' At this, the boy beamed and said, 'Oh, they're still back in the river. I am going back to catch them now.'"[4]

Denominations are not the only institutions promoting the tithe. Christian Broadcasting Network offers a teaching sheet on giving and tithing that draws on writings by its founder, Pat Robertson. In Robertson's view, the law of the tithe is not the only obligation at work; rather, there is also a law of reciprocity that is just as real. "Christ's admonition to 'Give and it will be given to you' defines a remarkable spiritual principle," Robertson asserts. "It can also be called the 'law of reciprocity,' which is quite evident in the physical world: for every action, there is an equal and opposite reaction. Smile at another person, and he'll probably smile back at you. Be critical of others, and they'll respond in kind. As you give, you will receive. Give generously, and you will receive in like measure." Why then should people tithe, especially since God owns everything and doesn't need the tithes? People need to give them, "for, in instructing us to tithe, God is helping us understand the law of reciprocity." Where, in the view of

CBN, should these tithes be rendered? Here it gets interesting. "In the Old Testament," the site says, "the Jews were instructed to take their tithes 'to the storehouse,' which was the temple—the center of religion for the entire country. Today, since the body of Christ has so many manifestations (churches, colleges, television and overseas ministries, hospitals, relief agencies, etc.), people can choose where their tithe should go." According to CBN, it is important for people to tithe to the place that "feeds you spiritually."[5]

Clearly, whether one believes that tithing means ten percent to a local church or ten percent to all Christian causes depends mightily on the nature of one's ministry. Meanwhile, the website of the St. James African Methodist Episcopal Church in Columbus, Georgia, teaches that tithing is a moral and spiritual obligation of the Christian for five reasons:

1. The law commands it. . . .
2. Stewardship includes it. . . .
3. Needs demand it. . . .
4. Love constrains it. . . .
5. Results justify it. . . .

An explanation and biblical citations are given for each reason. The biblical citations—Leviticus 27:30, Malachi 3:8, 1 Corinthians 16:2, 2 Corinthians 8:14, Luke 7:47, Luke 16:11, and Matthew 23:23—tend to group together the sorts of things that Christians are to do in the world and on behalf of the needy with divinely sanctioned rules about giving under a holistic understanding of tithing. Here, giving is more than God's command; it actually meets the needs of God's people.[6]

Though tithing is frequently addressed in conservative Protestant traditions, it has also been supported in the more liberal and mainstream Episcopal Church. After a successful attempt to improve poor diocesan giving patterns in the Diocese of Alabama by teaching tithing in parishes in the mid-1970s, the topic of tithing began to appear regularly in General Convention statements offered by the denomination at its national triennial meetings.[7] In 1982, tithing was affirmed as the "minimum standard for giving for Episcopalians," about which the standing commission on stewardship and development commented, "We understand this to mean giving at least ten percent of our income to the work of God." In true Episcopal fashion, the Convention Committee debated how one should construe the terms used in that statement and chose the middle route, deciding "intentionally not to give precise definitions of 'income' or 'the work of God,' but to leave these definitions as areas for personal decision." In 1988, another tithing statement was adopted; it directed that there be tithing within three years and called upon the church's bishops and deputies to the General Convention to sign the statement. In 1991, a tithing statement was again passed, and Episcopalians were asked to include in their wills bequests to the church, to the extent that they were able to do so. In 1994 and 1997, tithing statements were again adopted. In 2003, at the same General Convention that confirmed Gene Robinson to be the next bishop of New Hampshire, an act that in many respects required the bishops and deputies to eschew biblical literalism because of Robinson's avowed homosexuality, the delegates adopted a resolution on "holy habits" that read in part, "As Christian stewards and leaders of the Episcopal Church, we affirm that we are tithing or have adopted a plan to work toward tithing as a minimum standard for our giving."[8]

Episcopalians could be urged by their church leaders to tithe or to move toward the tithe, but anyone in any tradition who takes the Bible and tithing seriously may have questions about the practice. One can go to the "Ask Greg!" website, where concerns about giving and tithing are answered in the manner of the "Dear Abby" newspaper column. Tom, for example, asks, "I recently refinanced my home. If I follow the ten percent tithe, would I tithe on this whole amount or something different? Would this be considered income?" Another person wonders why Jesus did not directly preach on tithing. Diane asks, "Is it correct by God's standards to sew a seed of money and expect a harvest—either of money or something that may not be financial, such as sewing a money seed in order to get a husband or receive good health or to get out of debt? Please help me understand Galatians 6:7." When the Christian radio personality Greg Albrecht answers these and tens of other questions about tithing on behalf of the Plain Truth Ministries, he always gives some version of the same answer, namely, that tithing is not God's requirement of Christians under the new covenant of Jesus Christ. Albrecht encourages Christians to offer themselves generously in return for all that they have been given in God. What comes through clearly in these exchanges, however, is that while some ministers have a strong desire to compel a tithe, other, equally conservative Christians' doubt whether tithing requirements constitute a valid application of scripture.[9] For people like Greg Albrecht, questions about whether the tithe should be based on income before or after taxes, or after employer-required deductions, are quite beside the point.

Albrecht's view is shared by the dispensationalist Lee E. Warren, who argues that "Christendom makes tithing a work of salvation under the New Covenant, not realizing it is an ordinance of the Law of Moses under the Old Covenant." "This" he concludes, "is a grave dispensational error." Christ came not to institute the law but fulfill it. For those who continue to preach the tithe as

God's law, Warren has nothing but contempt. Referring to John, the author of Revelation, he writes, "In the eighteenth chapter he says that Mistress Babylon the Great Mother of Harlots, the abominations of the earth, would make merchandise of men's souls (Rev. 18:9–13). Former television evangelist Jimmy [*sic*] and Tammy Baker [*sic*] with their 'Praise the Lord' (PTL) show, and others, are excellent examples of this Harlot's religious frauds perpetrated on the masses." With only a little less outrage, he notes that those unable to give "large donations may be shunned by the pastor and other good standing members. Religious leaders use this form of mind control, psychology, and peer pressure on church-goers to manipulate both the giver and the size of the tithe. The manipulation that religious leaders use to get large tithes places an extra dose of condemnation on the congregation." Salvation, in short, is not predicated on giving "one dime to anybody."[10] Another dispensationalist, Ray Smith, asks, "How many untold tens of thousands of men will give account one day for teaching this verse (will a man rob God) in Malachi 3:8 totally out of context for their own sordid gain." Do these pastors have a right to quote scripture in this manner? No, Smith answers, and adds, "They themselves know better."[11]

What does all this back and forth over tithing really mean? Among other things, it means that religious leaders continue to preach the tithe in the face of massive resistance. Even in evangelical churches, according to statistics offered by the George Barna organization and the Southern Baptist Convention, 80 percent of the giving evidently comes from 20 percent of the people, just as in mainline congregations, while up to 50 percent of members in evangelical churches participate very little or not at all, a statistic even more disappointing than the roughly 25 percent of mainline church members who give financially little or nothing to their churches.[12] Joseph R. Miller speaks for the common wisdom of much of Protestantism when he argues that "you need to elicit more participants of obedience-based (not need-based) giving people. Train your people in Biblical principles of stewardship that are part of our primary occupation . . . encourage them to begin by practicing the tithe principle as first fruits giving to Christ . . . then encourage sacrificial gifts beyond the tithe."[13]

What has driven this insistence on the tithe as a minimum goal? Fear, hope, and greed. There is undoubtedly fear that if preachers stop preaching 10 percent giving, then people would give even less than they have been. Perhaps those few who truly tithe and constitute most of any church's support would stop giving if released from the obligation. Because many ministers are themselves tithers out of a belief in the work in which they are engaged, there is undoubtedly a hope that more church members may be inspired to give generously, with the thought that so much more could be accomplished through well-supported ministry. But undoubtedly some advocates of the tithe are motivated by a desire for more money to aggrandize ministries and enrich ministers.

RAISING MONEY BEYOND THE TITHE

Not every Episcopal congregation has gone to the mat for a whole tithe from its members, of course. Realists acknowledge implicitly that they could make do nicely on 2 or 3 percent of their member's incomes, as is evidenced by this set of questions and answers at the website of the Church of the Holy Comforter in Vienna, Virginia:

> What is proportional giving? It is making a commitment to give a specific percentage of your income to Holy Comforter. The appropriate percentage is up to you.
>
> How do I determine what percentage is right for me? Most importantly, ask for God's guidance. Consider what 2% or 3% of your income is and then determine whether you feel comfortable with that amount. Everyone's situation is different. Just like any significant goal in life, your financial pledge should be a stretch but should also be attainable. And consider trying to increase that percentage by a small amount each year.
>
> What is tithing? Tithing is the Biblical standard of giving God the first 10% of your income. While tithing is a worthy goal, it would be difficult for many people to achieve in one leap, which is where proportional giving comes in.
>
> Does my pledge really matter that much? Absolutely! Holy Comforter needs $1800 per member family to meet its operating budget. But not every family pledges and of those that do, not everyone is able to pledge $1800, which means that every pledge, no matter the size[,] matters. And it matters a lot.[14]

In that last answer, the vestry of Holy Comforter manages to communicate an expectation of support for the church on the part of all members, understanding of those who cannot afford the expected commitment, and a challenge to everyone to do what they can.

Raising money in the years since 1980 has by all appearances created no less anxiety than it did in earlier years. While denominational publishers continue to bring out stewardship books that provide theological approaches to giving, they also produce highly practical handbooks to help the clergy and lay leaders tackle the annual financial or building campaign for their church. These handbooks for church fund-raising are often physically distinct from their more theological counterparts because they are almost invariably in an 8½-by-11-inch format in order to incorporate lots of charts, tables, sample appeal letters, and even reproducible promotion and tally sheets. Illustrative of this are the goal-setting charts in Joseph D. Burnett's *Funds Campaign Manual for Churches*, published in 1980. One chart walks a congregation's leaders through the process of determining how much the church can expect to raise for a capital funds campaign based on the number of giving units, annual church current fund income, and a small coefficient of the total personal income of all church members. Just how realistic and detailed this estimation process is meant to be is indicated by the following suggested procedure: a particular church is to utilize anonymous cards collected from members at a meeting in order to extrapolate the total annual income of the congregation and to evaluate the percentage of income given by the congregation for current expenses and benevolences. A table listing all the tasks necessary to get from the initiation of a capital campaign to "Victory Sunday" takes up five pages in the manual. In all, fifty-six pages of tightly calibrated advice guide churches through a full-strength, successful capital funds campaign. Burnett warns those tempted to drop any steps that "to delete is to dilute! Experience has shown that the elements just described are basic to a sound collection program and that shortcuts of any kind will seriously lessen results."[15] Burnett's campaign manual closes with some general rules to remember:

> Don't threaten contributors who may fall behind in their payments. They resent this and rightly.
>
> Do compliment contributors whenever the opportunity arises. By making them aware of your appreciation, you create a normal desire to do more.
>
> Don't discourage contributors by emphasizing only what has not been accomplished. A negative approach breeds a negative response.
>
> Do call attention to what has been done because of their giving.
>
> Don't be dictatorial or apologetic. They are not clients who owe you money, nor is it necessary to beg from them.
>
> Do treat them as friends who love the church as much as you do.[16]

Apart from the word "church" in the last of Burnett's rules, the campaign manual's closing advice resembles nothing so much as a basic guide in business etiquette for the treatment of valued customers.

This is not to say that all campaigns have been bloodless and secular in approach. Kermit L. Braswell's guide, *Step by Step: A Financial Campaign for Your Church*, published in 1995, provides many instances of letters he says should be mailed out to various groups of leaders, workers, and members of a church.[17] Note how, in the following example, budgetary needs, an implicit doctrine of ministry, and a call to faithful discipleship are all marshaled to invoke a willingness to participate in the upcoming financial campaign:

> Dear John and Pat:
>
> St. John United Methodist Church is the church that we all love and where we find the opportunity for worship and the privilege of serving Christ. Our total commitment is needed as we move forward to meet the needs that have been determined by the committees and boards of the church.
>
> Please read the enclosed brochure explaining our objectives. The ministry of our church, done by the representative ministry—meaning all of us who profess to be Christians—is important. Thank you for your thankfulness.
>
> Yours in Christ,
>
> General Chairperson
>
> Pastor[18]

Although Burnett's and Braswell's capital campaign manuals were produced for and sold by mainline American Baptist and United Methodist publishing concerns, respectively, a contemporary version is just as likely to be purchased from an independent entrepreneurial source. TTB (Time to Build) is sold through www.pastors.com, which is the commercial online outlet for Rick Warren and his Saddleback Church megaministry. In short, what has so clearly worked to build Saddleback into a highly visible megachurch is now available in a step-by-step kit for churches like the one led by Pastor Tim Woody of St. Joseph, Missouri. Pastor Woody's testimony to the Time to Build plan goes as follows: "My church averages about 950 in attendance. I began to serve as the Senior Pastor only seven months ago and immediately found our church in great need for a new youth facility. I ordered the Time To Build kit and adapted the information to fit our church. We set a goal of 1.1 million dollars, and quite miraculously, we hit our goal, EXACTLY! The congregation is exuberant and it really has elevated me to a new level in their eyes. The small investment for the kit REALLY paid off!!"[19]

While tithing is the most popular way to talk about Christian giving to the church among conservative nondispensationalist evangelicals, the focus on money talk in liberal and mainline circles has adapted a theme from an earlier time, namely, a deep Christian concern for the uses of affluence by members of those churches and by American people of faith more generally. Some writers, like Herbert Mather, have preferred to go beyond legalism and advocate giving generously quite apart from a sense that God commands a specific percentage. Yet, writing in 1985, Mather noticed that low self-esteem constituted a major problem for many congregations in his own United Methodist Church. People were not prepared to give, insofar as they did not think the church was up to much good.[20] Others, like Douglas W. Johnson, have been prepared to go beyond improved self-esteem and have thought that the pastor has a role in "futuring" the mission of the church, whereby the congregation may see itself in mission that is relevant to the present and future, and not just a reflection of the past. Writing in 1986, Johnson affirmed that giving to causes in the name of one's Christian vocation outside the structures of the congregation was not only permissible but even advisable in a day and age when many of the charitable objectives of the ancient church were being achieved by governmental and not-for-profit agencies.[21]

THE NEW STEWARDSHIP AND OLD SCOLDS

John and Sylvia Ronsvalle lived simply and thought that the true nature of the American church was being revealed by its long-term giving patterns. Starting in the late 1980s and continuing into the 1990s, they became a prominent voice of doom about the state of American church giving by publishing several studies documenting a decline in giving as a percentage of personal income and a decline of total church dollars flowing outside congregations to benevolences and large-scale denominational activities. John Ronsvalle was a bright, self-effacing economist with a Ph.D. who applied econometric techniques to the churches' publicly reported giving statistics over a long period of time. Sylvia was his intense and passionate partner, a woman with years of firsthand experience caring for the poor in their hometown, Champaign-Urbana. Their combined efforts produced a book titled *The Poor Have Faces* that showed the impact of Reagan-era social program cuts on real individuals' lives. John's statistics and Sylvia's moral zeal in championing the least among the American people aimed at undercutting the vicious culture of program pruning that seemed to signal that people believed that society owed nothing to its poorest members.[22]

If government was the expression of society's unconcern in the 1980s for the Ronsvalles, the church was a source of even greater disappointment for them in the 1990s. Looking at the church (through the lens of Matthew 25 and the

Hebrew prophets), they expected to see something noble and unselfish to counter Reaganomics. Instead, they found its religious counterpart in largely middle-class churches, which kept more and more of their giving at home in the congregation. In successive studies, the most developed of which was their 1996 book, *Behind the Stained Glass Windows: Money Dynamics in the Church*, they projected that, in time, declining giving relative to income would starve the churches as meaningful social institutions, but not before lowered benevolence giving had starved the poor. The Ronsvalles thought that the churches stood in danger of losing their souls. " 'Discretionary income' is a reality for most of the population," they wrote, "and advertising agencies very intentionally have targeted that income, turning 'wants into needs.' " "In the new situation of widespread resources," the Ronsvalles continued, "when most people who come into church have income above basic needs, the contemporary church has, for the most part, been silent on the implications of these changed circumstances. Without a clear agenda for this new affluence being voiced from the church, members have absorbed the world's agenda of consuming and accumulating and then brought that agenda back into the void that was present in their congregations."[23]

Were things as bad in American Protestantism as the Ronsvalles suggested? In point of fact, their studies showed that overall real giving to churches (that is, adjusted for inflation) had risen significantly over the decades. But giving to churches had not grown as fast as personal incomes, which had soared in the postwar period. A good part of their analysis was based on a belief that the growth in real income should have led to a huge growth in church-based giving to ameliorate social deficits. John and Sylvia lived simply and gave generously. Increments to their own incomes led to even more generous giving on their part, so what they saw when they looked at other believers was weak belief and even weaker action. Greater affluence should have meant a greater capacity to eliminate poverty. *Behind the Stained Glass Windows* reads as a statistic- and guilt-crammed brief for making churches first and foremost generous agents of social transformation. To some extent the Ronsvalles deserve full credit for noticing what self-regarding institutions congregations could be, especially given the building boom that followed their book's publication in the 1990s. On the other hand, they missed both the intrinsic genius of religious congregations and the transformation that had taken place in most congregations' activities during the very period when churches were supposedly becoming less attentive to the needs of the poor.

As American political culture turned against the idea of the welfare state and the programs of the New Deal and the Great Society, congregations became more and more involved in hosting, sponsoring, and even initiating ministries to deal with the plight of the homeless, people recovering from mental illness, and Alzheimer's patients and other individuals with memory impairment who needed adult day care. Between the late 1970s and the mid-1980s, an extraordinary number of American congregations began programs to address those social needs while also starting food banks, senior-care and child-care programs, early education programs, Divorce Care programs, and Stephen's Ministries.[24] Congregations did this while continuing to adapt so as to provide ministry to families in transition, at the very time when the American family was being transformed by the increasing prevalence of divorce and single-parent households. What the Ronsvalles managed to show was that churches were keeping greater proportions of the dollars they raised in their local communities. Basing their studies on the denomination as the unit of analysis for giving and spending, however, they were not in a position to determine how well those dollars were spent.

On one reading, then, *Behind the Stained Glass Windows* could be understood as another screed by religious scolds about the use of money. For more than a century, since Washington Gladden's time, Christian observers who went beyond an account of why money should be given to the church usually expressed discomfort with the way the modern economy was arranged. By the early 1990s, however, there was just one contender for an advanced economic system; and it was not socialism, but rather market capitalism. *Behind the Stained Glass Windows* may be, therefore, the first truly post–market revolution stewardship book produced by Protestants. The Ronsvalles likened the church since 1945 to children permitted to be in a candy store after hours: "We've been able to try out new varieties and eat our favorites in an unrestrained way. However, after several decades, we are developing the toothaches and stomachaches that wiser counselors have warned us about. Our preoccupation has been understandable. But at some point a more constructive approach needs to be developed."[25]

Advanced consumer capitalism had made church life both a sweet experience and a dangerous one for the American church. The answer to the church's problems lay not in a repudiation of affluence, but rather in a determination to use that affluence in a Christian manner. "Money can accomplish great things," the Ronsvalles wrote; "to kill the goose laying the golden eggs hardly makes sense. The point is, as one leader advised, to give more of the eggs away." In their view, then, the church needed to stop (and read here "pastors needed to stop") objecting to the fact that creative people were rewarded in the marketplace with money for pursuing their careers. Instead, they argued, "the church is charged with the task of providing a broad, sweeping, vital vision that allows these talented people to also apply the fruits of their labor in magnificent ways."[26]

Periods of great affluence produce anxiety in Protestants and more generally in the societies they create. Max Weber observed in *The Protestant Ethic and the Spirit of Capitalism* that hardworking Protestants both wanted to prosper (thus showing that they deployed their God-given talents to maximum effect) and worried that they might be in an idolatrous relationship with their prosperity.[27] The stock market crash of October 1987, along with the insider trading scandals involving Ivan Boesky and Michael Milken, raised worries about whether the financial markets were even rewarding industry and thrift, or doing something genuinely insidious. In the 1987 Oliver Stone movie, *Wall Street*, the fictional financier Gordon Gekko serves as Stone's mouthpiece for a belief he finds repulsive, the view that all that drives humanity is greed. Michael Douglas, playing Gekko, addresses a shareholders' meeting for a company he is about to take over. His speech climaxes with these words:

> The point is, ladies and gentleman, that greed—for lack of a better word—is good.
> Greed is right.
> Greed works.
> Greed clarifies, cuts through, and captures the essence of the evolutionary spirit.
> Greed, in all of its forms—greed for life, for money, for love, knowledge—has marked the upward surge of mankind.
> And greed—you mark my words—will not only save Teldar Paper, but that other malfunctioning corporation called the USA.
> Thank you very much.[28]

In the late 1980s and 1990s, two themes emerged in theological discourse in clear response to the "greed decade," as the 1980s were called. The first was God's abundant intention in creation. The second was human generosity. Douglas Meeks, following biblical scholars like Richard Lowry and Walter Brueggemann, depicted God as an economist, one who set up a household where the basic paradigm was abundance and not the scarcity that drove the Gordon Gekkos of the world. Human beings erred theologically, therefore, by assuming that they lived in a world characterized by real scarcity. Robert Wood Lynn, meanwhile, took as his starting point God's abundance and gracious giving of life, joy, salvation, and the material means of sustenance. He argued in numerous speeches that the only theologically defensible reason to ask people to give was gratitude, a happiness for what had been done for them and given without price, that is, a desire to show one's thankfulness. Eugene Grimm and Herb Miller wrote a book, as did I, that tried to reframe the practices of church stewardship along these lines and argued that when the church sought its members' generosity only for itself, it was not faithful. Both books encouraged clergy to see it as their job to help form people who were more generous in all aspects of life. A team of sociologists led by Dean Hoge concluded that reciprocity with God lay at the motivational heart of most sincere and generous giving in churches. The sociologist Robert Wuthnow also spent the decade probing the sources of compassion, volunteering, thinking about money, and religious commitment, all of which centered on the problem of altruism. In these years, there was a remarkable amount of American Protestant thinking beyond the realm of "how-to" and within the realm of "why?" when it came to money and Christian life.[29]

AMERICAN KARMA

Far from mainline Protestant concerns about the corrupting influences of money and greed were the conservative, usually Pentecostal advocates of the Prosperity Gospel. The Prosperity Gospel, or the Gospel of Health and Wealth as it is sometimes called, burst into widespread public notice only in the closing years of the twentieth century. As noted in chapter 7, preachers like A. A. Allen had been preaching God's system for wealth and prosperity for many years prior to the emergence of black megachurch pastors like Creflo Dollar, who claim that a tithe to their ministries is a guaranteed route to health and wealth for givers. The line linking Allen's generation of southern prosperity preachers and Dollar's contemporary generation travels through evangelists Kenneth Hagin and Kenneth Copeland. Within Pentecostal and charismatic Christian circles, the belief that God blesses the faithful with physical health and financial prosperity was known as the Faith Movement, or, alternatively, the Word Movement. Hagin and his son Kenneth Hagin Jr., through their Rhema Bible Training Center spread this distinctive teaching throughout the world, but particularly in sub-Saharan Africa. In the United States, its most visible proponent was the television evangelist Kenneth Copeland. While other Faith Movement preachers tended to stress that health and prosperity were God's desire for believers, Copeland went further by citing Mark 10:29–30 to the effect that one could receive an actual "hundred-fold return" on one's contributions in faith to Christ's church; he freely called these contributions to God (and coincidentally to Copeland's television ministry) "investments."[30] God does not want sacrifice so much as he wants partners in the Copeland scheme of things. Meanwhile,

Creflo Dollar tells his followers that Jesus is coming back, but not to an indebted church; if they want to be there for the return, they need to clear up that debt to hasten his coming.[31]

As a form of fund-raising in Protestant churches, the Prosperity Gospel is a significant, even radical departure from the other motivations for giving that have been tapped in the history of the American churches. Necessity, shame, duty, biblical command, justice to God, guilt, gratitude, belonging, and the giver's psychological need to give are all themes that have been tapped, at one time or another, to get people to give to their churches. The reason for givers to give in the Prosperity Gospel scheme is in part to get, to be blessed not in a future state of rewards but in the here and now. God will not bless those who hold back even a portion from Him, but those who give a tithe or more will be abundantly blessed in return by getting back all of their monetary investment and more. Classical theorists of religion like Durkheim and Weber drew a more or less hard line between magic and religion and associated them with less developed and modern societies, respectively. What the gospel of wealth demonstrates is that contrary to classical theory, a human belief in something magical—that the gods can be manipulated by human activity into providing what human beings want—is still to be found in abundance in early twenty-first-century American Protestantism. But something beyond ordinary magic seems also to be afoot. The quid pro quo dimension of this practice somewhat resembles a system of karma—things happen for reasons and your actions catch up with you over time—but with a characteristically contemporary American twist. Whereas Buddhist and Hindu karma embraces moral acts and counsels detachment from the self and the material world as a means of escaping suffering, this American system of karma rewards giving up material things with a superabundance of material things.

In 2004, more than $88 billion were given to religious organizations.[32] The largest share of this sum went to Protestant congregations. Half of all American Protestants attend the 10 percent of congregations that can be classified as large in size; so the great bulk of the more than 300,000 Protestant congregations are small in size, and the average congregation's total annual budget hovers under $150,000 since there are so many congregations of fewer than two hundred members.[33]

The economic unit of the Protestant congregation, regardless of its size, therefore is not large relative to other corporate enterprises in American life. Large urban and suburban churches may individually occupy the same acreage as a big-box store like Walmart or Home Depot, but they do their business at one place, not at thousands of locations. Congregational enterprise is emphatically local enterprise. The support of these congregations is highly localized and spread among many individuals. Giving to religious causes still accounts for more than a third of all charitable contributions in contemporary American society. But unlike gifts to the arts, for example, gifts to religion are measured in the hundreds and thousands of dollars and not in the millions.

As the twenty-first century proceeds, American Protestants and their leaders continue to work as they always have to support their congregations. Though they all seek the means to continue ministry, they pursue that support in different ways with divergent emphases on what is important about money and giving toward the work of the church. These generalizations can be overdrawn, but it appears that conservative Protestants utilize the rhetoric of tithing as a serious biblical injunction, despite the fact that as generous as evangelicals can be relative to other groups, few actually tithe. While mainstream Protestants still talk about tithing occasionally, they tacitly encourage proportionate giving at lower levels that is adequate to meet the needs of extant congregations and commitments. Mainstream and evangelical Protestants alike worry about American affluence more than ever before, yet prosperity preachers offer something of an investment plan, aiming it mostly to congregations whose members have experienced too little affluence in their own lives. New and expanding ministries challenge their members to be part of something new for the sake of Christ's continuing work. Though each group within the American Protestant landscape asks for something slightly different, they each receive mostly what they are essentially after—enough to continue.

EPILOGUE

I happened soon after to attend one of his sermons, in the course of which I perceived he needed to finish with a collection, and I silently resolved he should get nothing from me. I had in my pocket a handful of copper money, three or four silver dollars, and five pistoles in gold. As he proceeded I began to soften, and concluded to give the coppers. Another stroke of his oratory made me asham'd of that, and determin'd me to give the silver, and he finish'd so admirably, that I empty'd my pocket wholly into the collector's dish, gold and all.—Benjamin Franklin on George Whitefield, in *The Life of Doctor Benjamin Franklin, Written by Himself*

Any claim that one's own time is unique naturally draws the suspicions of historians. Be they the best of times or the worst, one must be on guard not to assert that one's own experience represents a zenith or a nadir, precisely because it is the observer's own experience that is so described. With this warning in mind, then, I have arrived at a conclusion I have been slow to accept, but cannot reject: 250 years of voluntary support for religion and competition for the Almighty's dollar have transformed American Protestantism into a multifaceted, highly adaptive socioeconomic entity that is more ubiquitous than even McDonald's restaurants in contemporary American culture. Secularization theorists never predicted that early in the twenty-first century there would be so many new Protestant congregations or so many megachurch campuses in the suburbs, America's new center of demographic gravity. But the churches are there, and so too are the Borders and Barnes and Noble bookstores with their large religion, spirituality, healing, and self-help sections. Religion is, at this time, an expressive good. It allows people through participation (even by simply buying books they think they should read) to show what matters to them and why. Or at least it allows them to demonstrate the values they affirm—however little or much these values actually inform their behavior. Increasingly, as the dean of a university-based divinity school, I find it common for prospective students to list their religious traditions with what were formerly unlikely binary terms. "Buddhist-Presbyterian," "Unitarian-Catholic," and "UCC-Jewish" were just three of the self-proclaimed affiliations during the 2005 admissions season.

Religion as self-expression undermines religion as a prescriptive guide to living. This may come as a surprise to observers who marvel at just how moralistic contemporary religion's preacherly representatives can be. Make no mistake, the moral center of these particular locations in Protestantism is genuine. I do not doubt the sincerity of the ministers. Their strongly worded messages are, however, a crucial part of their sales pitch. They are "peddlers in divinity," a term perhaps first applied to George Whitefield at the beginning of this book's time frame. My point is that there is something about the voluntary principle of financing in the American religious context that turns every member of the clergy into a salesperson. In late twentieth- and early twenty-first-century consumer culture America, just how remarkable this development is in the long history of Christianity—indeed in all of the history of religions—is obscured. Religion thrives in part because it has so many highly differentiated outlets. In America you can have any kind of religion you are willing to pay for (and not a small amount of religion for no price at all).

Yet something is missing. The contemporary religious situation does not make for strong religion except insofar as individuals give their faith tradition shaping power in their lives. Ministers preach strong sermons, but usually to audiences that resemble the proverbial choir. The sanctity of families is preached nowhere more fervently than where it is already sacred. Inclusion is most often preached as Jesus' radical way where hearers desperately want radical inclusion. These days, freedom sermons work well in Republican congregations; peace sermons are better in liberal congregations that are Democratic Party strongholds. A preacher will sometimes test the limits of his or her congregation's tacit moral consensus, but a congregation faced with teaching about the limits of material abundance will typically nod acknowledgment about the virtues of the simple life and leave an hour later to pursue abundance. Two hundred years after they first became common, begging sermons continue. Set within the culture of abundance, they are less bothersome to give than perhaps at anytime in the past. Whether or not they admit it, today's preachers know they have to persuade and sell. The pursuit of the Almighty's dollar has never been easier. But finding the Almighty has never been more difficult.

APPENDIX A

Ministerial Support in the

Methodist Episcopal Church and the

United Methodist Church,

1880–2000

The ministerial salary data in the table below was compiled from *Minutes of the Annual Conferences of the Methodist Episcopal Church* (New York : Methodist Publishing House) and *General Minutes of the Annual Conferences of the United Methodist Church* (Evanston, Ill.: United Methodist Church) for the years given, with a correction post-1969 for the number of effective ministers reported by the denomination to the Office of Research, Evaluation, and Planning of the National Council of the Churches of Christ in the USA, *Yearbook of American Churches* (Nashville: Abingdon). The price index and real average salary figures for each year are derived from the historical price deflation method and the data in appendix B.

"Effective ministers" is the Methodist term used to designate clergy who are actually appointed to congregations and not to other ministries, retired, or disabled. "Total cash salaries paid" aggregates all actual salaries paid by congregations to their ministers, but does not include the value of church-owned parsonages. The "Nominal/pastor" column shows the amounts, on average, that pastors in the indicated years received in the funds of the day, while the "Real average salary (1860 base)" column removes the effects of price inflation/deflation to show the value of those average salaries in constant (1860) dollars.

Year	Effective ministers	Total cash salaries paid	Nominal/ pastor	Price index	Real average salary (1860 base)
1880	4,960	$3,273,337	$660	123	$537
1881	8,910	6,488,539	728	123	592
1882	8,675	6,995,860	806	123	656
1883	8,807	7,267,360	825	121	682
1884	9,094	7,702,441	847	118	718
1885	9,316	7,687,902	825	116	711
1886	9,497	7,924,513	834	113	738
1887	9,939	8,312,052	836	114	734
1888	10,130	8,684,330	857	114	752
1889	10,264	9,044,779	881	111	794
1890	10,044	9,366,658	933	109	856
1891	10,875	9,771,643	899	109	824
1892	11,158	10,063,795	902	109	827
1893	11,526	10,298,915	894	108	827
1894	11,802	10,714,161	908	103	881
1895	12,024	10,385,948	864	101	855
1896	12,391	10,413,141	840	101	832
1897	12,641	10,556,770	835	100	835
1898	12,756	10,769,216	844	100	844
1899	12,945	10,973,249	848	100	848
1900	12,865	11,261,353	875	101	867
1901	12,983	11,403,338	878	102	861
1902	13,070	11,751,286	899	103	873
1903	13,260	12,403,371	935	106	882
1904	13,376	12,588,637	941	107	880
1905	13,538	12,920,067	954	106	900
1906	13,710	13,539,774	988	108	914
1907	13,917	14,186,605	1,019	113	902
1908	14,005	14,657,283	1,047	111	943
1909	17,916	15,507,639	866	109	794

Year	Effective ministers	Total cash salaries paid	Nominal/ pastor	Price index	Real average salary (1860 base)
1910	18,879	16,023,742	849	114	745
1911	18,427	16,378,709	889	114	780
1912	18,337	16,835,179	918	117	785
1913	14,538	15,592,488	1,073	119	901
1914	14,580	15,976,831	1,096	120	913
1915	14,836	16,184,797	1,091	121	902
1916	14,872	16,636,608	1,119	130	861
1917	14,837	17,350,493	1,169	153	764
1918	14,602	18,138,194	1,242	180	690
1919	14,549	19,332,562	1,329	207	642
1920	14,534	21,944,613	1,510	240	629
1921	15,038	24,629,043	1,638	214	765
1922	14,829	25,456,382	1,717	200	858
1923	15,006	25,689,962	1,712	204	839
1924	15,175	26,467,009	1,744	204	855
1925	14,973	27,513,642	1,838	210	875
1926	14,854	28,165,755	1,896	211	899
1927	15,307	28,619,914	1,870	208	899
1928	15,037	29,035,584	1,931	205	942
1929	15,005	29,071,970	1,937	205	945
1930	14,836	28,759,818	1,939	200	969
1931	14,655	27,392,527	1,869	182	1,027
1932	14,590	24,086,942	1,651	163	1,013
1933	14,161	21,462,203	1,516	155	978
1934	13,771	20,934,443	1,520	160	950
1935	13,762	20,768,299	1,509	164	920
1936	13,705	21,039,963	1,535	166	925
1937	13,283	21,388,035	1,610	172	936
1938	13,157	21,805,961	1,657	169	981
1939	14,252	21,058,447	1,478	166	890
1940	23,924	31,114,170	1,301	168	774
1941	17,952	29,255,200	1,630	176	926
1942	18,436	29,538,883	1,602	195	822
1943	18,412	31,626,726	1,718	207	830
1944	18,269	35,034,599	1,918	210	913
1945	18,298	36,435,945	1,991	215	926
1946	16,930	40,065,379	2,367	233	1,016
1947	16,908	40,881,002	2,418	267	906
1948	16,707	46,798,765	2,801	288	973
1949	16,542	49,642,508	3,001	285	1,053

Year	Effective ministers	Total cash salaries paid	Nominal/ pastor	Price index	Real average salary (1860 base)
1950	16,320	52,202,343	3,199	288	1,111
1951	16,413	55,840,494	3,402	310	1,097
1952	16,554	60,263,489	3,640	317	1,148
1953	16,786	63,967,692	3,811	320	1,191
1954	17,070	67,702,196	3,966	321	1,236
1955	17,741	71,801,136	4,047	320	1,265
1956	17,786	76,411,758	4,296	325	1,322
1957	17,574	81,672,385	4,647	336	1,383
1958	17,964	86,178,641	4,797	346	1,387
1959	18,177	91,209,722	5,018	348	1,442
1960	18,471	96,214,457	5,209	354	1,471
1961	22,601	99,310,259	4,394	358	1,227
1962	19,329	104,179,795	5,390	362	1,489
1963	19,424	108,624,713	5,592	366	1,528
1964	20,192	110,299,651	5,463	371	1,472
1965	20,677	115,991,263	5,610	377	1,488
1966	20,600	118,524,986	5,754	388	1,483
1967	20,607	122,123,828	5,926	399	1,485
1968	20,849	129,404,493	6,207	416	1,492
1969	20,849	128,945,752	6,185	438	1,412
1970	20,619	140,250,600	6,802	464	1,466
1971	20,550	155,121,658	7,548	484	1,560
1972	20,518	165,324,972	8,058	500	1,612
1973	20,130	168,396,134	8,365	531	1,575
1974	20,222	214,685,406	10,616	590	1,799
1975	20,235	194,529,293	9,614	643	1,495
1976	20,235	209,993,715	10,378	680	1,526
1977	20,300	225,361,996	11,102	725	1,531
1978	20,357	241,417,566	11,859	780	1,520
1979	20,178	258,477,648	12,810	868	1,476
1980	20,558	278,177,557	13,531	985	1,374
1981	20,764	301,157,665	14,504	1,087	1,334
1982	20,781	329,125,204	15,838	1,154	1,372
1983	20,882	356,191,050	17,057	1,191	1,432
1984	21,430	379,991,792	17,732	1,243	1,427
1985	21,589	404,629,445	18,742	1,287	1,456
1986	21,201	427,961,916	20,186	1,311	1,540
1987	20,927	451,290,951	21,565	1,359	1,587
1988	20,844	473,403,833	22,712	1,415	1,605
1989	20,774	496,537,420	23,902	1,483	1,612

Year	Effective ministers	Total cash salaries paid	Nominal/ pastor	Price index	Real average salary (1860 base)
1990	20,607	517,513,985	25,114	1,563	1,607
1991	20,369	539,806,990	26,501	1,629	1,627
1992	20,342	563,236,150	27,688	1678	1,650
1993	20,450	580,241,768	28,374	1728	1,642
1994	20,573	600,694,138	29,198	1773	1,647
1995	19,880	617,786,120	31,076	1823	1,705
1996	19,560	632,543,920	32,339	1876	1,724
1997	19,570	648,488,228	33,137	1919	1,727
1998	19,580	666,057,372	34,017	1949	1,745
1999	19,726	714,547,206	36,224	1992	1,818
2000	19,650	741,029,134	37,711	2060	1,831

APPENDIX B

Historical Price Series Conversion Scale

The price series in the table below is based on John J. McCusker, *How Much is That in Real Money? A Historical Price Index for Use as a Deflator of Money Values in the Economy of the United States* (Worcester, Mass.: American Antiquarian Society, 1992), supplemented by the Consumer Price Index for 1991 to 2001. To get, for example, the value in 1991 of $100 in 1820 dollars, divide 1629 by 141 and multiply by $100: 1629/141 × $100 = $1,155; to find the value in 1820 of $100 in 1991 dollars reverse the numerator and denominator: 141/1629 × $100 = $8.65. McCusker's book also contains tables and methodologies for converting colonial-era pounds to post-Revolution dollars.

Year	Index	Year	Index	Year	Index	Year	Index	Year	Index	Year	Index
1700	130	1750	84	1800	151	1850	94	1900	101	1950	288
1701	141	1751	85	1801	153	1851	92	1901	102	1951	310
1702	136	1752	87	1802	129	1852	93	1902	103	1952	317
1703	118	1753	84	1803	136	1853	93	1903	106	1953	320
1704	108	1754	81	1804	142	1854	101	1904	107	1954	321
1705	104	1755	79	1805	141	1855	104	1905	106	1955	320
1706	111	1756	77	1806	147	1856	102	1906	108	1956	325
1707	119	1757	81	1807	139	1857	105	1907	113	1957	336
1708	126	1758	87	1808	151	1858	99	1908	111	1958	346
1709	116	1759	99	1809	148	1859	100	1909	109	1959	348
1710	100	1760	96	1810	148	1860	100	1910	114	1960	354
1711	105	1761	90	1811	158	1861	106	1911	114	1961	358
↓		↓		↓		↓		↓		↓	

Year	Index	Year	Index	Year	Index	Year	Index	Year	Index	Year	Index
1712	119	1762	95	1812	160	1862	121	1912	117	1962	362
1713	128	1763	95	1813	192	1863	151	1913	119	1963	366
1714	128	1764	88	1814	211	1864	189	1914	120	1964	371
1715	88	1765	89	1815	185	1865	196	1915	121	1965	377
1716	72	1766	98	1816	169	1866	191	1916	130	1966	388
1717	76	1767	95	1817	160	1867	178	1917	153	1967	399
1718	88	1768	90	1818	153	1868	171	1918	180	1968	416
1719	92	1769	93	1819	153	1869	164	1919	207	1969	438
1720	76	1770	100	1820	141	1870	157	1920	240	1970	464
1721	71	1771	96	1821	136	1871	147	1921	214	1971	484
1722	75	1772	109	1822	141	1872	147	1922	200	1972	500
1723	76	1773	101	1823	126	1873	144	1923	204	1973	531
1724	80	1774	97	1824	116	1874	137	1924	204	1974	590
1725	95	1775	92	1825	119	1875	132	1925	210	1975	643
1726	92	1776	105	1826	119	1876	129	1926	211	1976	680
1727	86	1777	128	1827	120	1877	126	1927	208	1977	725
1728	81	1778	166	1828	114	1878	120	1928	205	1978	780
1729	80	1779	147	1829	112	1879	120	1929	205	1979	868
1730	80	1780	165	1830	111	1880	123	1930	200	1980	985
1731	71	1781	133	1831	104	1881	123	1931	182	1981	1087
1732	67	1782	146	1832	103	1882	123	1932	163	1982	1154
1733	66	1783	128	1833	101	1883	121	1933	155	1983	1191
1734	67	1784	123	1834	103	1884	118	1934	160	1984	1243
1735	68	1785	117	1835	106	1885	116	1935	164	1985	1287
1736	65	1786	114	1836	112	1886	113	1936	166	1986	1311
1737	66	1787	112	1837	115	1887	114	1937	172	1987	1359
1738	71	1788	107	1838	112	1888	114	1938	169	1988	1415
1739	63	1789	106	1839	112	1889	111	1939	166	1989	1483
1740	66	1790	110	1840	104	1890	109	1940	168	1990	1563
1741	91	1791	113	1841	105	1891	109	1941	176	1991	1629
↓		↓		↓		↓		↓		↓	

Year	Index	Year	Index	Year	Index	Year	Index	Year	Index	Year	Index
1742	81	1792	115	1842	98	1892	109	1942	195	1992	1678
1743	71	1793	119	1843	89	1893	108	1943	207	1993	1728
1744	66	1794	132	1844	90	1894	103	1944	210	1994	1773
1745	64	1795	151	1845	91	1895	101	1945	215	1995	1823
1746	65	1796	159	1846	92	1896	101	1946	233	1996	1876
1747	71	1797	153	1847	99	1897	100	1947	267	1997	1919
1748	82	1798	148	1848	95	1898	100	1948	288	1998	1949
1749	84	1799	148	1849	92	1899	100	1949	285	1999	1992
										2000	2060
										2001	2136

NOTES

PROLOGUE

1 Edwards's salary, as reported by Patricia J. Tracy in *Jonathan Edwards, Pastor: Religion and Society in Eighteenth-Century Northampton* (New York: Hill and Wang, 1980), 156, is adjusted for differences in colonial pounds sterling, dollars, and price inflation as described in appendix B. Edwards's salary is also adjusted for standard of living differences by a factor of three, a conservative estimate. Clearly, although the colonial clergy, including Edwards, sometimes found it hard to collect their salaries in a timely fashion, the relative values of their incomes have never been equaled in subsequent history.

2 Quoted in "The Puritan Minister," *Atlantic Monthly* 12, no. 71 (September 1863): 272.

3 *Early Virginia Religious Petitions*, a collaborative project of the Library of Congress and the Library of Virginia, <http://memory.loc.gov/ammem/repehtml/repe home.html> (April 14, 2006): "November 7, 1785, Pittsylvania, Against assessment bill"; "November 7, 1785, Pittsylvania, In favor of assessment bill."

CHAPTER ONE

1 Lyman Beecher, *A Plea for the West* (Cincinnati: Truman and Smith, 1835).

2 Ibid., 11.

3 Ibid., 13.

4 Ibid., 17–18.

5 Kelly Olds, "Privatizing the Church: Disestablishment in Connecticut and Massachusetts," *Journal of Political Economy* 102, no. 2 (1994): 277–97.

6 Ibid., 279–81.

7 Ibid., 279.

8 Erskine Clarke, *Our Southern Zion: A History of Calvinism in the South Carolina Low Country, 1690–1990* (Tuscaloosa, Ala.: University of Alabama Press, 1996), 57–58, 152–55.

9 See William G. McLoughlin, *New England Dissent, 1630–1833: The Baptists and the Separation of Church and State* (Cambridge, Mass.: Harvard University Press, 1971).

10 Rhys Isaac, *The Transformation of Virginia, 1740–1790* (New York: W. W. Norton, 1988), 287–88.

11 Finney quoted in "The Best Seats in the House," *Christian History*, no. 20 (1997): 37.

12 Calculated using John J. McCusker, "How Much Is That in Real Money? A Historical Price Index for Use as a Deflator of Money Values in the Economy of the United States," *Proceedings of the American Antiquarian Society* 101, no. 2 (1991): 297–333; and Consumer Price Indexes (1991–2000), available from U.S. Department of Labor, Bureau of Labor Statistics, <http://www.bls.gov/cpi/>. See appendix B for a full conversion chart.

13 Charles Grandison Finney, *Lectures on Revivals of Religion* (New York : Leavitt, Lord, 1835), 383.

14 See John Carroll's letter to Charles Plowden, February 29, 1779, in Annabelle M. Melville, *John Carroll of Baltimore, Founder of the American Catholic Hierarchy* (New York: Scribner, 1955), 55; and Carroll's 1790 report to Cardinal Antonelli in *Documents of American Catholic History*, ed. John Tracy Ellis (Milwaukee: Bruce, 1956), 147.

15 Patricia Wittberg, *The Rise and Decline of Catholic Religious Orders* (Albany: State University of New York Press, 1994).

16 Robert Wood Lynn, unpublished, untitled manuscript (collection of writings on giving), 7.

17 Samuel Eliot Morison, *The Founding of Harvard College* (Cambridge, Mass.: Harvard University Press, 1935), 33.

18 Pharcellus Church, *The Philosophy of Benevolence* (New York: Leavitt, Lord, 1836). For this and subsequent quotations, I have not provided page references because I worked from an unpaginated typescript.

19 Parsons Cooke, *The Divine Law of Beneficence* (New York: American Tract Society, n.d. [1850?]).

20 Ibid., 22.

21 Ibid., 27.

22 Ibid., 28.

23 Ibid., 5.

24 Ibid., 6–7.

25 Ibid., 7–8.

26 Ibid., 11.

27 Ibid., 16.

28 Ibid., 16.

29 Ibid., 81.

30 Ibid., 85.

31 Edward A. Lawrence, *The Mission of the Church; or, Systematic Beneficence* (New York: American Tract Society, n.d. [ca. 1850]).

32 Ibid., 25.

33 Ibid., 37.

34 Ibid., 55.

35 Ibid., 25–28.

36 Ibid., 28.

37 Ibid., 116–18.

38 Ibid., 64.

39 Ibid., 76–107 passim.

40 Ibid., 104.

41 Ibid., 116–30 passim.

42 Ibid., 134–58 passim.

43 Samuel Harris, *Zaccheus; or, The Scriptural Plan of Benevolence* (New York: American Tract Society, n.d. [ca. 1850]).

44 Ibid., 6.

45 Ibid.

46 Ibid., 25.

47 Ibid., 38.

48 Ibid., 29.

49 Ibid., 26–29.

50 Ibid., 38.

51 Ibid., 39.

52 W. M. Prottsman, *A Practical Treatise on Church Finance with an Analysis of the Financial Plan of the General Conference of the Methodist Episcopal Church, South* (St. Louis: Methodist Book Depository, 1856).

53 Ibid., 17.

54 Ibid., 23.

55 Ibid., 24.

56 Ibid., 27.

57 Ibid., 38.

58 Ibid., 39.

59 Ibid., 42–44.

60 Ibid., 55.

61 Ibid., 73.

62 Ibid., 107.

CHAPTER TWO

1 *Christian Register*, April 29, 1837, 2.

2 See Rhys Isaac, *The Social Transformation of Virginia, 1740–1790* (New York: W. W. Norton, 1988); Thomas E. Buckley, *Church and State in Revolutionary Virginia, 1776–1787* (Charlottesville: University Press of Virginia, 1977); and Lyman Beecher, *Autobiography of Lyman Beecher*, ed. Barbara Cross, 2 vols. (Cambridge, Mass.: Harvard University Press, 1961).

3 For discussion of the social transformations and displacements wrought by a town's maturation and consequent division of all available land, see Kenneth A. Lockridge, *A New England Town: The First Hundred Years* (New York: Norton,

1970), and Philip Greven Jr., "Old Patterns in the New World: The Distribution of Land in 17th Century Andover," *Essex Institute Historical Collections* 101 (1965): 133–48. For attention to the religious impact of these processes, see John Coolidge, "Hingham Builds a Meetinghouse," *New England Quarterly* 24 (1961): 435–61, and J. M. Bumsted, "Religion, Finance and Democracy in Massachusetts: The Town of Norton as a Case Study," *Journal of American History* 57 (1971): 817–31.

4 See Oscar Handlin, *Adventure in Freedom: Three Hundred Years of Jewish Life in America* (New York: McGraw-Hill, 1954), 3–21; Jonathan Sarna, "The Evolution of the American Synagogue," in *The Americanization of the Jews: Reappraisals in Jewish Social and Intellectual History*, ed. Robert M. Seltzer and Norman J. Cohen (New York: New York University Press, 1995); and Leon A. Jick, *The Americanization of the Synagogue, 1820–1870*, (Hanover, N.H.: Brandeis University Press, 1976).

5 For the ways in which Puritans sublimated their longings for luxury into a refined but restrained beauty in devotionally related material culture, see John Wesley Cook, "Material Culture and Visual Arts," in *Encyclopedia of American Religion*, ed. Charles H. Lippy and Peter W. Williams (New York: Scribners, 1988), 1359–68.

6 Robert C. Broderick, *Historic Churches of the United States* (New York: Wilfred Funk, 1958).

7 Harold Wickliffe Rose, *Colonial Houses of Worship in America* (New York: Hastings House 1963), 204.

8 Ibid., 459–60.

9 Ibid., 465.

10 Ibid., 402.

11 Ibid., 299.

12 Ibid., 422.

13 Broderick, *Historic Churches*, 11.

14 Calder Loth and Julius Trousdale Sadler Jr., *The Only Proper Style: Gothic Architecture in America* (Boston: New York Graphic Society, 1975), 122.

15 Broderick, *Historic Churches*, 89.

16 In an examination of nineteenth-century Georgian Methodist buildings, Christopher Owen finds the same process at work as financial prosperity moved Methodists from log cabins to frame buildings and then to brick ones. Most interestingly, he tracks how slave balconies came down after the Civil War and gender-segregated seating gave way to family seating in the new neo-Gothic urban churches late in the century. Christopher H. Owen, "By Design: The Social Meaning of Methodist Church Architecture in Nineteenth-Century Georgia," *Georgia Historical Quarterly* 75, no. 2 (1991): 221–53.

17 There were instances of interfaith funds transfers running the other direction as well, particularly in strongly Roman Catholic Cincinnati and St. Paul, Minnesota. For the general pattern of interfaith cooperation in the development of the charitable sector in nineteenth-century communities, see James Hudnut-Beumler, "Religion and Philanthropy," *The Encyclopedia of Indianapolis*, ed. David J. Bodenhamer and Robert G. Barrows (Bloomington: Indiana University Press, 1994), 1107–9; and

Peter Dobkin Hall, *The Organization of American Culture, 1700–1900: Private Institutions, Elites, and the Origins of American Nationality* (New York: New York University Press, 1982).

CHAPTER THREE

1 Edward P. Gray, *The Apostolic Treasury: Its Nature, History, and Restoration* (San Francisco: Libby and Swett, 1871).

2 Ibid., 5.

3 See James Hudnut-Beumler, "Religion and Philanthropy," in *The Encyclopedia of Indianapolis*, ed. David J. Bodenhamer and Robert G. Barrows (Bloomington: Indiana University Press, 1994) 1107–9.

4 Gray, *Apostolic Treasury*, 32.

5 Ibid., 34.

6 Quoted in Gray, *Apostolic Treasure*, 58.

7 Ibid., 60.

8 Ibid., 62.

9 Ibid., 66–67.

10 Ibid., 68.

11 *Gold and the Gospel: Prize Essays on the Scriptural Duty of Giving in Proportion to Means and Income* (New York: Carlton and Porter, n.d.).

12 C. P. Jennings, *The Christian Treasury; or, The Church's Sources of Income* (Utica, N.Y.: Curtiss and Childs, 1878).

13 Ibid., 18.

14 Ibid., 17.

15 Ibid., 3.

16 *One-Tenth for All; or, Proportionate Giving God's Rule* (n.p., n.d. [ca. 1870]), 14.

17 Ibid., 15.

18 Alexander L. Hogshead and John W. Pratt, *The Gospel Self-Supporting* (Wytheville, Va.: D. A. St. Clair, 1873).

19 Ibid., 12.

20 Ibid., 13.

21 Ibid., 16.

22 Ibid., 28.

23 Ibid., 117.

24 Shepherd Knapp, *A History of the Brick Presbyterian Church in the City of New York* (New York: Trustees of the Brick Church, 1909), 543.

25 Church-owned publishing concerns such as the Hubbard Press, the Methodist Book Publishing Concern, and the Sunday School Board of the Southern Baptist Convention all vied with independent operations to supply congregations with this lucrative, and increasingly ubiquitous, church and Sunday school necessity. Indeed, this probably deserves to be called the great era of paper in American religious life.

26 W. W. W. Wilson, *The Model Benevolent System* (Freeport, N.Y.: E. A. Dorlon, 1895), 7–8.

27 Arlo D. Duba, "Offering and Collection in the Reformed Tradition," *Reformed Liturgy and Music* 16, no. 1 (Winter 1982): 26–32.

28 See Ernest Trice Thompson, *Presbyterians in the South*, 3 vols. (Richmond: John Knox, 1963–73), 1:519–29 and 2:420–26; and Stanley R. Hall, "The American Presbyterian Directory for Worship: History of a Liturgical Strategy" (Ph.D. diss., University of Notre Dame, 1990), 195–96.

29 Hogshead and Pratt, *Gospel Self-Supporting*, 206.

30 Ibid., 207.

31 Ibid., 213.

32 Wilson, *Model Benevolent System*, 5.

33 Ibid., 7.

34 Ibid., 15–16.

35 Ibid., 16–17.

36 Gilbert Monks, *Pastor in Ecclesia: A Practical Study in the Art of Money-Raising* (London: Elliot Stock, 1908).

37 H. Paul Douglass, *The Church in the Changing City: Case Studies Illustrating Adaptation* (New York: G. H. Doran, 1927).

38 William Leach, *Church Finance: Raising, Spending, Accounting* (Nashville: Cokesbury, 1928), 26.

39 Josiah Strong, *Our Country: Its Possible Future and Its Present Crisis*, rev. ed. (New York: Baker and Taylor for the American Missionary Society, 1891), 228–67.

40 Ibid., 228–29.

41 Ibid., 232–55.

42 Margaret Woods Lawrence, "Parish Ways and Means," in *Parish Problems: Hints and Helps for the People of the Churches*, ed. Washington Gladden (New York: Century, 1887), 96.

43 Ibid., 98.

44 John H. Vincent, "Sunday-School Benevolence," in *Parish Problems: Hints and Helps for the People of the Churches*, ed. Washington Gladden (New York: Century, 1887), 387.

45 John Wesley Duncan, *Our Christian Stewardship* (Cincinnati: Jennings and Graham), 1910.

46 Ibid., 13.

47 Ibid., 25–26.

48 Ibid., 27.

49 Ibid., 91.

50 Ibid., 63.

51 Ibid., 86.

52 Ibid., 91.

53 Ibid., 96–97.

54 Ibid., 99.

55 Harvey Reeves Calkins, *A Man and His Money* (New York: Methodist Book Concern, 1914), 13.

56 Ibid., 128.

57 Ibid., 132.

58 Ibid., 127.

59 Mary Askew, *Christian Stewardship: Six Bible Studies for the Women of the Southern Presbyterian Church* (Chattanooga, Tenn.: Stewardship Committee of the Presbyterian Church in the United States, 1920).

60 Ibid., 3.

61 Ibid.

62 Ibid., 14.

63 Ibid., 34.

64 Ibid., 35–36.

65 Ibid., 39.

66 Ibid., 51.

67 Ralph S. Cushman's first five books were all on the theme of stewardship: *Studies in Stewardship* (New York: New York Joint Centenary Committee, Methodist Episcopal Church, 1918); *Adventures in Stewardship* (New York: Abingdon, 1919); *The New Christian: Studies in Stewardship (revised)* (New York: Interchurch Press, 1920); *The Message of Stewardship: A Book for Daily Devotions and Class Study* (New York: Abingdon, 1922); and *Dealing Squarely with God: A Stewardship Primer* (New York: Abingdon, 1927).

68 Cushman, *Message*, 9.

69 Ibid., 53.

70 Ibid., 67.

71 Ibid., 70.

72 Ibid., 192–239.

73 Julius Earl Crawford, *The Call to Christian Stewardship* (Nashville: Publishing House of the Methodist Episcopal Church, South, 1926), 8–9.

74 Ibid., 33.

75 Ibid., 37–39.

76 Ibid., 73.

77 Duncan, *Our Christian Stewardship*, 118.

78 Ibid., 119.

79 Ibid., 119–20.

80 George A. E. Salstrand, *The Story of Stewardship* (Grand Rapids: Baker, 1956), 42–45, 54–55; see also E. B. Stewart, *The Tithe* (Chicago: Winona Publishing Co., 1903).

81 Duncan, *Our Christian Stewardship*, 120–21.

82 Derived from Charles H. Fahs, *Trends in Protestant Giving* (New York: Institute of Social and Religious Research, 1929), 13.

83 Crawford, *Call to Christian Stewardship*, 47–48.

CHAPTER FOUR

1 John Adams, *Diary and Autobiography*, ed. Lyman H. Butterfield, Leonard C. Faber, and Wendell D. Garrett (Cambridge, Mass.: Belknap Press of Harvard University Press, 1961), 1:73.

2 See Timothy D. Hall, *Contested Boundaries: Itinerancy and the Reshaping of the Colonial American Religious World* (Durham, N.C.: Duke University Press, 1994).

3 Cotton Mather, *A monitory letter about the maintainance* [sic] *of an able and faithful ministry. Directed unto those people, who sin against, & sin away the Gospel, by not supporting the worthy preachers of the Gospel* (Boston, 1700), 7; see also Increase Mather, *A discourse concerning the maintenance due to those that preach the Gospel: in which, that question whether tithes are by the divine law the ministers due, is considered, and the negative proved* (Boston: B. Green, 1706).

4 Patricia J. Tracy, *Jonathan Edwards, Pastor: Religion and Society in Eighteenth Century Northampton* (New York: Hill and Wang, 1980), 157.

5 Ibid., 55.

6 See Otto Lohrenz, "Unobtrusive Rector of Hamilton Parish: James Craig of Eighteenth-Century Virginia," *Fides et Historia* 28, no. 3 (1996): 25–39, for a cleric who continued to adapt and get paid; and Otto Lohrenz, "The Reverend John Wingate: An Economic Casualty of Revolutionary Virginia," *Journal of American Culture* 18, no. 4 (1995): 43–49, for one who did not manage as well and left the ministry. The charged political nature of the Virginia situation is well portrayed in Shrady A. Hill, "The Parson's Cause," *Historical Magazine of the Protestant Episcopal Church* 46, no. 1 (1977): 5–35. For New England, see Louise Chipley, "The Financial and Tenure Anxieties of New England's Congregational Clergy during the Early National Era: The Case of William Bentley, 1783–1819," *Essex Institute Historical Collections* 127, no. 4 (1991): 277–96, which tells the story of Bentley's ministry at the East Church of Salem, Massachusetts, during the most dramatic years of his denomination's loss of clerical status; the article also discusses his constant worries about his income and the difficulties of collecting it. In "Income and Ideology: Harvard-Trained Clergymen in the Eighteenth Century," *Eighteenth-Century Studies* 13, no. 4 (Summer 1980): 396–413, Stephen Botein explores the difficulties of clergy in the eighteenth century when currency inflation devalued their stated salaries.

7 John Tufts, *Anti-ministerial objections considered, or The unreasonable pleas made by some against their duty to their ministers, with respect to their maintenance answered. Together with an answer to that question, Who are oblig'd to endeavor a reformation in this case? In a letter to Richard Kent, Esq; one of His Majesty's justices of the peace for the county of Essex, and a member of the Honourable House of Representatives* (Boston: B. Green, 1725), 12.

8 See Kelly Olds, "Privatizing the Church: Disestablishment in Connecticut and Massachusetts," *Journal of Political Economy* 102, no. 2 (1994): 277–97, for a thor-

ough account of what the introduction of competition did to demand for minis-terial services (it increased, particularly for former dissenters), clergy income (it increased), and financing (it became highly demand elastic).

9 See Samuel Haber, *The Quest for Authority and Honor in the American Professions, 1750–1900* (Chicago: University of Chicago Press, 1991), for a treatment of how physicians and lawyers worked at licensing restrictions to improve their standing at the very time clergy embraced the democratic freedom that diminished theirs—the freedom to preach wherever and whenever they chose.

10 Nathaniel S. Haynes, *History of the Disciples of Christ in Illinois, 1819–1914* (Cincinnati: Standard Publishing Company, 1915) 521–22.

11 See Donald M. Scott, *From Office to Profession: The New England Ministry, 1750–1850* (Philadelphia: University of Pennsylvania Press, 1978), 55–56, on the growing number of young ministers from the ranks of the poor; and E. Brooks Holifield, "The Penurious Preacher? Nineteenth-Century Clerical Wealth: North and South," *Journal of the American Academy of Religion* 58, no. 1 (1990): 17–37, on the ways many nevertheless became gentlemen and people of means over time.

12 *Annual Report of the Board of Missions of the General Assembly of Presbyterian Church in the United States of America* (1853), 17.

13 *Annual Report of the Board of Missions of the General Assembly of Presbyterian Church in the United States of America* (1856), 24.

14 Ibid., 25.

15 *Annual Report of the Board of Domestic Missions of General Assembly of Presbyterian Church in the United States of America* (1859), 19.

16 "Statistical Reports," *Minutes of the General Assembly of Presbyterian Church in the United States of America* (1872), 198–434.

17 United States, Bureau of the Census, *Historical Statistics of the United States, Colonial Times to 1957* (Washington, D.C.: Superintendent of Documents, 1960), Series D-718–721.

18 Susan B. Carter, Roger L. Ransom, Richard Sutch, and Hongcheng Zhao, Codebook and User's Manual: Survey of 230 Male Wage-Earners in Ohio in 1879, reported in the *Third Annual Report of the Ohio Bureau of Labor Statistics* (Berkeley: Institute of Business and Economic Research, 1993).

19 Susan B. Carter, Roger L. Ransom, Richard Sutch, and Hongcheng Zhao, Codebook and User's Manual: Survey of 500 Women Wage-Earners in Indianapolis, 1893, reported in the *Fifth Biennial Report of the Indiana Department Statistics* (Berkeley: Institute of Business and Economic Research, 1993).

20 "Statistical Reports," *Minutes* (1872), 198–434.

21 See Joshua Rosenbloom, "One Market or Many? Labor Market Integration in the Late Nineteenth-Century United States," *Journal of Economic History* 50 (March 1990): 85–107.

22 Bureau of the Census, *Historical Statistics,*, Series D-735–738.

23 Susan B. Carter, Roger L. Ransom, Richard Sutch and Hongcheng Zhao, Codebook and User's Manual: Survey of 347 Teachers in Iowa, 1884, reported in the *First*

Biennial Report of the Iowa Bureau of Labor Statistics (Berkeley: Institute of Business and Economic Research, 1993).

24 The ELCA Lutherans are the only large denomination in today's terms that is excluded from analysis; their predecessor parts at the time of the censuses would alone have doubled the length of our table.

25 Bureau of the Census, *Historical Statistics*, Series D-765–778.

26 Paul Howard Douglas, *Real Wages in the United States, 1890–1926* (Boston: Houghton-Mifflin, 1930), 385–88; see also Edward L. Thorndike and Ella Woodyard, "The Effect of Violent Price-Fluctuations upon the Salaries of Clergymen," *Journal of the American Statistical Association* 22, no. 157 (March 1927): 66–74.

27 A methodological note on the Methodist data series: because aggregate data from the Methodist recapitulations are employed, year-to-year definitional glitches and additions to the data base by virtue of denominational mergers can be observed. Rather than dwell on tracing only those from some predecessor stream forward (an impossible task given the available record), I have chosen instead to generate a series that represents the United Methodist Church's ordained ministry as it evolved. The payoff of this decision lies in the trend lines that emerge over long periods of time.

Before 1969, the Methodist Episcopal Church used a figure of "total effective ministers" as its basis for counting the number of Methodist ministers in its work force who were available for appointment. After the merger with the Evangelical United Brethren in 1968, the church moved to defining its ministerial number on the basis of full conference membership. This definitional difference resulted in nearly 10,000 retired and disabled ministers being added to the definition of the number of ministers the church counted in its workforce. For the purposes of this study, I have continued to utilize the prior definition of "total effective ministers" by shifting to the figure reported by the United Methodist Church to the National Council of Churches for its *Yearbook of American and Canadian Churches*. That reported figure corresponds to the number of ministers actually serving churches—a number that most closely corresponds to the universe of people receiving the cash payments made to pastors of churches that the Methodist Church reports.

28 Report of the Board of Ministerial Pensions and Relief, *Minutes of the Convention of the United Lutheran Church in America* (1940), 346–47, in Archives of the Evangelical Lutheran Church in America, Chicago, Ill.

29 "The Money Job Rankings," *Money*, March 1994, 72–73; Internal Revenue Service, *Statistics of Income Bulletin* (1994), Sole Proprietorship Returns.

30 "The Pastor's Salary: A Leadership Survey," *Leadership* (Carol Stream, Ill.), Fall 1988, 57.

31 See William C. Bonifield and Edgar W. Mills, "The Clergy Labor Markets and Wage Determination," *Journal for the Scientific Study of Religion* 19 (1980): 146–58; Dean R. Hoge, Jackson W. Carroll, and Francis K. Sheets, *Patterns of Parish Leadership: Cost and Effectiveness in Four Denominations* (Kansas City: Sheed and Ward, 1988); and Becky R. McMillan and Matthew J. Price, *How Much Should We Pay the Pastor?*

A *Fresh Look at Clergy Salaries in the 21st Century* (Durham, N.C.: Duke Divinity School, 2003).

32 Malcolm Getz, unpublished MS, 2003.

33 Matthew J. Price, "Fear of Falling: Male Clergy in Economic Crisis," *Christian Century*, August 15–22, 2001, 18–21.

CHAPTER FIVE

1 Charles H. Fahs, *Trends in Protestant Giving: A Study of Church Finance in the United States* (New York: Institute of Social and Religious Research, 1929), 60–67.

2 Ibid., 63–64.

3 Ibid.

4 John M. Versteeg, *The Deeper Meaning of Stewardship* (New York: Abingdon, 1923), 13.

5 Ibid., 14.

6 Ibid., 64.

7 Ibid., 72.

8 Reinhold Niebuhr, "Is Stewardship Ethical?" *Christian Century*, April 30, 1930, 555–57.

9 Ibid., 556.

10 Cited in William Herman Leach, *Church Finance; Raising, Spending, Accounting* (Nashville: Cokesbury, 1928), 74.

11 Ibid.

12 Samuel A. Stein, *A Guide in Church Finance* (Columbus, Ohio: Lutheran Book Concern, 1920), 12.

13 Ibid., 12–17.

14 Ibid., 33.

15 "Important Announcement to the Members of St. Pauls Church," *St. Pauls Bote* 30, no. 4 (April 1919): 121.

16 "Members of St. Pauls Church," *St. Pauls Bote* 30, no. 5 (May 1919): 147.

17 "Members of St. Pauls Church," *St. Pauls Bote* 30, no. 11 (November 1919): 373.

18 "The New System," *St. Pauls Bote* 35, no. 2 (March 1924): 51.

19 "Members and Friends of St. Pauls Church," *St. Pauls Bote* 38, no. 10 (October 1927): 501; "Annual Report of the Pastor," *St. Pauls Bote* 51, nos. 1–2 (January–February 1939): 2.

20 "Eight Thousand Master Churchmen," pamphlet published by the Protestant Episcopal Church in the United States of America.

21 H. C. Weber, *The Every Member Canvass: People or Pocket-Books* (New York: Fleming H. Revell, 1932).

22 Ibid., 12.

23 Ibid., 36–37.

24 Quoted in Leach, *Church Finance*, 10.

25 Herbert A. Bosch, *Not Slothful in Business* (Garden City, N.Y.: Doubleday, Doran, 1928), 6.

26 Ibid., 7–8.

27 Bosch, *Not Slothful in Business*, 13.

28 Ibid., 34.

29 Ibid., 37.

30 Ibid., 43–44.

31 Ibid., 61.

32 Ibid., 64.

33 Ibid., 81–82.

34 Ibid., 89.

35 Leach, *Church Finance*, 11.

36 Ibid., 29.

37 Ibid., 44.

38 Ibid.

39 Harvey Reeves Calkins, *A Man and His Money* (New York: Methodist Book Concern, 1914); Julius Earl Crawford, *The Call to Christian Stewardship* (Nashville: Publishing House of the Methodist Episcopal Church, South, 1926); David McConaughy, *Money the Acid Test: Studies in Stewardship, Covering the Principles and Practice of One's Personal Economics* (New York: Missionary Education Movement of the United States and Canada, 1918).

40 Leach, *Church Finance*, 48.

41 Ibid., 49.

42 Ibid.

43 Ibid., 72.

44 Ibid.

45 Julius Earl Crawford, *Financial Recovery for the Local Church* (Nashville: Cokesbury, 1934), 57.

46 William H. Leach, *Here's Money for Churches and Societies* (Nashville: Cokesbury, 1936), 17, 36–38, 40–41.

47 George L. Morelock, *Spiritualizing Church Finance* (Nashville: General Board of Lay Activities, Methodist Episcopal Church, South, 1936), 8–9.

48 Ibid., 10.

49 Harry Emerson Fosdick, "Stand by the Church," in *Successful Fund-Raising Sermons*, ed. Julius King (New York: Funk and Wagnall's, 1953), 50.

50 George E. Lundy, "Raising Money for Church Purposes," in King, *Successful Fund-Raising Sermons*, 4–5.

51 Ibid., 10.

52 Ibid., 11.

53 George Arthur Buttrick, "A New Day For Our Church," in King, *Successful Fund-Raising Sermons*, 32. Though Buttrick's sermon and several others date from the early 1950s, they still reflect the kind of preaching that belonged to the pulpit in the

days before television cut attention spans and helped reshape religious rhetoric and cause-selling technique.

54 Ibid., 34.

55 Ibid., 36.

56 Albert A. Chambers, "That Your Love May Abound," in King, *Successful Fund-Raising Sermons*, 40.

57 Charles H. Hagedorn, "The Subject Jesus Talked about Most," 54–60, and J. Wallace Hamilton, "What is Devotion Worth?" in King, *Successful Fund-Raising Sermons*, 66–74.

58 Lewis M. Hirshon, "To Be Found Faithful," in King, *Successful Fund-Raising Sermons*, 86.

59 John P. Jockinsen, "And Thou Shalt Teach Them Diligently," in King, *Successful Fund-Raising Sermons*, 102.

60 Ibid.

61 Robert James McCracken, "On Giving Hilariously," in King, *Successful Fund-Raising Sermons*, 109.

62 Ibid., 112.

63 Richard Pacini, "No Sidelong Glance," in King, *Successful Fund-Raising Sermons*, 142–48.

64 George Francis O'Pray, "Five Barley Loaves and Two Small Fishes," in King, *Successful Fund-Raising Sermons*, 149.

65 Ibid., 151.

66 Ibid., 156.

67 Samuel S. M. Shoemaker, "The Privilege of Giving," in King, *Successful Fund-Raising Sermons*, 192.

68 Anson P. Stokes Jr., "Stewardship," in King, *Successful Fund-Raising Sermons*, 209.

69 Ralph W. Sockman, "Bonds That Do Not Break," in King, *Successful Fund-Raising Sermons*, 200, 207.

70 Peter Marshall, "A Tip or a Tithe," in King, *Successful Fund-Raising Sermons*, 134.

CHAPTER SIX

1 For a lively account of the differential development of social ideals and industrial development in British and North American cities, see Paul T. Phillips, *A Kingdom on Earth: Anglo-American Social Christianity, 1880–1940* (State College: Pennsylvania State University Press, 1996).

2 James L. Doom "Church Architecture," in *Encyclopedia of Religion in the South*, ed. Samuel S. Hill (Macon, Ga.: Mercer University Press, 1984), 48.

3 Alexander Crummell, *Charitable Institutions in Colored Churches* (Washington, D.C.: B. L. Pendelton, 1892), 7–10.

4 See Jeanne Halgren Kilde, *When Church Became Theatre: The Transformation of Evangelical Architecture and Worship in Nineteenth-Century America* (New York:

Oxford University Press, 2002), for the many ways in which these massive churches were Victorian mansions religiously writ large.

5 While there is a slight bias against large churches for member financial support on a per capita basis, this is more than offset by the economies of scale achieved by large institutional churches either in the early twentieth century or today. Therefore, a few more members are always to be preferred since the total amount of congregational activity grows faster with membership gained than when member giving declines.

6 For an analysis of institutional churches that survive and more that do not, see James W. Lewis, *At Home in the City: The Protestant Experience in Gary, Indiana, 1906–1975* (Knoxville: University of Tennessee Press, 1992).

7 Charles Eden Carroll, *The Community Survey in Relation to Church Efficiency: A Guide for Workers in the City, Town, and Country Church* (New York: Abingdon, 1915); and Nancy T. Ammerman, *Congregations and Change* (New Brunswick, N.J.: Rutgers University Press, 1997).

8 Edmund de Schweinitz Brunner, *The New Country Church Building* (New York: Missionary Education Movement, 1917), x.

9 Ibid., ix.

10 Clarence W. Hall, "The Churches Rise Again" *McCall's,* June 1955, 34–37.

11 Ibid., 112; see "The New Churches," *Time,* December 26, 1960, 28–33, for a retrospective view of the architects involved in ecclesiastical design in the 1950s and the styles they employed.

12 John Knox Shear, *Religious Buildings for Today* (New York: F. W. Dodge, 1957), 2.

13 Not all consumption of the built environment is strictly speaking the result of fresh choices about what to build. Trickle-down church possession is a pattern, especially for urban areas, that dates back to the earliest days of the nation. Jay Dolan's *The Immigrant Church* (1975) is a splendid introduction to how many times and in how many ways a particular church building can be reused, utilizing the case of the Catholic Church in New York City. But even if you are worshiping in a style that you did not choose to build, you are still consuming it in much the same way that people consume particular used car types according to their submarket tastes and preferences. (Although, to be fair, a hierarchy of needs does operate here more than in the market for used cars, since geography is a limiting factor.)

CHAPTER SEVEN

1 Roy L. Smith, *Stewardship Studies* (New York: Abingdon, 1954), 36.

2 Ibid., 44.

3 George L. Hunt, *There's No Place Like Home for Stewardship* (Philadelphia: Committee for Stewardship Education, Board of Christian Education, Presbyterian Church in the U.S.A., 1949), 9.

4 Ernest F. Scott, *Man and Society in the New Testament* (New York: Charles Scribner's Sons, 1946), 187.

5　Hunt, *There's No Place*, 19.

6　Wesner Fallaw, *The Modern Parent and the Teaching Church*, (New York: Macmillan, 1946), 24.

7　Gladys Fitzsimmons MacGee, "Who Gives," in *Yearbook of Philanthropy, 1947–48*, ed. John Price Jones (New York: Inter-River Press, 1948), 12–14.

8　Hunt, *There's No Place*, 56.

9　Richard Byfield and James P. Shaw, *Your Money and Your Church* (Garden City, N.Y.: Doubleday, 1959), 20.

10　Ibid., 22, 74–76.

11　Hunt, *There's No Place*, 73.

12　Weldon Crossland, *How to Increase Church Income* (New York: Cokesbury, 1947).

13　Ibid., 40, 45.

14　Ibid., 45.

15　Ibid., 54.

16　Ibid., 63–64.

17　William F. McDermott, *Everlasting Treasures* (Chicago: General Board of Lay Activities, Methodist Church, 1948), 6.

18　Ibid., 8.

19　Ibid., 12–13.

20　Lawrence E. Brooks, *Better Church Finance* (Anderson, Ind.: Warner Press, 1960), 61.

21　Ralph Seaman, *101 Ways to Raise Money for Your Church* (New York: Frederick Fell, 1952), 7.

22　Ibid., 19.

23　Ibid., 40.

24　Ibid., 42.

25　Ibid., 63.

26　W. E. Grindstaff, *Developing a Giving Church* (Westwood, N.J.: Fleming H. Revell, 1954), 7.

27　Ibid., 12.

28　Ibid., 22.

29　Ibid., 23.

30　Ibid., 38.

31　Ibid., 38–39.

32　Ibid., 43.

33　Ibid., 138–39.

34　Ibid., 165.

35　Ibid., 186–87.

36　Ibid., 189.

37　Costen Jordan Harrell, *Stewardship and the Tithe* (New York: Abingdon-Cokesbury Press, 1953), 36.

38　Ibid., 59.

39　Ibid., 16–17.

40 Brian Keith Rice, *What Is Christian Giving?* Studies in Ministry and Worship (London: SCM Press, 1958), 23.

41 Ibid., 31.

42 Ibid., 37.

43 Ibid., 40.

44 Ibid., 42.

45 Ibid., 45.

46 Quoted in Brooks, *Better Church Finance,* 24.

47 Charlie W. Shedd, *How to Develop a Tithing Church* (New York: Abingdon, 1961), 15.

48 Ibid., 35–37.

49 Ibid., 65.

50 John S. McMullen, *Stewardship Unlimited, a Cooperative Text,* Faith for Life Series (Richmond: John Knox, 1962), 11.

51 Ibid.

52 Ibid., 13.

53 Ibid., 14.

54 Ibid., 60.

55 Helen Kingsbury Wallace, *Stewardship for Today's Woman* (Westwood, N.J.: Revell, 1960), 17.

56 Ibid., 24.

57 Ibid., 35.

58 Virginia Ely, *Stewardship: Witnessing for Christ* (Westwood, N.J.: Revell, 1962), 82–84.

59 Luther P. Powell, *Money and the Church* (New York: Association Press, 1962).

60 Ibid., 191.

61 Ibid., 183–200.

62 Charles Harry Atkinson, *How to Finance Your Church Building Program* (Westwood, N.J.: Revell, 1963), 7.

63 Ibid., 9.

64 Ibid., 13.

65 Ibid., 26.

66 David W. Thompson, *How to Increase Memorial Giving* (Westwood, N.J.: Revell, 1963), 25.

67 George W. Harrison, *Church Fund Raising* (Englewood Cliffs, N.J.: Prentice-Hall, 1964), 14–15.

68 Ibid.

69 Ibid., 17.

70 Described in Thomas K. Thompson, *Handbook of Stewardship Procedures* (Englewood Cliffs, N.J.: Prentice-Hall, 1964), 45.

71 Ibid., 51.

72 Ibid., 56.

73 Quoted in T. K. Thompson, *Handbook,* 106.

74 Robert F. Casemore, *There Were Twelve: A Collection of Twelve Stewardship Plays* (New York: Dept. of Stewardship and Benevolence, National Council of the Churches of Christ, 1964.)

75 Waldo J. Werning, *The Stewardship Call: An Approach to Personal and Group Stewardship Based on the Concept of Christian Vocation* (Saint Louis: Concordia, 1965), 20, 25, 33, 37, 40, 45–46.

76 Ibid., 42.

77 Lukas Vischer, *Tithing in the Early Church* (Philadelphia: Fortress Press, 1966), xi.

78 A. A. Allen, *Send Now Prosperity* (Miracle Valley, Ariz.: A. A. Allen Revivals, 1968), 18.

79 Ibid., 19.

80 Ibid.

81 Ibid., 22.

82 Ibid., 60.

83 Raymond E. Balcomb, *Stir What You've Got! And Other Stewardship Studies* (Nashville: Abingdon, 1968).

84 Carl W. Berner, *The Power of Pure Stewardship* (St. Louis: Concordia, 1970); David W. Crockett, *Sound Financial Stewardship* (New York: Morehouse-Barlow, 1973).

85 Bartlett L. Hess and Margaret Johnston Hess, *How to Have a Giving Church* (Nashville: Abingdon, 1974) , 11.

86 Ibid., 17–18.

87 Ibid., 18, 22, 25, 29, 41.

88 Ibid., 52.

89 Wallace E. Fisher, *A New Climate for Stewardship* (Nashville: Abingdon, 1976), 34.

90 Ibid., 36, 35, 41.

91 Ibid., 42–43, 46.

92 Ibid., 69, 71.

93 Ibid., 96, 98.

94 Ibid., 118.

95 Richard B. Cunningham, *Creative Stewardship* (Nashville: Abingdon, 1979), 83.

CHAPTER EIGHT

1 *The Minister's Wife; or, What Becomes of the Salary* (Boston, James M. Usher, 1861).

2 A. H. Redford, *The Preacher's Wife* (Nashville: Publishing House of the Methodist Episcopal Church, South, 1877).

3 Mary Orme Tucker, *Itinerate Preaching in the Early Days of Methodism* (Boston: B. B. Russell, 1872), 99–100.

4 See Jon Butler, *Becoming America: The Revolution before 1776* (Cambridge, Mass.: Harvard University Press, 2000), particularly chapter 4, "Things Material," for an illuminating account of how well off the average American was in the eighteenth century relative to Europeans of the same period.

5 Leonard I. Sweet, *The Minister's Wife: Her Role in Nineteenth-Century American Evangelicalism* (Philadelphia: Temple University Press, 1983), 73.

6 Ibid., 74.

7 Quoted in ibid., 75.

8 Margaret Woods Lawrence, "Dues Not Donations," in *Parish Problems: Hints and Helps for the People of the Churches*, ed. Washington Gladden (New York: Century, 1887), 41–42.

9 Ibid., 43, 46.

10 Ennen Reaves Hall, *One Saint and Seven Sinners* (New York: Thomas Y. Crowell, 1959), 8.

11 Lawrence, "Dues Not Donations," 146.

12 Cleland Boyd McAfee, *Ministerial Practices: Some Fraternal Suggestions* (New York: Harper and Brothers, 1928), 168.

13 Frances Sandys Elson, *Quiet Hints to Ministers' Wives* (Boston: Stratford, 1934), 10, 25, 28, 31, 32, 51.

14 Carolyn P. Blackwood, *The Pastor's Wife* (Philadelphia: Westminster, 1950), 20.

15 Ibid., 182.

16 Welthy Honsinger Fischer, *Handbook for Ministers' Wives* (New York: Woman's Press, 1950), 13–14.

17 Mabel H. Case, *The Singing Years* (New York: Vantage Press, 1953), 101.

18 Lora Lee Parrott, *How to Be a Preacher's Wife and Like It* (Grand Rapids, Mich.: Zondervan, 1956), 72–75.

19 Ruth Truman, *Underground Manual for Ministers' Wives* (Nashville: Abingdon, 1974), 121.

20 Ibid., 122.

21 Ibid., 128.

22 Ibid., 138.

23 John H. Morgan and Linda B. Morgan, "Wives of Priests" (Notre Dame, Ind.: Parish Life Institute, 1980), 22.

24 Charlotte Ross, *Who Is the Minister's Wife?* (Philadelphia: Westminster, 1980), 62–63.

25 Ibid., 65.

26 Mary Owens Fitzgerald, *The North Carolina Conference Parsonage System: Insights and Alternatives* (n.p., 1979), 1, 8.

27 Robert W. Bailey and Mary Frances Bailey, *Coping with Stress in the Minister's Home* (Nashville: Broadman Press, 1979), 87. See also Frederick Leonard Smoot, "Self-perceived Effects of the Parsonage System on United Methodist Clergy and Spouses' Sense of Becoming and Growth in the Parish Ministry" (Ph.D. diss., Claremont School of Theology, 1978), for a full account of the negative psychological effects of continuing the parsonage system into the late twentieth century.

28 Cameron Lee and Jack O. Balswick, *Life in a Glass House: The Minister's Family in Its Unique Social Context* (Grand Rapids, Mich.: Ministry Resources Library, 1989), 273–75.

29 Claire Eva, "Balancing the Budget," *Ministry*, January 2000, 10–13.

30 Kay A. Fuller, "For Richer or Poorer," *Connecting*, Spring 2001, BGC Women in Ministry, <http://www.bgcworld.org/newsstand/connect/conn_spg.htm> (November 1, 2004).

31 Edward C. Lehman Jr., *Gender and Work: The Case of the Clergy* (Albany: State University of New York Press, 1993), 184–189.

CHAPTER NINE

1 "New Hope Community Church History," <http://www.newhopechurchtn.org/about/history.htm> (June 17, 2005).

2 "The History of The Living Word Community Church," <http://tlwcc.org/History.php> (June 17, 2005).

3 "Tithing," <http://www.ag.org/top/beliefs/christian_doctrines/gendoct_06_tithing.cfm> (July 1, 2005).

4 "Sermon Illustrations: Tithing," <http://www.cogstewardship.cc/devotiongiving.htm> (June 22, 2004).

5 "CBN Teaching Sheets, Giving and Tithing," <http://cbn.org/spirituallife/cbnteachingsheets/giving_and_tithing.asp> (June 17, 2005).

6 "Good Reasons For Tithing," <http://www.netministries.org/see/churches/http//netministries.org/see/churches.exe/ch06797> (June 20, 2004).

7 "Experience of the Episcopal Church in Improving Stewardship: One Person's View," <http://members.aol.com/stewdship/experience.htm> (May 15, 2005).

8 "On Holy Habits," <http://www.fwepiscopal.org/augfour.html> (September 9, 2003).

9 "Tithing and Giving—Ask Greg! Questions," <http://www.ptm.org/uni/QandA/Tithing.htm> (June 20, 2005).

10 Lee E. Warren, "Can Tithing Cause Blessings?" <http://www.plim.org/tithing.html> (June 25, 2005).

11 L. Ray Smith, "Tithing Is Unscriptural under the New Covenant [A Scriptural Exposition on the Fraudulent Fleecing of the Flock]" <http://bibletruths.com/tithing.html> (June 25, 2005). See also Ernest L. Martin, *The Tithing Dilemma* (Portland, Ore.: ASK Publications, 1997), for a dispensationalist account of how churches should be financed without a reliance on tithing.

12 For Barna's findings, see George Barna, *How to Increase Giving in Your Church: A Practical Guide to the Sensitive Task of Raising Money for Your Church or Ministry* (Ventura, Calif.: Regal Books, 1997); and "Research Archive about Stewardship," <http://www.barna.org/FlexPage.aspx?Page=Topic&TopicID=36> (January 20, 2005).

13 Joseph R. Miller, "Funding the Local Church" <http://churchconstruction.com/articleresults.php?id+5> (January 20, 2005).

14 "Giving Back," <http://www.holycomforter.com/discipleship/givingback.htm> (July 1, 2005).

15 Joseph D. Burnett, *Capital Funds Campaign Manual for Churches* (Valley Forge, Penn.: Judson Press, 1980), 10, 12, 56.

16 Ibid., 56.

17 Kermit L. Braswell, *Step by Step: A Financial Campaign for Your Church* (Nashville: Abingdon, 1995).

18 Ibid., 32.

19 "Time To Build Testimonies," <http://www.pastors.com/pcom/stewardship/ttbte stimonies.asp#8> (June 30, 2005).

20 Herbert Mather, *Becoming a Giving Church* (Nashville: Discipleship Resources, General Board of Discipleship, United Methodist Church, 1985).

21 Douglas W. Johnson, *Finance in Your Church* (Nashville: Abingdon, 1986).

22 John Ronsvalle and Sylvia Ronsvalle, *The Poor Have Faces: Loving Your Neighbor in the 21st Century* (Grand Rapids, Mich.: Baker Book House, 1992).

23 John Ronsvalle and Sylvia Ronsvalle, *Behind the Stained Glass Windows: Money Dynamics in the Church* (Grand Rapids, Mich.: Baker Books, 1996), 29–30.

24 See Cynthia Woolever and Deborah Bruce, *A Field Guide to U.S. Congregations* (Louisville, Ky.: Westminster John Knox, 2002), 59, for an estimate of the scale and range of community service undertaken by American congregations.

25 Ronsvalle and Ronsvalle, *Behind the Stained Glass Windows*, 302.

26 Ibid., 303.

27 Max Weber, *The Protestant Ethic and the Spirit of Capitalism*, trans. Talcott Parsons (New York: Charles Scribner's Sons, 1958).

28 "Gordon Gekko: Address to Teldar Paper Stockholders," from the movie *Wall Street* (1987), quoted in <http://www.americanrhetoric.com/Movie Speeches/moviespee chwallstreet.html> (June 26, 2006).

29 M. Douglas Meeks, *God the Economist: The Doctrine of God and Political Economy* (Minneapolis: Fortress, 1989); Eugene Grimm and Herb Miller, *Generous People* (Nashville: Abingdon, 1992); James Hudnut-Beumler, *Generous Saints: Congregations Rethinking Ethics and Money* (Bethesda, Md.: Alban Institute, 1999); Dean R. Hoge, *Money Matters: Personal Giving in American Churches* (Louisville, Ky.: Westminster John Knox, 1996); Dean R. Hoge, Patrick H. McNamara, Charles E. Zech, and Loren B. Mead, *Plain Talk about Churches and Money* (Bethesda, Md.: Alban Institute, 1997); Robert Wuthnow, *Acts of Compassion: Caring for Others and Helping Ourselves* (Princeton, N.J.: Princeton University Press, 1991); R. Wuthnow, *God and Mammon in America* (New York: Free Press, 1994); R. Wuthnow, *Poor Richard's Principle : Recovering the American Dream through the Moral Dimension of Work, Business, and Money* (Princeton, N.J.: Princeton University Press, 1996); and R. Wuthnow, *The Crisis in the Churches : Spiritual Malaise, Fiscal Woe* (New York: Oxford University Press, 1997).

30 For a complete account of the rise of the Prosperity Gospel, see Bruce Barron, *The Health and Wealth Gospel* (Downers Grove, Ill.: InterVarsity Press, 1987).

31 Kelefa Sanneh, "Pray and Grow Rich; Letter from Atlanta," *New Yorker*, October 11, 2004, 48.

32 Debra Blum and Holly Hall, "Americans Donated $248.5-Billion to Charity in 2004, as 2.3% Rise," *Chronicle of Higher Education*, June 24, 2005, A27.

33 Adelle M. Banks, "Massive Survey Looks at Religious Life at Local Church Level," Religion News Service, May 15, 2002, available at <http:www.uscongregations.org/rns-article-massive-survey.htm> (June 1, 2006).

INDEX

Bodenhamer, David J., 242 (n. 17), 243 (n. 3)

Boeringer, James, 177

Boesky, Ivan, 224

Bombeck, Erma, 194

Bonifield, William C., 248 (n. 31)

Bosch, Herbert A., 111–16, 118

Botein, Stephen, 246 (n. 6)

Brainerd, David, 127

Braswell, Kermit L., 220

Broderick, Robert C., 38, 242 (nn. 6, 13, 15)

Brook, Lawrence E., 161

Brown, Dan, 211

Browning, Elizabeth Barrett, 70

Bruce, Deborah, 258 (n. 24)

Brueggemann, Walter, 224

Brunner, Edmund de Schweinitz, 140–41

Buckley, Thomas E., 241 (n. 2)

Budgeting as an aid to stewardship, 116–17

Buildings, religious, increased community use and size of, 147–49

Bumsted, J. M., 242 (n. 3)

Burnett, Joseph D., 219–20

Business methods in church practice, 27, 59, 110, 119

Butler, Jon, 255 (n. 4)

Butterfield, Kenyon, 97

Butterfield, Lyman H., 246 (n. 1)

Buttrick, George Arthur, 125–26

Byfield, Richard, 153–54

Calkins, Harvey Reeves, 65–67, 117

Campolo, Tony, 207

Capital and building campaigns, 163, 177, 218–20

Capital investments of churches, 32–33, 138–41, 148–49

Carey, William, 127

Carnegie, Andrew, 61

Carroll, Charles Eden, 252 (n. 7)

Carroll, Jackson W., 248 (n. 31)

Carroll, John, 13

Carter, Jimmy, 181

Carter, Susan B., 247 (nn. 18–19, 23)

Cary, William, 24

Case, Mabel H., 193

Casemore, Robert F., 177

Caulkins, Harvey, 165

Chambers, Albert A., 126

Chipley, Louise, 246 (n. 6)

Church, Pharcellus, 15–19

Clarke, Erskine, 239 (n. 8)

Class, 2, 3, 12, 16, 49, 76–78, 82–83, 88–89

Clergy: anxiety about income, xii, xiv, 3–4, 60, 78–97, 167–68, 196, 198; opposition to economic life and practices, 28–30; status of, 76

—wives and husbands of, 187–98; status and deprivation of, 188–89; as counsel to others, 189–94; and expectations of sacrifice, 190; and children, 191–92, 195–96; and spending, 194; and home, 194, 196

Cohen, Norman J., 242 (n. 4)

Collections during worship, 55–56, 58

Colleges: compared organizationally to religious congregations, xii

Community churches, 202–4, 207

Competition, 36; between religions, xv, 4; between religious causes, 18, 48–49; within Protestantism for adherents, 33–36

Conservative Protestantism and giving, 177–82, 227–29

Constable, Henry, 51

Constantine, 14

Consumer churches, 141–49

Consumer culture, 26, 30, 68–69, 128–29, 152–53; and church consumption patterns, 141; and capitalism, religiously assessed, 220–25

Consuming religion, 143–47, 208–11, 229

Cook, John Wesley, 242 (n. 5)

Cooke, Parsons, 19–22, 25–26